TEACHERS' TEAMING HANDBOOK

A Middle Level Planning Guide

TEACHERS' TEAMING HANDBOOK

A Middle Level Planning Guide

John Arnold
North Carolina State University

Chris Stevenson
University of Vermont

Harcourt Brace College Publishers
Fort Worth Philadelphia San Diego New York Orlando Austin San Antonio
Toronto Montreal London Sydney Tokyo

Publisher: Earl McPeek
Acquisitions Editor: Jo-Anne Weaver
Product Manager: Don Grainger
Project Editor: Laura Miley
Art Director: Don Fujimoto
Production Manager: Andrea A. Johnson

Cover credit: Dan Bryant Photographs

ISBN: 0-15-503072-8
Library of Congress Catalog Card Number: 97-068444

Address for orders:
Harcourt Brace & Company
6277 Sea Harbor Drive
Orlando, FL 32887-6777
1-800-782-4479

Address for editorial correspondence:
Harcourt Brace College Publishers
301 Commerce Street, Suite 3700
Fort Worth, Texas 76102

Web site address:
http://www.hbcollege.com

Printed in the United States of America

8 9 0 1 2 3 4 5 6 016 10 9 8 7 6 5 4 3 2

To Edward Yeomans
and Vincent Rogers,
our mentors,
whose vision,
encouragement,
and love have
profoundly
influenced
our lives.

Acknowledgments

We are deeply grateful to the thousands of students, teachers, administrators, and colleagues who have been our mentors over the past thirty years. These include middle level students we have taught; teachers with whom we have teamed or with whom we have served as principal; teachers in countless workshops; undergraduate and graduate students; and colleagues in schools, universities, and institutes. What we know about teaming we have learned primarily from these sources of firsthand experience.

Especially, we are indebted to the teachers and administrators whose practices are cited in this book. They have been a particular inspiration to us, and we appreciate their cooperation in verifying or correcting our attempts to accurately describe their work.

We wish to thank Jo-Anne Weaver at Harcourt Brace College Publishers for her encouragement and support. We thank the editorial staff at Harcourt Brace who worked on this text. These include, Linda Blundell, editorial assistant, Laura Miley, project editor, Andrea Johnson, production manager, and Don Fujimoto, art director. We also thank Christine Terwilliger and Jenny Parish for their help in preparing the manuscript.

Foreword

by

Ross M. Burkhardt

"Be the change you seek," Gandhi declared. John Arnold and Chris Stevenson are living examples of that exhortation. Their lives reflect wholehearted dedication to the education of young adolescents. Partners in many middle level activities over the years and close personal friends as well, Stevenson and Arnold have done us a great service with this book, one that passionately embraces the notion that "interdisciplinary teams . . . build a sense of community and promote curriculum integration" (*This We Believe,* NMSA 1995). We are fortunate to have the benefit of their collective wisdom in this handbook.

Written with experientially based clarity, *Teachers' Teaming Handbook: A Middle Level Planning Guide* represents the distillation of more than sixty years of combined experience as teachers, administrators, consultants, and university instructors in middle level education. In unambiguous language Arnold and Stevenson spell out the possibilities and the pratfalls of teaming for the beginning teacher as well as for the experienced practitioner. Their bias is clear—teaming works; in fact, it works magnificently for young adolescents when done properly: "Organizing by teams enables a few teachers to create an educational community in which students are known and understood, taught in ways that complement their abilities and enable them to be successful and supported in multiple ways as they grow through the challenges of contemporary adolescence." Further, the authors emphasize that "it is not possible to overrate the importance of teaming as an organizational format that lends itself to matching students' abilities and interests with developmentally appropriate curriculum and pedagogy."

Illustrated with telling anecdotes and honest examples culled from hard-won experience, this practical handbook is must reading for any serious middle level educator who is on a team, about to join a team, considering teaming, or even working solo (it may move that individual to seek out advantageous teaming partnerships!). Using a chapter structure that offers several scenarios followed by commentary on those scenarios, then by guiding principles accompanied by planning guidelines, caveats, and actual team documents, Arnold and Stevenson address the importance of planning, the crucial role of the principal in nurturing teams, the development of a team vision, team governance, organization and procedures, the creation of a team identity, communication among team members, curriculum, accountability, and interpersonal relationships. The authors argue that "the majority of teams in most middle schools do not come close to maximizing their potential" because they fail to create "a sense of community" among their students. Stevenson and Arnold underscore the value of rituals and traditions and the need to "form caring relationships that promote a spirit of personal belonging," astutely observing that "disrespect destroys community." They also call for more *role taking* on the part of young adolescents, who are celebrated as learners and for whom "a desire for competence is always present."

This can be daunting stuff—the authors set high standards for what teaming can and ought to be. They present a vision of excellence for middle schools, yet they temper their admonitions with realism and hard truths—results take time, there are many roads to good teaming, not all teams look alike, be wary of overzealous team competition, it won't all be accomplished in the first year. Nevertheless, their premise is clear: "The overarching goal is to create an educational experience for young adolescents that matches better with their nature and needs than does the traditional alternative." What do we want our "intentional impact" to be on the teams that we create and serve? As teachers, we need to be intentional about where we are going and how we intend to get there. This handbook provides a refreshing road map.

Among other issues, Stevenson and Arnold stress the importance of human relationships: Although hard work, planning, and commitment are necessary factors for teaming to flourish, "positive relationships are the single most important element" in fully realized teams. Those readers who have worked on successful or unsuccessful teams know the truth of this assertion. The authors also voice strong support for "the importance of freedom for self-determination for children and for educators." Teachers need to have autonomy in their classrooms to make the best decisions that they can in behalf of their charges. Similarly, students should have a strong voice in determining many aspects of life in the classroom, including governance and curriculum issues.

Arnold and Stevenson agree that teachers deserve to play a significant role when decisions are made about which colleagues are going to be on the team. In fact, they state it plainly: "It is foolhardy to expect teachers who don't like each other to team successfully." Hence, common goals for a team, developed by the teachers on that team, are essential. And, "if the team is to genuinely grow and develop, there must be considerable continuity of basic goals and values." Hence, the authors support longevity on teams, noting that "the continuity of adult relationships is an extremely important ingredient" for the eventual success of a team. Teaming is an evolutionary process that just takes time—a fact that building administrators need to remember in their hurried world of do-it-now directives from the district office. Also, common planning time for teams of teachers is an absolute necessity. Without it, a teaming enterprise is doomed to failure. And the authors do not understate matters when they assert: "A textbook is not an appropriate curriculum for young adolescent learners. At best it is one resource among many for the kind of learning that empowers our students." Amen!

Many specific examples of developmentally appropriate schooling are cited from around the country, only adding to the power of the text. We learn about engaging activities and practices in the Paradise Project, Burlington, VT; the Watershed

Team, Radnor, PA; the Gator Team, Camp Lejeune, NC; the Songadeewin Family, Swanton, VT; the Alpha Team in Shelburne, VT; Sidwell Friends Middle School in Washington D.C.; the Unit Team, Fayerweather Street School, Cambridge, MA; Mt. Jefferson Junior High School in Lee, ME; and Western Middle School in Alamance County, NC, to name but a few. The work that educators in these and other schools are doing is testimony to the efficacy of teaming as a major component of middle level education.

I have taught on many teams and with many colleagues since I began my career in 1962. Experience tells me that most of what Arnold and Stevenson lay out is right on the money. If "two heads are better than one," then people working in concert toward an end larger than any one of them will produce a better result. We live in a pluralistic society. What better way of preparing the nation's youth for "the real world" than by educating them in team settings? As the authors so eloquently put it, "team organization should always be seen as a serious opportunity for students to grow toward more adultlike forms of personal accountability under the guidance of teachers who appreciate the special opportunities that teaming provides."

Ross M. Burkhardt
Wading River, New York

Introduction

"Teaming" is particularly American. There is something about it that is closely akin to our democratic heritage. A few professional sports teams even declare themselves to be "America's Team." And by some estimates, 50 percent of all employees in the United States will operate as members of some type of team (Rayer 1993). Although various applications of the general idea of teaming have appeared in America's schools over the years, the context of teaming that is the focus of this book is very explicit: interdisciplinary team organization in middle level schools.

The materials that comprise this book derive from both formal research and from empirical observations and experiences of the authors, both of whom have taught young adolescents, one of us as a team leader; have been principals in teamed middle level schools; have taught courses and institutes on teaming; and have worked with teachers on teams in hundreds of schools across the country.

Our constant goal while writing this book has been to provide both a conceptual framework and *a practical guide for team planning.* We believe that experienced team members who may have had to invent themselves without much external guidance will find this book useful as they continue their evolution, refining and/or expanding their practice. Teachers just starting out, who need to know the widest range of possibilities before creating a team plan, should find this book especially helpful. Because team organization may require principals and assistant principals to revisit their school's decision-making process, every building administrator in a middle level school where teaming already exists or where it is being contemplated can derive value from this book. Every chapter has direct and implicit advice for these crucial school leaders. We further hope that district administrators and school board members will want to gain a better understanding of teaming in order to support it within the larger community and will find this book a concise, explicit resource for their important decisions. In addition to its use by practicing educators, this book may also serve as a text for graduate or undergraduate college classes and especially as a focus for in-service preparation.

In our effort to make this book true to actual practice and as user-friendly as possible, we have organized most of the chapters around several teaming scenarios drawn from actual schools. These scenarios are followed by an analytical commentary, a delineation of selected principles of teaming, recommended guidelines for planning, additional possibilities, caveats to keep in mind, and illustrative examples and displays shared by teachers on effective teams. The majority of the scenarios describe the actual practice of specific teams; in such instances, the school name and location are given, and the accuracy of the descriptions have been verified by the teachers or administrators involved. Other scenarios are drawn from the composite practice of several teams or individuals. In these situations pseudonyms are used with no school name given.

Overview of the Book

Chapter 1 defines the nature of teaming, places it in the larger school organizational context, and explains why it is such a vital strategy for engaging young adolescents in a developmentally responsive manner. It especially emphasizes the benefits for students, teachers, parents, and the school as a whole. Further, it advocates developing small "partner teams" where feasible.

Planning and developing viable teams are, of course, not as simple as following principles and guidelines. There are requisite conditions that need to be in place for a team plan to have a reasonable chance of success, and these are discussed in chapter 2, "Considerations in Planning." Readers are advised to thoroughly explore all issues raised in that discussion, expressing ideas, concerns, and needs with colleagues in those positions of authority that are able to help them achieve the support they will need.

No individual has more potential for positive influence on the promise of teaming than the principal. Teachers look to their leaders for moral direction and support as well as for considerations of time, space, and materials, and budgetary provisions. Clearly the path to successful teaming is made infinitely smoother by informed, trusting, supportive leaders. Chapter 3 examines pertinent issues within the principal's sphere of influence and authority, and both teachers and administrators are urged to read and candidly discuss those issues. Where both parties are willing to trust each other and support each other's needs, teaming stands on firm ground.

It has already been implied that conventional school organization falls short of tapping the full potential of young adolescent learners. It may also inhibit the growth and development of teachers. When one's educational vision transcends common practice, however, new, better, and more far-reaching possibilities are realized. Chapter 4 appeals to teachers to look well beyond convention, imagining for students and for themselves possibilities that come within reach after they are able to look and see beyond what is and has been. Building upon a substantive team vision, reasonable, achievable goals for all can be developed through thoughtful planning and negotiated collaborations.

Chapters 5, 6, and 7 address a host of practical, operational issues—the myriad so-called nuts and bolts of teaming. At the heart of the matter is freedom for self-determination for children and for educators. We cannot overstate this essential point. Although there is no single recipe for creating an effective team, there are many procedures and practices relative to governance, organization, and team identity that must be incorporated if the team is to be sufficiently comprehensive. These chapters detail many of those important operational particulars.

Young adolescent learning is in very large measure about communication, and teams have a particularly rich opportunity to build strong, clear connections among the teachers and students on a team and between the team and its interested constituents: principal, parents, and other teams. Perhaps teaming's greatest benefit to teachers is young adolescents' readiness and ability to shoulder some of the responsibilities for communication, and chapter 8 spells out concrete ways to promote quality discourse among all constituents.

Chapter 9 conveys some of the particularly promising opportunities for curriculum and pedagogy that complement the various ways that young adolescents go about learning. Although an entire book could be devoted to the curricular aspects of teaming, this chapter emphasizes ways to personalize and integrate curriculum. It also makes broad suggestions that can be selectively undertaken by even a novice team as an initial step toward curricular evolution.

If or when a small group of teachers forms a challenging, responsive educational program for a distinct group of students, it is reasonable to expect improvements in students' responses to their educational opportunities. It is professionally prudent, therefore, to consistently maintain comprehensive records pertaining to students and their performance. Chapter 10 stipulates some simple but highly important ways to collect data on a continuous basis that will help adults and students to understand how well the team is functioning as well as to identify possibilities for future development.

Although every chapter contains vital information about successful team organization and operation, chapter 11 is arguably the most crucial. In its treatment of the acute matter of interpersonal relationships, the authors draw heavily from firsthand experience with teamed teachers who work conscientiously at establishing and maintaining effective relationships with each other, their students, off-team colleagues, and parents. We are not psychologists or specialists in group dynamics, so we do not presume to analyze personalities. Rather, our emphasis is on initiatives that any and all individual teachers can take to support each other and in turn to find reciprocal support.

Because we hope that many teams who use this book will develop a *written* team plan, we have provided a postlogue that includes two team plan outlines that were written by teachers in summer teaming institutes.

Many, many successful teams—a number of which are described in this book—are a direct result of teachers who committed themselves to a vision of working in new ways with each other and with their young adolescent students. Their special genius and determination have motivated us to describe their advances and to share their insights in hopes that many, many others will follow their lead.

An Important Qualification

This book has been organized to guide all interested educators in developing a viable team plan for more fully and effectively educating young adolescent students. Such work, however, is as much of the heart as it is of the mind. As is true in every visionary initiative, much of the planning will require rational contemplation and shared responsibility. Working as closely with other teachers as teaming requires is very different than what most of us have known in the past. In all likelihood, compromises will be required. In order to preserve and strengthen teamed teachers' solidarity, individuals may at times need to support initiatives that they do not personally fully embrace. Such is the nature of compromise and each individual's decision to be a part of any group's *esprit.* Through all the deliberations and planning, however, there must be a crucial constant: each team member's personal commitment. This work initially requires faith, energy, time, and resourcefulness that go beyond what most teachers have been accustomed to in the past. However, recognition of the great benefits of teaming to all concerned and commitment to one another will provide the energy and drive necessary for success. To paraphrase an observation credited to Mark Twain, "If you believe you can do it together, or if you believe you cannot—you're right."

Brief Table of Contents

Table of Contents

TEACHERS' TEAMING HANDBOOK

A Middle Level Planning Guide

BACKGROUND AND RATIONALE

A small group of committed people can change the world; and indeed, it's the only thing that ever does.
Margaret Mead

Traditionally schools have been organized around academic disciplines. Institutions of higher education appoint instructors and organize departments according to academic specialties. High schools, junior high schools, and to some extent elementary schools have followed suit; students and teachers follow daily schedules that generally allow an hour or less to each academic domain. Thus teachers and students have been organized around subject matter requirements, with little or no consideration given to designs that would be more complementary to the natural human learning processes of the students being affected.

From the beginning of the movement to reconceptualize junior high schools and to develop educational programs around what has become referred to as "the middle school concept," an abiding emphasis has been on designing programs that are responsive to the developmental needs and interests of the students. Such a need is for "small communities of learners" (Carnegie Council on Adolescent Development 1989). Interpretations of "smallness" have invariably called attention to youngsters' need to belong to groups in which it is possible for them to know their classmates and teachers well and in which teachers know a great deal more about youngsters than just their names. For adults to be able to respond effectively to their students' academic and personal needs, they need to have continuous daily interactions with a single community of students who comprise a subset of the larger school. Organizing a school by such teams enables a few teachers to create an educational community in which they know and understand students, teach them in ways that complement their abilities, enable them to be successful, and support them in multiple ways as they grow through the challenges of contemporary adolescence.

Thus interdisciplinary team organization—or "teaming," as used throughout this book—is the key structural component of exemplary middle schools. It has enormous *potential* to meet the academic and social needs of young adolescents as well as to increase the effectiveness, enjoyment, and professional development of their teachers. Teaming further offers a greater capacity for engaging parents more meaningfully in their children's education and for enhancing the climate and functioning of an entire school.

Whereas the definition and conditions of teaming may vary from school to school, most often teams are organized so that from two to five teachers representing various disciplines work together with a common group of students, share a common block schedule, and have common planning time. Team teachers include those who teach all of the core academic subjects (language arts, social studies, mathematics, and science), and in some instances special subject or special education teachers may be included. Where possible, their classrooms are in close proximity to one another, helping to define particular spaces as that team's home territory.

This format contrasts distinctly with that of the conventional junior high school, where teachers are organized by departments, operate on an externally mandated bell schedule, have little or no control over student groupings, and seldom have time to plan and coordinate instruction or other programs with colleagues. In such organizational arrangements students frequently must deal with up to ten different teachers weekly, scurry among classrooms often spread throughout the school building, and face forty-five-minute classes composed of highly diverse students with classroom procedures and expectations that reflect individual teachers' particular idiosyncrasies. In bygone years when our society was more stable and cohesive, perhaps the majority of students could function satisfactorily in schools organized along these lines. But given the increased fragmentation of contemporary society, it makes little sense to place students in such scattered and impersonal school environments.

It is important to note that interdisciplinary team organization is not synonymous with "team teaching." The latter term refers to two or more teachers who join together strictly for an instructional purpose (e.g., coteaching a traditional subject or a cross-disciplinary course or unit, sometimes in the same room) but who don't necessarily share the same students and schedule for the rest of the day. However, types of team teaching, especially those involving integrative curriculum, are sometimes used in conjunction with the more comprehensively developed interdisciplinary team.

Although various forms of teaming exist in some elementary and high schools, interdisciplinary team organization is most closely identified with the middle school movement. Since the 1960s, virtually every authority on middle level education has considered teaming as the key organizational component for restructuring schools for young adolescents. The Carnegie Council on Adolescent Development's *Turning Points: Preparing American Youth for the 21st Century* (1989) and the National Middle School Association's *This We Believe: Developmentally Responsive Middle Level Schools* (1995) stand as especially precise and forceful contemporary statements on the importance and propriety of teaming in middle-level schools.

Recent studies show accelerated utilization of teams in middle level schools. Alexander and McEwin (1989) found that 33 percent of the schools surveyed had implemented teaming, whereas Epstein and McIver (1990) set the figure at 42 percent, with an additional 28 percent responding that "they planned to develop teams within the next three years." A 1993 study by Valentine and others found that 57 percent of the schools had teaming arrangements in place. McEwin, Dickinson, and

Jenkins (1996) show that teaming is more prevalent in sixth grade (about 60 percent) than in eighth grade (about 45 percent).

Over 90 percent of the schools deemed "exemplary" in one study (George and Schewey 1994) were organized into teams. George and Schewey also concluded that students learn more, behave better, feel more positive about school and teachers, and interact better with each other, even if the school represents two or more sizable ethnic groups.

Most significantly, perhaps, most comprehensive investigation to date into the effects of teaming and other aspects of the middle school concept (Felner et al., in press) shows that the more fully innovations are implemented, the greater is student achievement. Students' positive attitudes toward themselves, each other, and the school also correlate highly with the degree of implementation of the middle school concept. In addition, an analysis by Strahan and others (1997) of thirty data-based studies of teaming published within the past nine years details a wide variety of gains for both students and teachers engaged in teaming. In sum, it seems abundantly clear that teams are increasing rapidly in schools serving ten to fourteen year old students in this country and that students are benefiting in fundamental ways.

In spite of this trend, however, additional studies (Alexander and McEwin 1989, Dickinson and Erb 1997, Felner et al., 1997) plus the authors' personal observations indicate that the majority of teams in most middle schools are not coming close to maximizing their full potential. Some of the difficulties are due to administrative or structural inadequacies, such as insufficient leadership and support; inadequate initial preparation and ongoing common planning time for teamed teachers; lack of site-based control over scheduling and grouping; and a general paucity of team autonomy. Yet, even where proper structures and supports are provided, many teams still fail to capitalize on the opportunities available to them. They fail to create a full sense of community with and among their students. Team philosophy, mission, and standards are often unclear or are not understood, especially by students. Use of planning time is often only marginally effective. Separate subjects continue to be taught on a bell schedule in a didactic manner, and curriculum integration is infrequent or even nonexistent. Students are often grouped by imprecise measures of ability, much in the manner of conventional departmentalized schools. There are too often too many disturbing signs that professional utterances about "teaming" are just so much old wine in new bottles.

What most distinguishes the *exemplary* teams we have known is a blend of vision and volition on the part of teachers. Where the educational world of young adolescents and their teachers has most substantially and successfully changed is because of their common commitment to a vision of schooling that transcends the ordinary. A partnership between child and adult generations, based on mutual trust and interpersonal bonding, has created a synergy that enables everyone involved to go well beyond what could occur in conventional settings. When anyone is privileged to observe such a community, it is readily apparent that the work and the way of life manifest are truly making a difference.

In the ensuing discussion of potential advantages and opportunities associated with effectively planned and implemented teams, it is assumed that at the very least the school community is receptive to this particular organizational change. Chapter 2 gives details about attitudes and conditions that are essential if teaming is to develop successfully.

STUDENT NEEDS FOR PERSONAL IDENTITY AND BELONGING

Perhaps the major reason why effective teams are urgently needed today is that so many young adolescents feel isolated and alone. Too many of them have numerous unfulfilled needs for a positive, optimistic view of themselves and for a sense of belonging to something that gives them pride. Schools and external activities tend to be fragmented, and the deterioration of family life contributes to students' feelings of dissociation from the traditionally central institutions in their lives. Due to the virtual loss of the extended family, high divorce rates, one-parent families, two parents often working full-time and at hours that remove them from their children, plus a host of other factors, many families lack the togetherness that developing adolescents need. Seldom do families work or play together, and meals are often a catch-as-catch-can affair. In addition, many young people receive inadequate supervision. One of our graduate students conducted an inquiry project that showed that 70 percent of the seventh graders in a rural school did not regularly have an adult at home when they left for school in the morning and when they returned in the afternoon. Another such inquiry indicated that less than 40 percent of the parents monitored the television programming that their children watched. Lack of adult supervision has always been detrimental to young adolescents, but it is especially so in our media-driven culture where they are bombarded with choices that promise immediate gratification but work against long-term growth.

Successful middle school teams work hard at creating community spirit and team identity that address students' growing-up needs. They work diligently at building strong bonds with and among students, utilizing team names, logos, mottoes, rituals, and traditions. They work together, and they play together, engaging in activities that engender the caring relationships that promote a spirit of personal belonging. They cultivate student initiative and responsibility, and they celebrate their students' accomplishments in much the same way that families need to do.

Another key ingredient in feeling a sense of belonging and identity is the opportunity to participate in and contribute to a group. Yet, many students attend large, impersonal schools that offer them little opportunity to participate in school life. By breaking a school up into a number of semiautonomous units, "smallness out of bigness" can be accomplished. Each team can have its own newsletter, plays, assemblies, intramural sports teams, student council, and so on. Virtually any activity previously offered only on a whole school basis (drama, music, publications, etc.), and thus limited to relatively few students, can become available to every student. Thus there are far more opportunities for participation, leadership, planning, and decision making in teamed schools than in conventional departmentalized ones, and every student on the team is encouraged and expected to participate. In this regard, it is especially important to remember that developmental psychologists regard *role-taking* opportunities as *key ingredients* in fostering all aspects of adolescent development: intellectual, social, emotional, physical, and moral. Effective teams rely on high levels of student participation for their success.

A particularly significant research finding is that teaming has much potential to foster racial harmony. A study by Damico (1982) concluded that black and white students in teamed schools, when compared to those in nonteamed schools, had a more positive attitude toward the opposite race, had more cross-racial friendships, and felt more positively about their schools. Four decades ago Allport (1958) in his classic, *The Nature of Prejudice,* set forth three conditions necessary for racial harmony to exist within a group: (1) desire for harmony on the part of its leaders, (2) shared goals, and (3) mutual interdependence. These are precisely the characteristics of a good team, and perhaps they explain Damico's findings.

In sum, it is abundantly clear that teaming can promote positive interpersonal relationships. Where people work together as a community, there is much greater opportunity for them to know each other better. Students are more likely to develop friendships with peers and to have meaningful contact with adults.

INTELLECTUAL AND ACADEMIC BENEFITS TO STUDENTS

The advantages of teaming from the students' perspective are not limited to the social and emotional realm, however. Effective teams also promote young adolescents' intellectual development and enhance their opportunities for academic success. By frequently discussing the needs and performance of students whom they know well in team meetings, teachers learn from each other as they share insights about students' strengths, weaknesses, interests, and abilities. It becomes far easier and more immediate for teachers to respond professionally and effectively when they are thus informed about their constituents. Some of the chief academic benefits to students are:

- Individual learning styles, interests, and dimensions of intellectual development are better understood by teachers and thus can be more effectively supported by responsive teaching/learning strategies.
- Students are helped to become better organized learners because of far greater consistency with regard to teachers' expectations, standards, and procedures.
- Students' academic progress can be monitored more efficiently, and, where they are experiencing difficulty, contracts and other interventions can be developed and administered by teachers. Moreover, students receive more cogent and frequent assessment of their progress.
- Their specialized personal interests can be better accommodated through teachers' planning of minicourses, special interest studies, independent projects, and the like.
- They can be easily moved from one class to another according to need because their teachers establish instructional groups and student placement rather than

leave such crucial decisions up to "the office" or some external computer scheduling program.

- Knowledge becomes increasingly connected, relevant, and holistic through curriculum integration that entails correlated activities planned by their teachers.
- Exceptional students in particular can be better accommodated through teaming. When teachers plan together daily, the possibilities for accommodating individual differences are greatly enhanced. Gifted students and those with handicapping conditions can both be challenged appropriately through independent study and unique projects. Appropriate mainstreaming is easier to manage, and the variety of curricular offerings makes pullout programs for both gifted and handicapped students much less necessary. Common planning time allows for frequent, convenient discussions with consultants and special education teachers, enabling the latter to function more efficiently and effectively.
- Students' time is used more effectively due to the flexible block schedule that is largely controlled by teamed teachers. Minimal time is lost to changing classes, and blocks of time lead to a far more seamless student engagement in learning.
- Students become much more actively involved in planning and managing their own learning, setting personal as well as team learning goals and planning and assessing their own progress as well as that of the team. These are the opportunities for taking initiative and demonstrating responsibility that are so vitally important to the development of young adolescents growing steadily toward more adultlike self-sufficiency. At their best, students are learning to become capable, adaptable, self-reliant young women and men.

TEACHER EFFECTIVENESS AND PROFESSIONAL DEVELOPMENT

Virtually all of the teaming benefits to students just mentioned are benefits to teachers as well. Where students' social and academic needs are being thoughtfully addressed through teaming, teachers enjoy their work more and develop a stronger sense of themselves as professionals (Gatewood et al. 1992). Indeed, the primary motivation for teachers entering their profession is to make a difference in students' lives, to help them learn, grow, and develop as competent, confident young citizens. Teaming done well ensures an academic and social context in which young adolescents learn how to be good students and good citizens, increasing the probability of their continuing that lifestyle as older adolescents and adults. The primary focus is on responsible learning and relationships, reducing the necessity for emphasis on rules and external discipline.

There are also direct and specific advantages of teaming to teachers. Teaching can be a lonely affair. In many conventional schools, teachers are largely isolated from interactions with colleagues that are meaningful and satisfying. Outside of occasional departmental meetings or in-service sessions, their contacts with colleagues are generally limited to brief encounters in the lunchroom or faculty lounge. They generally plan, teach, evaluate, and try to provide for their students' well-being on their own. We have heard numerous teachers in such situations say, in effect, "Kids are great, and I like to be with them. But it's hard, day in and day out, to be with only students. I crave more contact with my colleagues." Teaming provides teachers with the opportunity to develop *close* colleagues and an evolving organizational structure within which meaningful relationships may grow. When teachers talk and work together daily, sharing goals, exploring each other's ideas, exchanging insights about the same students, and jointly planning strategies, genuine camaraderie and friendship can flourish.

Moreover, there is opportunity to capitalize on each other's distinctive skills, abilities, and personalities. One colleague may have great insight into students' needs or learning styles, another may be excellent in building community and handling discipline, and still another may have strong skills and empathy for working with parents or administrators. Not only do these conditions provide a better education for students, they also allow teachers to mentor to and learn from one another in a natural way. Where colleagues are having difficulties, trying out new ideas, or enjoying a personal success, a support system exists. Over time, a genuine spirit of "pulling together" emerges. This network of sharing ideas, skills, and concerns is particularly helpful to new teachers as well as to student interns, providing them with continuing orientation, support, and an optimistic view of teaching.

In terms of curriculum, teaming allows teachers to develop a far more comprehensive and cohesive approach than can be accomplished when working in isolation. Because teachers share ideas about students and materials and operate in a flexible framework, they are better able to provide learning experiences that are appropriate for the students they share.

Three types of curriculum are facilitated particularly well by teaming. First, there are opportunities to meet students' and teachers' individual interests and needs through the creation of minicourses, independent studies, apprenticeships, service learning programs, and enrichment and remedial units.

Second, there is an ideal framework for creating integrative curriculum. All the necessary structural ingredients are provided by team organization: Team teachers embrace all of the core academic disciplines, teach the same groups of students, and have joint planning time. Where this structure is used by capable, committed teachers who have considerable knowledge of students' needs and interests, the potential for the most powerful and effective types of curriculum for young adolescents is greatest.

Third, substantive advisory activities can be developed. By sharing the planning of such activities, advisors can help alleviate the time crunch felt by most teachers and can capitalize on team members' knowledge of individual students as well as on their curriculum development skills.

Because of all these advantages and opportunities afforded by teaming, teachers develop a stronger sense of professional efficacy and personal empowerment. They have the authority to make important decisions about students and curriculum; they have greater control over their own scheduling and grouping; they have colleagues for support and stimulation. In many schools, teams also have a strong say in hiring decisions and have team budgets that they administer. In brief, they are treated like professionals.

In conditions such as these, a type of synergy occurs in which the whole (the team) becomes greater than the sum of its parts (individual teachers). Teachers revel in the fact that by pursuing common goals together, they accomplish a great deal more than by working alone. And they enjoy it more.

TEAMING AND PARENTS

Many parents feel a good bit of uncertainty about the schooling that their children are experiencing today. Effective teaming provides parents with opportunities for greater, more meaningful communication and involvement than typically happen in nonteamed settings. Because teachers understand their individual students more fully, they are also better able to communicate effectively with parents about individual children's needs, interests, and growth. In turn, teachers can learn a great deal more about their students by listening to the adults who know them most intimately. Thus informed, teachers can provide detailed assessment of a child's overall progress as well as make suggestions for helping at home. If an urgent need arises, all team teachers can meet with parents at the same time during common planning time. By having each advisor on a team responsible for communicating with his or her advisees' parents, teams can have more frequent home contact through notes, telephone calls, and conferences than can departmentalized teachers, who typically have daily responsibility for one hundred or more students.

Because team teachers have more control of time and curricular options, they can also utilize parents as teachers. On many teams parents may serve as tutors, minicourse leaders, independent study or apprenticeship mentors, service learning coordinators, guest presenters, or aides. Parents can also participate more effectively in supporting team events such as special celebrations, culminating events for curriculum projects, back-to-school nights, field days, and the like. Sometimes parents are enlisted in a formal capacity to promote parent understanding, participation, and support.

In the best of circumstances, teachers and parents work together on the education of the children whose care they share. Having just a few effective parent participants in the life of a team has a noticeable effect. And when parents are favorably disposed toward the work taking place with their children, word spreads as surely as when a vocal parent is unhappy with the school. Utilizing parents and developing constructive partnerships with them is a high and achievable priority for teamed teachers. When both adult groups agree on expectations and standards for young adolescents, students are much more likely to flourish.

TEAMING AND SCHOOL CLIMATE

Where the needs and concerns of students, teachers, and parents are being met through teaming, it follows that the climate and functioning of the entire school will improve. Simply put, well-teamed schools work well. Their purposes are clear to everyone. Teams are the primary groups that students and parents feel connected to. They are the most logical and effective units of school organization for developing and following through on policies and procedures. There is greater and more meaningful faculty involvement with far less need for "top-down" decision making. Administrators, especially those in large schools, can involve faculty in policy development and other decision making through regular meetings with team leaders. Conversely, administrators can stay abreast of school functioning by attending meetings with team leaders and by visiting common planning time and team meetings. Teams are also the natural units for building school spirit. Intramural programs, problem-solving contests, in-house television announcements and programs, assemblies, holiday observations, "fun days," and a host of other activities can be built around team participation.

Further, teams help create a more orderly school environment. Because classes within teams change according to their own rhythms rather than according to an arbitrary bell schedule, corridors are not periodically filled with students clamoring and rushing to the next class. Visitors frequently comment about how calm schools are where effective teaming is in place.

A consistent finding among teamed schools is that student behavior improves markedly and that disciplinary problems decline. The greater the degree of implementation of authentic middle school principles, the greater the effect (Felner et al, 1997). A key seems to be that in successfully teamed schools, teachers and students know each other better. They work together on issues related to discipline, and where rules are needed they forge them together and enforce them consistently. Instead of routinely sending students to the principal, teams handle the great majority of discipline problems themselves. Successfully teamed schools show a substantial decrease in referrals to the office and suspensions. Further and as noted earlier, students spend less time in hallways, where problems more frequently occur.

The key organizational components in most successful middle level schools are teams, advisory programs, flexible block schedules, and an exploratory curriculum. Of these, effective teams contribute most conspicuously to the overall growth and development in any school because it is in these primary groups that adults and children share their ideals, interests, and energies. It is appropriate, even, to think of a single middle level school as a composite of several effectively operating small schools (teams). Again, the vision of "smallness within bigness" associated with middle level education is realized.

In sum, teams greatly help middle level schools meet their mission of being "unique and transitional" (George and Alexander 1994). That is, they help meet the unique needs and interests of young adolescents and their teachers and parents by providing a vital program that effectively enables students to move initially from elementary school and then on to high school and the world beyond in due course. In so doing, they well illustrate Dewey's timeless admonition that "the best way to prepare children for the future is to have them live fully in the present" (1938).

ADVANTAGES OF SMALL TEAMS

Although this book is written for various team configurations, we believe that small "partner teams" consisting of two or three teachers and forty to seventy-five students have some distinct advantages over larger groupings. There are, of course, successful larger teams, but there is a marked tendency for such teams to divide the day into periods of less than an hour and to teach their subjects separately, thus replicating the junior high school departmental format that deters curriculum integration. We suspect that teaming in general and curriculum integration have not advanced as quickly as one would hope is in no small part because of the preponderance of large teams.

With partner teams virtually all of the potential advantages of teaming discussed in this chapter are magnified. In these smaller teams people get to know each other better and find agreement more easily. Because a two-teacher team has on average half as many students as a four-teacher team, there is a greater potential to create a strong spirit of belonging and community. Curriculum can be more easily attuned to students' interests and needs. Indeed, a great deal of the most innovative curriculum work we've seen has occurred in partner teams in which teachers and students apparently have been able to plan and organize their studies relatively easily. Comprehensive student-centered assessment appears to be more easily accomplished. Occurrences of student self-government are notably more frequent and more highly developed among smaller teams, and students appear to take initiative and accept responsibilities more easily in these groupings. Discipline is also less external, rule-bound, and adversarial, and student advising appears to occur more naturally throughout the day.

From the teachers' standpoint, partner teaming brings the advantage of more efficient communication between adults. Having fewer adults seems to make it easier for teachers to find agreement about philosophy and curricular planning. If those two or three teachers have their students for most of the day, it becomes much easier for them to flex the schedule and to accommodate the irregular time requirements of a more integrated curriculum. Because all partner team members often share the teaching of the core literacy and mathematics skills, their collaboration in accommodating particular student needs is easier to accomplish. Instruction and assessment in writing, reading, and mathematics, for instance, occur continuously. If there is a downside to this design from a teacher's perspective, it is likely that it has to do with the broader responsibility for cultivating students' scholarly skills in everything—not just in one's preferred subject area.

Of course, teachers on small teams must meet state licensing requirements. And simply being a small team does not guarantee success. If the partners are not compatible, conflicts may be magnified. If one teacher lacks fundamental competence, the workload will be inequitable. On a small team it is much less possible to "hide" a weak teacher. The aforementioned risks notwithstanding, the advantages of partner teaming appear to outweigh the disadvantages considerably, as long as the teachers choose to work together and are committed to the same general direction for their students and themselves.

MULTIAGE, MULTIGRADE, AND MULTIYEAR TEAMS

Although multiple year relationships do not *characterize* teaming at the middle level, we are increasingly encountering this arrangement, particularly in regard to partner teams in which students stay on the team for two or three years. In some versions students are age- and grade-mixed in classes; in other versions they may be separated into team classes by grade levels for particular activities or subjects. We have observed math classes on three-year multigrade teams, for example, in which advanced sixth graders work successfully alongside eighth graders. Chief among the many benefits of multiage team groups is that teachers have fewer new students each year than do teachers in grade-level teams. It follows that teachers and students who have established effective working partnerships in the previous year lose much less time in working out teacher-student relationships and curricular strategies. Multiyear teaming appears to be far more efficient than changing grades annually. The potential for maintaining continuous progress is a particularly attractive advantage of this arrangement.

There is presently little formal data that show the effects of multiyear teaming at the middle level, but our informal observations are that students of two or three years' difference in ages appear to work very well together and that older students fulfill teachers' expectations that they exert more positive and responsible leadership with their younger classmates. The spirit of ownership and togetherness in these teams cannot be denied, and we expect that the future will bring continuing growth and refinement of these multiyear partner teams. It is no accident that many of the exemplary teams cited in this book are organized in this manner. We hope that some users of this book will develop their teams along these lines and share their insights and suggestions as team organization at the middle level continues to evolve.

A little-used but interesting version of multiyear teacher-student relationships at the middle level is known as "student-teacher team progression" or "looping," whereby a team of teachers "moves up" with the same students, teaching them a second, and sometimes third, year in order to build on already established relationships and maintaining curriculum and assessment continuity. After the first year, looped teachers would have no new students other than the occasional transfer student. Preliminary reports (George, Spreul, and Moorefield, 1987; Lynch, 1990; Grillo, 1992) indicate that this arrangement is positively associated with students' personal and academic growth.

We recognize, however, that multiyear teacher-student relationships are not for everyone, especially teachers and parents who are less comfortable with such a significant departure from traditional organizational paradigms. In fact, given the variety of ways we have seen teams configured, it seems clear that there is no single pattern that is appropriate for all schools. And indeed, various configurations may often be used effectively within the same school. Whatever team design people may choose, we hope that the commitment to schooling that enhances children's sense of personal efficacy and their actions as learners and citizens will be considerably enhanced. The material that has been included in the following chapters was selected for its relevance to *all* teaming arrangements. Particular examples cited may or may not fit precisely with specific local conditions, but the principles apply to all teams, regardless of size.

CONSIDERATIONS IN PLANNING

What understandings and attitudes are necessary?
What decisions need to be made?
What kinds of structures and support are required?
What kinds of preparation are needed?
How long will it take us to work together successfully?

Scenario 1

A steadily deteriorating interpersonal and academic climate has beset Midville Public School System's "intermediate schools" to the point that many teachers, parents, and administrators are near desperation. Student misbehavior is at an all-time high, and there are frequent clashes among students and between students and adults. Already marginal test performance has slipped even further. Teachers have not been able to agree about causes or possible remedies for this erosion of quality and spirit, and their morale is uniformly low. Parents have complained so much to the school board that in mid-February it instructed the superintendent in no uncertain terms "to straighten things out."

After a consultant advises that each of the system's five schools be reorganized into interdisciplinary teams, the superintendent calls key central office administrators and principals together to develop a teaming strategy for the next fall. Two after-school workshops for teachers as well as an evening meeting for parents are held in late spring to explain the forthcoming changes. During the summer the principals and assistant principals in each school form grade-level teams of four core teachers (math, science, English, social studies) and one special subject teacher (foreign language, music, art, health, or physical education) to work with groups of 100 to 125 students. During the summer teachers learn by letter who their teammates will be and that schedules and class lists will be handed out when they return for an in-service session at the end of August. The letter further implies that teaming will be instituted for a year "to see how it works in Midville."

Scenario 2

Members of the four-teacher Pathfinder Team, who began their work together with high hopes two years ago, are quite frustrated. With great interest they have read about and have visited teams that promote student growth and achievement, develop curriculum, and collaborate as professionals in exciting ways. Yet, somehow teaming isn't working for them quite that way. After weeks of discussion, they decide to list their specific concerns with an eye toward discussing them with Ms. Carson, the principal. The list includes the following items:

- The two periods per week that we have for common planning are not enough. Though we meet after school when we all can, we are not able to keep up with student needs or initiate any new types of curriculum very effectively.
- There is growing tension between students in different classes that you assigned on the basis of achievement tests and past grades. Students are quite aware of their group status, and they see each other in terms of pecking orders. Also, some students in the same class don't get along well. We would like to be able to separate some of them, but we can't do so under present grouping policies.
- Because the bell schedule is set, we can't alter the length of classes as we need. In particular, we need more time for science labs and various curriculum projects, plus a less disruptive way to arrange guest speakers and plan special events.
- Pullouts for gifted and special education programs are especially exasperating. Because pulled-out-of-class students miss key ideas and experiences, we have to repeat assignments or give them extra work. In addition, it is extremely difficult to find any time to meet with special education teachers. We would prefer to have them work with students in our classes rather than have them pulled out.
- There is no time to meet with the unified arts and other special subject teachers who work with our students, so we don't have much communication with them. We would like to correlate some of our efforts with theirs and collaborate with them on an interdisciplinary project.

Scenario 3

Scott and Marie teach self-contained sixth grades in adjoining rooms at Joyce Kilmer Middle School. During a fall faculty meeting about teachers' curriculum plans for the year, they learn that they are both planning in the spring to teach units about their state of Maryland. Because Scott's interests and educational background are in environmental studies, he is planning to emphasize the Chesapeake Bay estuary and its ecosystems. Marie's specialization in social studies is naturally leading her to emphasize the rich history and culture of the area. Their idea exchanges lead to, "What if we teamed our students for these units and taught together?" Although these units would not be taught for several months, Scott and Marie's conversation takes on a new intensity. Both quickly recognized the benefits to their students that could come from the other teacher's knowledge and expertise. They begin to think about the potential for combining and grouping their students for other parts of the curriculum as well. They grow increasingly excited about the prospects inherent in teaching together. Very soon their questions about how to proceed in this emerging new collaboration outstrip their answers.

Scenario 4

Many of the teachers at Cutting Edge Middle School pride themselves on their reputation for professionalism in their community. For a decade they have been organized into interdisciplinary teams of five to six teachers with approximately 125 students organized around a seven-period school day. The school also has a teacher advisory program that meets once a week. Parents in their affluent community have high expectations for their children and the school, and Cutting Edge benefits from their generous financial as well as moral support.

Several teachers and the administrators have expressed their concern, however, that although students do well in terms of grades and standardized test performance, something seems to be missing. Although students generally do what they're assigned to do and behave themselves reasonably well, they also exhibit an indifferent, even mindless, attitude about their schooling. Inquiries by teachers confirm their suspicion that even their most successful students see little in the curriculum that they regard as authentic and relevant in their lives. Yet, they seem to be comfortably conforming to the school's expectations in apparent faith that they are doing what is expected of them.

One segment of the faculty accepts the school as "good enough," and those teachers are generally satisfied with their own circumstances. Others believe, however, that young adolescents have an even greater potential for gaining intellectual and academic engagement, for developing personal initiatives and responsibilities, and for giving back to both their school and the larger community. In a rare and exemplary professional initiative, members of this core of teachers challenge their colleagues to join them in dialogue to look beyond the best of what they are already doing in their school.

Scenario 5

Because a pilot three-teacher team at Sidwell Friends Middle School in Washington, D.C., has been so successful, members of the entire faculty decide that they want to form teams also. A primary consideration is, "How should teachers be grouped?" All teachers wish to work with colleagues with whom they are philosophically compatible, but they also realize that maintaining balance in terms of skill, experience, gender, and other variables is important.

As professionals in a Quaker school, faculty members are accustomed to making key decisions that affect teaching and learning. They decide to appoint a "teaming committee" composed of the principal and four teachers to make teaming recommendations for the faculty to consider. They direct the committee to first ask faculty members to name confidentially several people with whom they would especially like to work and any others with whom they would not like to work.

Two weeks later, the committee presents a proposed slate of teams during faculty meeting. A lively discussion follows. "This team is too strong" and "This team has too many young teachers on it" and "This team all has one teaching style" are some of the comments heard. A few alternative suggestions are offered, and some teachers volunteer to move to other teams. The teaming committee goes back to the drawing board. The next week, a second slate of teams is presented, but once again, faculty members are not satisfied. Suggestions are again noted, so the committee comes back the third week with still another slate. Though this final slate does not perfectly satisfy everyone, all agree that this is the best that can be done for the good of the whole. Consensus is achieved.

COMMENTARY

The dogmas of the quiet past are inadequate to the stormy present. . . . As our case is new, so we must think anew and act anew.

Abraham Lincoln

These scenarios reflect a decision-making continuum that represents a range of actual practices in our schools. From Midville's top-down mandate to Sidwell Friends's teacher-vested authority, the central concern is about who makes what decisions and how they are accomplished. We believe that the most sensible and promising way to prepare for any substantial school innovation is to seek a partnership that includes everyone who will be affected by the change. That means that the process may be more gradual than many of us would like, and it often requires reconsiderations about authority. However, recognizing that people want to have some say in their destiny, prudent folk look for ways to collaborate in planning changes.

Scenario 1 about the Midville School System is all too familiar. Schools and teachers have long suffered from such well-intended, top-down, knee-jerk responses to problems and needs. It sometimes seems as if our accepted but unofficial slogan is, "We'll try anything for a year." But rarely do such thoughtless approaches work well or last very long.

The Midville administration obviously knows little about the intricacies of teaming and is looking for a quick fix. It has rushed into a complex and important restructuring of its middle level schools with woefully inadequate planning, and the very people who are expected to implement the changes have been excluded from the planning process. None of the conditions necessary to support teaming is in place, and teachers have had only the meagerest staff development.

The best that one could hope for from Midville would be that arbitrarily grouped teachers discover that they enjoy collaborating and decide to do some activities together. They might then commit themselves to a more enlightened collaboration that would grow into a viable team program. A far more probable and regrettable outcome, however, is that teams so belatedly informed and inadequately prepared will continue to struggle with the same problems they already know, and after a year or so everyone will concur either that "teaming doesn't work" or perhaps more mordantly that "teaming doesn't work for *our kids.*"

To reorganize people abruptly in such a superficial way tells teachers that the change is not an important one. After all, who knows better than teachers that authentic change is usually complex and requires careful thought and planning? They also know deep down that more than anything else change depends on the combination of their personal and collective commitment balanced by strong conviction and support from their administration. Parents are likely to interpret the change to teaming at first as a commitment on the administration's part to address their concerns about their children. But when and if the conditions that precipitated their original actions persist, they will become disillusioned. In either case, kids' perceptions of it all—teaming and education in general—will continue to depreciate the quality of attitude, expectations, and accomplishments of which they are capable. Everyone loses.

Although the Pathfinder teachers in Scenario 2 are well motivated, understand the potential of teaming, and have good ideas, they are highly frustrated by inadequate support. Insufficient common planning time, little control over scheduling and grouping, and isolation from special subject teachers are staggering problems, and the teachers lack the authority to make their team really work.

Unfortunately, this is another all-too-common situation that belies poor preparation. Apparently key decision makers haven't realized the scope of teamed teachers' needs. In such situations, teaming often reverts to the teaching of separate subjects on a bell schedule. Fortunately, the Pathfinders are aware of the bind that the lack of supporting structures places them in, and they are taking the first step toward ameliorating their situation by informing the principal of specific difficulties.

The evolution of interest in collaboration and questions about teaming evidenced by Scott and Marie in Scenario 3 bodes well for them. On their own they have already recognized some promising opportunities, and given their reciprocated respect, the common sense of further collaboration already appeals to them. They want to build on their own individual strengths as well as each other's, and they appear ready to explore some new collaborative opportunities. In order for them to see the full range of possibilities, it is important that they visit successfully functioning teams in other schools and exchange perceptions and ideas for their own team. Ideally they will be able to learn how other teachers have addressed some of the issues and questions that they confront. They will also benefit from reading about team organization. It will also be important that they gain the support of colleagues, parents, and students by communicating the emerging plan and their commitment to it to each other and to the students they will share. Likewise crucial to their ultimate success are the trust, advocacy, and concrete support of their school administration. Principals *must* see their professional role in terms of doing what they can to support teachers like these who are seeking to create the very best matches possible with their students. It is teachers such as Scott and Marie who have pioneered successful teaming and provided so much of the data for this book.

The developing state of affairs at Cutting Edge Middle School in Scenario 4 is particularly hopeful because of the teachers' vision and commitment to go beyond the best of the school's current practice. It would be foolhardy to assume that every teacher would be equally enthusiastic about such things as the schoolwide student indifference that teachers have observed. Although not all faculty are involved, a core of concerned teachers is *looking beyond* the program that it is responsible for and *looking directly at* the effects and results of adolescent life in its school community. Such teachers exhibit professional expectations of themselves that should characterize every school. Assuming a responsive administration, this situation bodes well for meaningful, enduring evolution relative to how their school is organized and will function.

Scenario 5 about Sidwell Friends Middle School illustrates several key principles in selecting teachers who will work together on teams, a very crucial consideration in planning: (1) Faculty, the people who are going to carry out teaming, should play a major role in determining teams. In forming a teaming committee, the principal was willing to give up considerable "control," and teachers were accepting responsibility for the outcome. (2) To the greatest extent feasible, teachers should choose the colleagues with whom they would like to team. (3) A balance relative to faculty expertise, experience, teaching style, leadership, rapport with students, gender, race, and a host of other variables must also be taken into account. (4) A good bit of communication and collaboration between the principal and faculty members is necessary.

It should be noted that the selection process took time. A process was set up whereby everyone's opinions could be heard both individually and collectively, and there was time for reflection and reconsideration. By having faculty so involved in the process, there was no mumbling or grumbling about the outcome. All faculty members did not get exactly what they wished for, but everyone realized that that was impossible and that the results were equitable and best for the school as a whole.

Not every school, of course, can use a process such as this one. Where schools are large, or new schools are being created, or several are being consolidated, faculty members may not know each other well enough to guide the entire process. Nevertheless, the principles set forth earlier should guide team selection. (See Example 1 at the end of the chapter for a continuum of team selection possibilities. See Example 2 for a teacher preference form.)

With regard to schools where teaming is already in place, circumstances can require some teams to be reconfigured. These circumstances may include a changing number of students in a grade level, personality clashes, or imbalances among teams. However, unless there are compelling reasons to make changes, we strongly prefer to keep existing teams intact. It takes several years for teams to function optimally, and changes in membership can slow progress considerably. Unfortunately, due to the circumstances just mentioned plus the mobility of teachers generally, there are relatively few "mature teams" whose members have worked together five or more years. Where such teams exist, they often serve as models and mentors for other teams.

The preparation for planning that is needed to support teaming will vary somewhat from place to place. For example, where a single alternative team within one school is being formed, little if any planning on the part of an entire school *system* is necessary. On the other hand, where a whole system is establishing teams (usually as a major part of the conversion to middle schools from junior high or K–8 schools), detailed planning is essential.

In the former case, teachers who wish to work together or who are aware of teaming can collaborate with the principal to create a plan. After ensuring school board support, they can develop a design according to their priorities. The students and parents who elect to become part of the alternative team are the ones who most need to be well informed and included in a planning process that complements the teachers' initiatives.

In the latter case, however, an ideal systemwide plan may involve a steering committee, task forces, a planning document, extensive staff development, and a great deal of community education. (See Example 3.) It is crucial that all constituents understand and be involved in the planning process: school board members, central office administrators, building administrators, teachers representing established specializations, parents, and students. It is also necessary to allow plenty of time for the change, ideally two years in a large system. Finally, *everyone* needs to be kept informed.

Regardless of the scope of the transition to interdisciplinary team organization, a number of key supportive conditions or structures need to be in place if teaming is to approach its potential and achieve teaming's considerable potential (Arnold 1997).

Teachers must have considerable say in deciding about the size as well as the composition of teams. Their voice is important in forming new teams as well as in shifting faculty among existing teams. As chapter 1 indicates, we have found that two or three teachers teamed with forty to seventy students seem to evolve more rapidly and completely than large teams. The great strength of small "partner" teams is that students and teachers work closely together and therefore know each other more intimately. Small team arrangement may not always be possible, however, owing to teacher preference and experience, licensing restrictions that vary from state to state, and other considerations. Various teaming patterns may exist within the same school.

Core teachers must have common planning during the school day; this provision is an *absolute necessity*. Time for these meetings usually occurs while students are attending special subject classes such as art, music, and physical education. Often schools can provide just a single planning period that must accommodate both individual and team planning. Even if the schedule allows a daily planning period, it will not be uncommon for teachers to meet before or after school as well as to talk on the telephone from time to time. In order to achieve the coherence and continuity that teaming promises, we urge that whenever possible two periods be provided: one for individual preparation and one for joint planning. Increasingly, schools that are serious about teaming are providing these two periods. (The National Commission on Teaching and America's Future reports that in Germany,

Japan, and China, teachers spend fifteen to twenty hours per week working with colleagues, observing other teachers, and participating in study groups. These teachers state that they could not succeed if forced to work under conditions prevalent in most American schools [cited by Holland, 1997].)

To the greatest extent possible teams must have control over student groupings and scheduling. More than anyone else in the school, core teachers know best how time can be used effectively and who should be grouped with whom for various purposes. An ideal master schedule (Example 5) ensures large blocks of time that teamed teachers can apportion in ways they deem most appropriate in order to address their students' needs and academic goals. Teachers can lengthen or shorten periods as needed; create extra periods for labs, projects, speakers, films, and so forth; rotate the order of classes; or use an entire block of time for an activity. Administrators planning school master schedules should avoid "pullout problems" to the greatest extent possible. In addition to causing dissension and making students feel singled out, pullouts destroy block schedules because teachers have to plan around pullout periods. If such programs must occur, they are best scheduled at the beginning or end of the block.

With regard to grouping, teams are ideally given a heterogeneous mix of students whom they can group in accordance with individual and team goals, moving students from one class to another according to needs. They can also create special groupings for minicourses, projects, interdisciplinary work, skill development, simulations and dramas, and so forth. The essence of this issue is that teachers are in the best position to determine how to organize their students and apportion time in order to accomplish their educational goals. In initially assigning students to teams, it is wise to give teachers who taught them previously a strong voice in assignments. In the late spring of subsequent years, team teachers may assign their students to teams at the next level.

When teams work best, teachers are exercising a good bit more authority in conceptualizing, organizing, and implementing an educational program than when they are departmentalized. Their responsibilities are not limited to "covering curriculum," but they are supported in bringing about a program that complements their students' needs and interests and that in turn engenders students' responsibility and performance. Their authority is also extended to decisions about curriculum, instruction, and evaluation. Accordingly, there should be flexibility for teachers to develop their own ideas and strategies about how best to achieve their students' skill and concept development. In our experience, committed teachers rise to this opportunity, applying their insights and ideas to bring about productive partnerships with each other and their students. It is vital that everyone understand this change from conventional expectations and requirements, confident that with appropriate and ample preparation and continuing support, schooling for young adolescents can be transformed to better accommodate their developmental circumstances.

Because virtually everyone has attended conventional schools, we probably tend to think in terms of students being organized by age into what are called "grades," daily schedules based on units of forty-five minutes, and curriculum organized as separate core subjects and electives. Given our familiarity with this paradigm, it will be difficult for some of us to envision a form of schooling that transcends this model. Some of us may even reject outright the suggestion that there is a better way to organize schools for young adolescent learners. And even the most visionary of us needs to examine and question thoughtfully both the tenets of team organization as well as individual examples of teaming.

When confronted with descriptions of teams, many will understandably have questions such as those that introduce this chapter. For example, we may wonder about students' working the majority of their time with two or three teachers who not only bring a special subject expertise, but who also may be generalists in teaching basic academic skills. We may naturally speculate about differences in content coverage on a team compared with programs organized around a more traditional separate subject schedule. And it is common for parents to wonder how their children will handle high school if they've spent their middle grades on a team. Therefore, laying the groundwork for successful teaming requires a dual process of research and invention.

At a bare minimum teachers must understand the concept and central principles of team organization if their own eventual design is to be well conceived. Reading, visiting already established teams, and discussing are natural ways of exploring the concept both in theory and in practice. In the best of circumstances, teachers will grow into true colleagues who are

> "working together, debating about goals and purposes, coordinating lessons, observing and critiquing each other's work, sharing successes and offering solace, with all the triumphs of their collective efforts far exceeding the summed accomplishments of their solitary struggles." (Johnson 148)

For a long time there has been a good bit of public and professional dissatisfaction with the effects of schools, and the momentum for change in practice comes from multiple sources. Countless initiatives—many of them quite useful and effective—have emerged from our schools. What ultimately changes the ways schooling evolves, however, is how teachers work together toward common purposes. Team organization as described in this book stipulates crucial aspects of planning that professionals who are serious about undertaking fundamental change should incorporate in their process. All of the other initiatives and educational models that proliferate become particularly relevant when they are considered by teachers working in a context and relationship that they have designed together and to which they share commitment.

PRINCIPLES

- **Participating teachers, principals, and their supervisors understand and are committed to team organization for educating adolescent students.**

It is crucial that everyone closely involved comprehend the central elements of teaming and the structural requirements of time, space, and autonomy necessary for teachers to develop a viable program. Teachers must be committed to pursuing educational designs based on a sound knowledge of the nature and needs of young adolescents and team organization, and they must be assured of the support of their supervisors. The kinds of changes sought in teaming require understanding and support from all professionals associated with the school.

- **Teaming requires significant structural changes and allowances in schools previously organized according to the traditional junior high or K–8 school paradigm.**

  Elementary schools are usually organized around self-contained classrooms, and secondary schools are typically organized by departments. Successful middle level schools evolve an organizational framework that affects teachers' responsibilities, the master schedule, curriculum organization, and much of the administration of school regulations such as homework and testing schedules and classroom management procedures.

- **Teaming necessitates greater decision-making authority and responsibility for teachers.**

  Although teams may develop programs that resemble each other, responsibility for developing them is vested more in the teamed teachers than in the school administration, which was almost totally relied upon in the past. When teams develop rapidly and function well, teachers have substantially increased control over their daily schedule in order to create larger blocks of instructional time. They are also assured of daily time for team planning, and they must have the authority to organize curriculum, group students, and develop governance procedures as long as those decisions are compatible with their system's or school's mandated policies.

- **Everyone recognizes teaming as an evolutionary process.**

  Such substantial changes in how any school is organized to better serve its students do not happen quickly. Letting go of old ways of doing things takes time and cumulative experience for teachers and students. Teams that have endured for more than a few years have *evolved.* Their current practices are rooted in an earlier time, but they also show evolution from their initial iteration. The first year establishes a basic format for how the team will begin functioning, and it is natural to find through firsthand experience that some ideas and designs work better than others. In subsequent years the team will show continuity from the beginning with contemporary refinements and changes. Truly dynamic teams evidence incremental growth over time, and everyone needs to understand and expect that kind of program evolution.

PLANNING GUIDELINES

1. *To everyone concerned:* **Inform yourself**!

   Exercise your own curiosity and scholarly dispositions for inquiry and exploration by finding out what other teams do. Read, visit other teams and schools, consult with teamed teachers for guidance, talk among yourselves, exchange visions and ideas about how teams might be configured in your school. Get to know the practices associated with effective teaming so that your planning will be as thoroughly informed as possible. Just as if you are planning a move into another culture, investigate in every way possible to become as well informed as possible for the team that you will be part of. A list of print and video resources is included at the end of this book.

2. *Involve teachers in decisions about team assignments and put together teachers who want to work together.*

   People who choose to work together can accomplish remarkable things, but it is foolhardy to expect teachers who don't like each other to team successfully. Although teams often flourish as a result of differing teacher specialties and teaching styles, common goals are an *essential precondition.* Contrasting goals will likely turn into conflicting goals. Therefore, teachers should be as fully involved as possible in decisions about how team membership will be configured and especially about with whom they will be teamed. Although the principal must of necessity take responsibility for the ultimate decision, teachers should be as involved as possible in deciding who will be teammates. (See Examples 1 and 2.)

3. *Clarify authority and grant teams considerable autonomy.*

   If teachers are to have responsibility for creating a successful team, they must also have the freedom and authority to make the decisions that will enable them to do so. In brief, it is vital that teachers be authorized to establish team goals and to define team policies that are consistent with schoolwide and systemwide goals and policies. It is also appropriate that they be able to organize teaching time, grouping practices, and the curriculum so that they may pursue their stated goals and policies. The issue of team governance is thematic to this book, especially in chapter 5 ("Governance"), but suffice it to say that for teachers to create a viable team organization, they must have the authority and support to do what needs to be done. Teachers who are not trusted to make significant decisions about their work are unlikely to give students many opportunities to assume responsibility for their own learning. Every school administrator must examine issues of authority and autonomy openly and conscientiously so that there will be no confusion about the conditions under which teachers are expected to function. There should be no doubt or uncertainty on this point. Where entire schools or school systems are establishing teams, it is advisable to put team expectations in writing. (See Example 3.)

4. *Provide the organizational structures necessary to support effective teaming.*

   Develop a comprehensive plan where an entire system is changing to teamed middle schools. A heterogeneous group of students, common planning time, a flexible block schedule, and control over grouping, as noted earlier, are essential if teaming is to realize its potential. Also, be wary of "pullout" programs. See Example 5 for an ideal block schedule that facilitates various aspects of learning.

5. *Allocate necessary time and resources for planning.*

   The opening scenario of this chapter is a blueprint for disaster. Mandates, no matter how enlightened they may be, will not assure that teachers are disposed or able to produce what is being sought. A complete team plan delineates an array of policies and procedures that reflect an evolutionary, negotiated process. As such, it should be developed over a period of months as a reflection of the natural evolution of goals and strategies. In all-school and all-system transitions to teaming, extensive in-service work is a must. Although an individual plan may or may not be written down according to the format recommended in this book, the abundance of issues that require an agreed-upon design is such that teachers need time and opportunity to work together to come to the design that they can support and implement. As will be shown later, this design is expected to evolve according to shifting priorities and agendas that necessitate ongoing evaluation and follow-up planning.

6. *Have each team develop its own, unique* ***written*** plan.

   This plan, which should include provisions for the topics discussed in chapters 4–11, is extremely helpful in enabling teachers to think through important issues and to have an organized, comprehensive approach to teaming. Beginning teams with written plans in hand will be able to hit the ground with their feet moving; experienced teams will be able to refine and elaborate their current practice by developing such plans. Appendix I presents an extensive team plan written by teachers in one of our summer institutes on teaming.

7. *Commit to teaming for the long haul.*

   Although lots of teams have functioned remarkably well early on, in all likelihood the greatest benefits for everyone will become more evident in the second and third years. It is not uncommon for a team's initial plan to be somewhat uncertain, even ragged. Therefore, it is essential that everyone understand that just as with any new experience, everything won't work as smoothly as it was designed to do. It is similarly important to remember that students don't understand teaming yet because they have never experienced it. Given their limited experience of how school should work, they may even initially challenge the whole idea. Give the process time and unwavering support; you will need to grow together. Avoid as much as possible changing teachers on a team more frequently than is absolutely necessary. Teachers need time to grow and change *together,* and the continuity of adult relationships is an extremely important ingredient in success. Team organization is an evolutionary process that takes time.

8. *Keep others informed.*

   Public and professional interest in schooling is at an all-time high, so any innovative plan will generate curiosity. Chapter 8 addresses communication strategies and urges that the plan for teaming include ways to communicate with multiple constituencies outside the immediate membership of the team, especially parents, colleagues, central office, and interested public. Students will be able to handle most of the writing and publishing activities of a team newsletter and the school paper. Periodic formal presentations about the team by teachers and students promote the quality of understanding that will help generate the confidence of others.

CAVEATS

Organizing middle level teachers and young adolescent students into "small communities for learning" makes possible a promising new opportunity for academic and pedagogical advances as well as for healthy socialization and growth toward good citizenship (Carnegie Council on Adolescent Development 1989). Although this vision of schooling is based on a recognition of students' developmental needs, it also reflects an optimism and confidence in the students themselves. Two hundred years ago young adolescents were forced by the survival circumstances of eighteenth-century life to accept quite a lot of responsibility for themselves and for others, especially family members. Although few of us would choose to return to that era, we are well advised not to underestimate the extent to which young adolescents can and should take greater responsibility for themselves today. Team organization should always be seen as a serious opportunity for students to grow toward more adultlike forms of personal accountability under the guidance of teachers who appreciate the special opportunities that teaming provides.

Given the contrast of teaming to departmental and self-contained school organization, it is crucial that adequate attention be given to learning how various teams work as well as to the planning that teachers must do to create a team plan that has the greatest prospect for success. A year of consistent study and planning is reasonable preparation, but if a whole school or system is not involved, it is also possible to get ready in less time. Some of the most effective teams we have seen were designed over the summer months and implemented in the fall term. Teachers who are positively disposed toward teaming and who are able to work with chosen colleagues are capable of surprising accomplishments. The keys are disposition, preparation, and support.

Finally, the importance of understanding and commitment to team organization by all constituents cannot be overly stressed. School board members, superintendents, administrators, teachers and other staff, and students and their parents must understand how teaming differs from the traditional paradigm of schooling that virtually all adults experienced when they were emerging adolescents. With support from all these interested groups and a special commitment to ideas, time, and energy by teachers, remarkable educational advances can be accomplished.

EXAMPLES

1. Team Selection Criteria/Strategies

(Authors)

Factors to Consider

- Personal and philosophical compatibility
- Areas of licensure
- Competence

– Experience
– Relationship with students
– Discipline/community-building skills
– Creativity
– Arts/making/doing skills
– Leadership/organizational skills
– Learning styles

Continuum of Selection Strategies

Faculty committee decides	Faculty input to principal (preference surveys, sociograms, learning style inventories)	Principal alone decides

2. Team Preference Form (see p. 27–28)
(Authors)

Your preferences and the information you supply are very important in forming teams for our school. Please fill out this form thoughtfully and frankly; it will be kept *confidential.*

We will try to put together teams that (1) have teachers who are compatible with one another and (2) are reasonably balanced in terms of experience, gender, race, and so forth. Teams do not have to be the same size. We probably will have a mixture of two-, three-, and four-teacher teams. Although it is impossible for all teachers to be teamed with exactly whom they want, we will strive to make selections based on "the good of the whole."

3. Framework For Team Planning
(Danville, VA Middle Schools)

Scheduling—There will be a core block schedule which team teachers can "flex" at their discretion. Classes do not have to be taught in any particular order for any set length of time. Teachers may agree to lengthen or shorten classes to accommodate labs, speakers, films, special projects, etc. Overall, however, there is the expectation that the schedule will be balanced, with each subject given sufficient time. Two exploratory courses, during which time team and individual planning occurs, will be scheduled back-to-back on a grade-level basis by the office.

Grouping Students—Each team will be assigned a heterogeneous group of students, balanced for race, gender, achievement, and personal characteristics. (The one exception will be the Bonner AG teams—one per grade level.) Within the team, it is important to provide appropriate challenges for all students. Students will be grouped and regrouped continuously throughout the year based on their academic performance, interests, or personal characteristics. Whatever the grouping pattern

TEAM PREFERENCE FORM
(Confidential)

Name ____

(circle) Sex: M F Race: Black White Hispanic Other

Years of teaching experience _______ Years teaching 11–14-year-olds _______

Current school ______________________________________

Areas of certification/endorsement ___________________________

1. Person I'd *most* like to have on my team ______________________

2. Others I'd be interested in teaming with ______________________

____

____

3. Name of person(s) I would *not* like to team with ________________

____

4. Size of team I would most prefer (rank order 1–4; 1 = first choice)

   2 teachers_____ 3 teachers_____ 4 teachers______ 4+ teachers_______

5. Subjects I'd most like to teach (rank order; 1=first choice)

   Language Arts_____ Social Studies_____ Math______ Science______

   Other (specify and include in ranking)___________________

6. How interested are you in gaining an endorsement in another subject if funding is available? (circle)

   Not Interested Somewhat Interested Very Interested Definitely Plan To

7. If you do seek another endorsement, in what subject? _______________

8. How do you feel about teaming in general? (circle)

   Not Interested Slightly Interested Interested Very Interested

9. Have you had experience in teaming? If so, please describe it briefly.

10. What do you consider to be your greatest strengths as a teacher?

11. What concerns about yourself, if any, do you have in reference to teaming?

12. Briefly, how do you hope that your team will function?

Additional comments, if any (continue on back if necessary):

employed, teachers will develop and use a variety of ways for differentiating and personalizing curriculum and teaching/learning strategies. All students will be expected to master the revised Standards of Learning (SOLs) and to achieve at the highest level possible. The rigor of the SOLs in each subject area is comparable to or exceeds the course of study for classes previously designated as advanced.

Common Planning Meetings—Since team teachers are provided two planning periods–one team and one personal—it is expected that they meet jointly for at least an average of 45 minutes per day. Usually this will amount to one period daily. However, on occasion teams may wish to plan together for a double period one day and skip the next day. Tending to personal affairs is to be done during the personal planning period, not team planning. Grade-level meetings during common planning time will be held about once a month.

All-Team Meetings—All-Team Meetings, which include students and teachers, should be held at least once every two weeks, probably using an extended advisory period.

Team Log—Notes/minutes of common planning and all-team meetings should be kept in a team notebook.

Team Leaders—will be chosen by the teams.

Team Leader Meetings—will be held with the principals once every two weeks.

Curriculum—Each team is expected to develop and teach at least one substantive interdisciplinary unit this first year. In addition, teams are to seek ways to make the day-to-day curriculum as interrelated as possible. Teachers are to provide appropriate academic and developmental focus, personalized challenge and support for all students, and applied learning through exciting, interest-based activities.

Relations with Exploratory Teachers—One or two exploratory teachers will be *affiliated* with each team. They will have advisees from the team, and efforts should be made to keep them informed of pertinent team issues. In addition, team teachers are urged to work as closely as possible with their student's exploratory teachers, searching for ways to correlate/integrate material, share insights about students, etc.

Special Education—Depending upon numbers, one special education teacher will work with several teams on a "consultative teacher" model basis and will meet for common planning with team teachers as much as possible. Special education students will be members of a team and an advisory group and will attend all-team meetings.

4. Steps in Systemwide Transitioning to Middle Schools
(Adapted from High Point Public Schools)

1. Have a vision and commitment, based primarily on early adolescent needs.
2. Form a steering committee representing all constituencies.
3. Secure a knowledgeable consultant.
4. Place a knowledgeable and respected person in charge of the transition.
5. Develop a written philosophy and comprehensive plan for curriculum and instruction, organizational structure, that the school board officially approves.
6. Set up subcommittees for curriculum, organization, facilities, personnel, and other components with goals and timelines.

House					
6th* Grade House	**A/A**	CORE SUBJECTS, LUNCH			**Exploratory Courses** Indiv. and Team Planning
7th* Grade House	**A/A**	**Exploratory Courses** Indiv. and Team Planning	CORE SUBJECTS, LUNCH		
8th* Grade House	**A/A**	CORE SUBJECTS	**Exploratory Courses** Indiv. and Team Planning	CORE SUBJECTS, LUNCH	

* Houses could be multi-age

[shaded] = Exploratory Teachers Individual & Team Planning + Lunch

7. Formulate an extensive plan for staff development.
8. Implement the program.
9. Provide an on-site master teacher to help teachers if possible.
10. Develop an ongoing plan for maintenance and improvement, including orientation for new faculty, staff development, and parents.

• *Tips*

– Allow plenty of planning time.
– Keep everyone informed.

THE VITAL ROLE OF THE PRINCIPAL

What is the principal's role in organizing teams?
What will be his/her relationship to teams? To team leaders?
What kinds of support and guidance will teachers need?
How will authority and decision making be affected?
What problems are likely to arise?
How can harmful competition be avoided?

Scenario 1

Russell Clarke, principal of Greenville Junior High School, organizes a program improvement committee (PIC) composed of interested parents and teacher volunteers for the purpose of examining middle level innovations such as team organization, teacher advisory programs, integrated curriculum, and the like. Although the committee has no authority to make policy, it exists as an efficient way for interested volunteers to explore new possibilities and report what they find to the whole staff. The committee gets under way by meeting two to three times a month during the fall term. Initially committee members talk a lot, exchanging perceptions and ideas from a variety of readings about exemplary practices. Clarke sits in on most of the meetings, listening intently, raising pertinent questions from time to time, and thanking people for their contribution. By the end of the fall term several PIC members offer to make one-day visits to schools where teams are well established. Clarke arranges substitutes for teachers who want to participate, and on one occasion he joins a visitation group to learn more about how teaming works from the principal's perspective. After reports from visits to just three sites, there is widespread interest within the PIC about introducing teaming to Greenville. Clarke publicly compliments the PIC, expresses his personal enthusiasm for teaming, and proposes that the faculty begin planning a transition to team organization.

Scenario 2

For several years some teachers at the Tuttle Middle School in South Burlington, Vermont, have been aware of teaming in other schools. Their discussion is peppered with expressions of apprehension and doubts as well as with genuine interest in what teaming might be like in their school. Dave Ford, Tuttle's new principal, decides to take the initiative during the fall term by meeting privately with all faculty members to ascertain their interest in and understanding of the dynamics of teaming. Further, promising complete and absolute confidentiality, he asks all teachers with whom they would like to work as well as with whom they would *not* like to work in the close relationship that teaming requires. For several weeks Ford makes trial configurations of teams that take into consideration teachers' personal preferences, teaching styles, and certification. On the Friday marking the beginning of a week-long school holiday, he presents each teacher with a sealed envelope containing an explanation of the selection process he has followed and a *tentative* team assignment for that teacher for the next school year. He further asks that teachers reflect on his proposal over the vacation week and let him know their reactions upon their return. Virtually every teacher expresses satisfaction with his or her assignment, thus team planning for the next year is able to begin at midyear and continue through the summer.

Scenario 3

Every Thursday morning either Principal James Morgan or Assistant Principal Diane Causby attends the forty-minute daily planning meeting of teachers on the Wildthings Team. They also make a biweekly review of the Wildthings Team book, in which daily team activities and decisions are documented. One Thursday meeting focuses on individual students. In their discussion teachers report that several students have unusually strong mathematics abilities. Because a similar realization had surfaced in another team a few days earlier, Principal Morgan volunteers to inquire about students with unusual capacities on all teams. This initiative fuels a subsequent discussion at the Team Leaders' meeting about offering special support across teams for students with exceptional abilities in mathematics.

Scenario 4

The fifty-five students and two teachers on the Wings Team are hosting the culminating event for a six-week study of family history and futures called "Roots and Shoots." Students have studied their own families by collecting information, photos, and lots of stories from and about family members. A team survey has produced additional information about family members' hobbies, pets, travels, and favorites (books, food, movies, music, etc.) that students have published in booklet form. The evening's agenda includes some formal presentations by students about what they have learned, speculations about their own future lives, refreshments made from favorite family recipes, and a demonstration of music and dance favorites of their parents and grandparents. Dr. Spence, the principal, moves through the crowd of guests in a perceptive and sensitive way, complimenting students for their work, welcoming parents and other family members, congratulating them for their accomplishments and contributions. The following morning Spence delivers a brief note of formal congratulations and appreciation to be read at the Wings Team meeting.

Scenario 5

Jefferson Middle School organizes its intramural sports program around its six interdisciplinary teams. The students on the All-Americans Team are proud of having won intramural championships in soccer, volleyball, and flag football. Because two of their teachers, Mike and Tom, are skilled coaches, the All-Americans' athletic performance has improved dramatically under their tutelage. In the flush of these successes, Mike and Tom get caught up in some good-natured ribbing with colleagues, boasting about their students' athletic prowess. In short order, the teasing spreads to their students, who increasingly tease students on other teams that are less successful athletically. What started as a benign rivalry becomes intense and confrontational. Principal Judy Nowell is disturbed by the divisiveness, in regard to both individual relationships and impact on the overall school climate. She ponders how to respond to the situation. After thoughtful conversations with several of her colleagues who are uncomfortable about addressing the issue with Tom and Mike, she asks to attend an All-Americans' common planning meeting. There she describes what she has observed, explains that she understands how easy it is for good-natured fun to get out of hand, and then presents the teachers with four specific things they can do to defuse the situation. In closing she smiles, offers to help in any way needed, and closes cheerfully with, "Okay. Let's get over it. Today."

Scenario 6

At their annual June planning retreat, Sandra Caldwell, principal of Middle School of the Kennebunks in Kennebunk, Maine, and the four team leaders consider schoolwide goals for the coming year. For the past several years, they have emphasized all-school themes. A recent theme has been "Connections," a series of initiatives that connected the students with several different constituencies in their Maine community, especially senior citizens. An earlier theme emphasized personal wellness, and teachers practiced what they preached by dieting and by organizing their own aerobic and exercise classes. In addition to engaging students in stimulating projects, these ongoing themes build schoolwide unity, a major emphasis of Caldwell's leadership in facilitating teams. At this particular spring retreat, the team leaders and the principal agree to concentrate during the coming year on the concept of multiple intelligences. They commit themselves to studying its theory and research over the summer and to beginning to explore ways to apply their insights and ideas in the fall. Their plans include interviewing students and then offering them minicourses specially designed to match their cognitive specialties as identified by multiple intelligences theory. This new initiative ensures that the school is unified by a common professional emphasis, and it also justifies their claim that their program is "research-based."

Scenario 7

In October, Ron Parrish, previously a high school principal, is named principal of the newly consolidated Broad Creek Middle School in Carteret County, North

Carolina, scheduled to open the next fall. Although he once taught in a junior high school, Ron's understanding of contemporary middle school philosophy and practice is limited. He is nonetheless excited about the opportunity, but he is also understandably apprehensive. He begins to read, visit reputable middle schools, and pick people's minds. In the spring and summer, he arranges an assortment of workshops on teaming during teacher workdays. Focusing on teachers' preferences but also being sure to mix faculty from the three schools involved in the Broad Creek consolidation, he makes team assignments. He also persuades the school system to hire a consultant to work with teams on a weekly basis. In the first meeting of Broad Creek's new faculty in August, he states, "I don't know exactly how to do all this, but I'm working at it. We are all in this together; we can teach and learn from each other. We'll learn to do it right. I'm here to help you in any way I can. All I ask is that you show that you care about kids, and give it your very best effort."

Scenario 8

Wilma Parrish (not related to Ron Parrish in the preceding scenario), founding principal of Western Middle School in Alamance County, North Carolina, has been a remarkable teacher and principal for many years. She makes a point of knowing the names of each of the eight hundred students at Western plus the names of most of the parents. She is also very familiar with the full curriculum at each grade level of the school. She visits classrooms daily, sometimes teaching an impromptu lesson, often helping an individual student with an assignment.

Parrish may also be seen picking up bits of paper in the halls of the building, which is fourteen years old but new-looking and graffiti-free—modeling the care and attention that she expects from students and teachers. The many visitors who come to Western are invariably treated to some of Wilma's homemade cookies during an extended information session and tour of the school. They are also introduced to the custodians as key members of the staff; they all are a family who has been with the school since it opened.

In organizing teams Wilma has *not* insisted that they all look alike. Teachers are not expected to conform to a set pattern. They work in two-, three-, and four-teacher groupings as well as in a few self-contained classrooms. Some teams are organized by grade level, whereas others are multiaged. Some teams stay together for many years, whereas others reconfigure periodically. Teacher preference for partners and for team size is given the highest possible preference in these matters. Teams are naturally expected to meet system and state requirements for curriculum, but they are strongly encouraged to develop imaginative ways of doing so. Innovative, effective curriculum designs light up Wilma's eyes, and most teams avail themselves of her support. A staunch advocate of interdisciplinary learning, she often sits in on teams' curriculum planning sessions, contributing ideas about both content and process.

Parrish has initiated a number of evening programs on adolescent issues for parents, in addition to all-school themes such as the week of the Atlantic Coast

Conference basketball tournament, known in the area as "ACC Week." She provides an ongoing staff development program based upon teachers' expressed needs and desires. She also frees her talented faculty to make presentations for professional conferences, other school systems, and universities. On most weekends she can be found tutoring children at a housing project near the school, often inviting them into her home for some of those ubiquitous cookies.

COMMENTARY

It's easy to get good players.
Getting 'em to play together—
that's the hard part.

Casey Stengel

In our view there is no more challenging and heroic work than that of a principal who is committed to a responsible evolution of progressive student-centered educational practices and who leads that process by personal example. Public schools especially are buffeted by cries for modernization from one camp and for a return to traditional practices from another. Teachers are often stymied by appealing theory, research, and exemplary practice while facing day-to-day survival amid an increasingly alienated adolescent constituency. Politicians rarely miss an opportunity to claim commitment to "excellence in education" and "higher standards for students and teachers." More than any other professional person, the principal has the considerable, often formidable task of leading responsible, coherent program development in the face of withering criticism from both within and without the school community.

Perhaps the most notable dimension of exemplary leadership as illustrated in the preceding scenarios is each principal's realization about the urgent importance of teachers' participation in the school's authority and decision-making processes. Principals who accomplish this complex task embody a special genius, and they merit respect and emulation of their living example of enlightened leadership. How extraordinarily valuable to the improvement of education are principals such as those described in the scenarios!

Each of these principals projects a sensitivity to teachers' colleagues' needs and a wisdom in guiding decision making that is appropriate to each situation. In Scenario 1, Russell Clarke recognized the potential of teaming from the beginning, but rather than *decree* its implementation, he led important other constituencies toward a shared realization that teaming would better serve the children and teachers of their school. He was careful to support that initiative by forming a PIC, by arranging professional time for teachers to participate, and by participating firsthand in the PIC process.

As a newly appointed principal, Dave Ford (Scenario 2) knew from the outset that his credibility in teachers' eyes would be established early in their relationship. Consequently he conveyed his personal advocacy for teaming indirectly and through confidential conversations with teachers that kept the focus on their ruminations about how they could see themselves functioning on teams. Ford's sensitivity to his new colleagues' concerns and the trust he demonstrated in working with and in consideration of their priorities amply demonstrated his wisdom and professional responsibility to them. He also modeled an unambiguous standard of interpersonal relationships for everyone.

All teachers need to believe in the principal's advocacy of their work. In the cases of the Wildthings and Wings teams (Scenarios 3 and 4), the chief administrators' presence in the day-to-day rigors of their work and special team events speaks volumes about the degree to which they support their teams. By keeping up with the nuts and bolts of their team via the Wildthings' team book and by following a predictable schedule for attending team planning meetings, principal Morgan and assistant principal Causby are able to know a great deal more about the lives of both the teams and individual students and teachers on them. Morgan subsequently showed the extent to which he listened, trusted, and responded to his teacher colleagues. He acted on a need that they had identified as an opportunity to benefit all teams and the whole school. Such knowledge of issues enables leaders to act in need-driven ways that are relevant to the actualities of their schools, enhancing their personal credibility in everyone else's eyes.

The principal's mere presence at the Wings' culminating event adds importance to the occasion in the perceptions of students, their parents, and other guests. But Dr. Spence was not content merely to be in attendance. She used the occasion to help everyone feel welcome and his or her attendance valued, and she conveyed her advocacy of an innovative curriculum project by word and action. She later formalized her commendation in writing, an emulation of "leading by example" that was appreciated by everyone.

Teachers sometimes get caught up in doing things that they don't approve of their students doing. So it was in the case of Jefferson Middle School (Scenario 5), where athletic competition generalized into teasing that was beginning to be harmful. It is easy in our culture, with its great emphasis on sports, for any designation of "team," to immediately and naturally invoke such competitiveness. New principal Judy Nowell showed courage in addressing a problem that was noticeably deteriorating the school's climate. In addressing that problem, however, she was careful to be explicit without offending, and she wisely offered teachers help in the form of four specific suggestions plus a standing offer of further assistance. Later that initial year she proposed to her colleagues that they reconsider the wisdom of pitting interdisciplinary teams against each other in sports. Their subsequent decision to mix students from all teams for intramurals essentially eliminated a rivalry that in all likelihood would in time have become more seriously damaging.

The deliberateness with which Sandra Caldwell, a highly experienced principal (Scenario 6), addresses issues in her schools clarifies for all members of the school community just where they stand. In addition to leading her colleagues in a process of establishing and assessing schoolwide themes, she acknowledged the value of the team leaders' work and insights through the ritual of a retreat conducted much like corporate, political, or other professional leaders might utilize to take stock of their institutions. She also wisely showed that by an ongoing process of assessment and planning, their school innovations would be based on sound, relevant research.

It is very rare for principals to have been teachers on teams such as those described in this book. Most principals taught in elementary, junior high, or high schools, and although they may have gained lots of valuable experience, the teaming that teachers are pursuing today is generally well outside the realm of principals' firsthand experience. To his enormous credit, Ron Parrish (Scenario 7) both acknowledged his limitations and committed himself to learning with and from his colleagues. His school went on to become an outstanding one as they learned together. Parrish's humility and determination are exemplary; most of us can learn an important leadership lesson from his example.

Wilma Parrish (Scenario 8) is without doubt one of a kind. Few of us can match her ability to learn and remember students' and parents' names. Yet, each of us is capable of emulating her remarkable devotion to her colleagues, students, and profession. Note the simple but profound wisdom of her realization that all teams do not have to look alike. Her interest in interdisciplinary curriculum heartened and reassured teachers for whom such a challenge represented a discomforting departure from tradition. Her wisdom from years of reflection on her experience brought stability and direction to a dynamic school, and all educational leaders would do well to remember Wilma Parrish as an exemplar of the principal's potential.

In each of these brief scenarios is evidence of the vital characteristics of successful middle level principals. We might think of these characteristics as "attributes of professional character" as manifested in educational leaders. Consider these elements of leadership style. First, it is important to emphasize that decision-making authority *must* be shared between administrators and teachers—wherever possible and whenever appropriate. Whether teachers or parents or students are asked outright for an opinion or vote or whether their views are gathered more subtly, these principals do not see their work in terms of mandates and arbitrary declarations. They see themselves as important partners in a decision-making process that is grounded in the professional community.

A second distinct attribute of these principals is that they lead by example. In adolescent vernacular, "They walk the walk." One's credibility as a leader in a middle level school is much more often the product of what one says *and does* than of just what one says. All of the principals in these scenarios acted consistently with what they avowed.

Another notable attribute of these principals is their resolve to support their colleagues' initiatives with sometimes seemingly mundane but often crucial arrangements: schedule, physical space, planning time, and especially the authority to create a teaming plan and curriculum responsive to their students. One principal observed that, "My job is to do what I can to make it possible for teachers to do the very best work of which they are capable." The principals described here consummate that attitude and spirit.

Finally, although these principals had prior experience teaching young adolescents, few of them had expertise in the actualities of an evolving modern middle school; they had not personally experienced much of what they were leading their colleagues toward becoming. They did not position themselves as experts. They were not afraid to acknowledge what they did not know. However, their manner of thoughtful, responsive leadership provided reassurance and encouragement that would enable their colleagues to move beyond what had heretofore been accepted practice.

More than any other contemporary educational innovation, team organization embodies the potential to move practice beyond the mire of controversy that bogs down so many otherwise promising initiatives. The savvy principal recognizes that team organization moves greater authority and responsibility for planning and decision making to teachers—those who are closest to the day-to-day issues in education. Teaming also enables more responsive, efficient adjustments and adaptations to student needs because necessary authority is vested in those who are able to be most accountable for what is happening in any student's educational program. In brief, principals come to realize that successful teams enable a school to more efficiently address and accomplish its mission.

Teaming involves changes in how teachers organize, plan, and teach; those processes are the focus of this book. But teaming also requires changes in the traditional role of principals. In order for a school to become more intimate, and more responsive to students' and teachers' needs through teaming, the principal has to let go of the traditional authoritarian role in favor of collaboration, facilitation, coordination, and synergy. Mandates are supplanted by collaborative decisions. The necessity for impersonal decisions declines, and issues that have important consequences for individuals are accomplished with greater sensitivity to individual circumstances. Detachment and isolation are replaced by concrete knowledge of what is going on in classrooms. The unhappy task of being a school's ultimate disciplinarian declines substantially when interpersonal conflicts are more frequently resolved between antagonists within their teams.

It is impossible to overstate the importance of how principals go about working with teamed teachers. When teachers dare to go beyond conventional ways of doing things in order to better accommodate their students' needs, it is essential that principals likewise show teachers multiple forms of support. When the going gets rough, teachers who feel unsupported are tempted to back down and return their practice to a more perfunctory and ordinary style. But when teachers enjoy affirmation, encouragement, and reassurance in the form of tangible support and personal encouragement, real progress is possible. Principals who accept such responsibility and who commit themselves to supporting teachers who are engaged in team development are heroic leaders indeed.

PRINCIPLES

The *principles* listed in this section are everyone's responsibility, but they are of special concern to *principals*. How principals approach these dimensions of school administration has enormous impact on the successful growth of teaming.

- **Advocacy of young adolescents is fundamental.**
  The principal must constantly remind everyone, through word and deed, that providing an education that supports students' healthy personal and academic growth and development is the primary business of the school. Sometimes this advocacy involves challenging negative attitudes or stereotypes about young adolescents; always it involves an insistence that decisions be made with this question foremost in mind: "Is this good for our students?" A large banner hanging over the principal's office suite in one school that reads, "We Care About Kids Here" says it all.
- **Knowledge about adolescents, teaming, and middle level education in general informs all programs and decisions.**
  Effective middle level principals are engaged in not only remaking a school, but also in remaking themselves as leaders and ongoing learners. Like their teachers, most principals have had little specialized preparation for teaming and other middle school features. They have not attended middle schools as children, have not had middle level courses in college, nor were they required to take them for principal certification, and have not taught on a middle level team. Given this situation, it is imperative that principals take advantage of the increasingly available sources of knowledge about middle level education. Principals surely do not have to be walking textbooks, but they do need to evidence a desire to learn if they are to earn faculty respect and develop a viable school.
- **Decision making is shared.**
  As the sanctioned authority in a school, the principal has by far the most to say about how decisions are accomplished. Wise principals realize that as much as possible, those closest to the teaching/learning situation need to make important judgments pertaining to it and affecting their students and themselves. For teachers to assume ownership and responsibility for a team program, they must be able to organize time, curriculum, team procedures, and routines with as much freedom as possible. It is likewise important that students also be involved in decision making, especially within teams. There may be no more advantageous place than within a team to teach by example that democracy is active, responsible citizenship. More is offered on this subject in chapter 5, but the principle of shared decision making merits repeated mention.
- **The principal leads.**
  Shared decision making in no way implies passivity. Principals are responsible for seeing that teams reflect the school's overall philosophy and that teams put it into practice. Effective principals help select teachers who genuinely care about kids, have expertise, and make sound decisions. They help teachers establish procedures that "make teams work" as well as challenging and developmentally responsive programs. Although they do not dictate, they often suggest, persuade,

and work for consensus. They help set specific expectations for students and teachers and then provide ways for expectations to be met.

- **Structures to support teaming are in place.**

  As the previous chapter makes clear, teaming efforts are severely hampered where supporting structures are missing or inadequate. In the best of circumstances, the principal does everything possible to provide time, space, and resources for teachers to carry out the very best education of which they are capable.

- **A positive school climate is continuously being developed.**

  A positive school climate is grounded in respect for *all* people. Diversity is recognized as a strength to be celebrated. Positive climates are characterized by caring, community, cooperation, clear communication, and good spirit (see chapter 8). Racism, sexism, excessive competition (especially between teams), put-downs, and mean spiritedness can poison the best-laid plans. Invariably the principal, by virtue of position, must establish by actions and words the appropriate tone for a middle school. Realizing these truths, good principals are especially supportive of teams, the building blocks of positive school climate, and work with them to create an atmosphere where all feel welcomed and respected.

- **Program assessment and evaluation form the basis of ongoing planning and improvement.**

  Curricular innovations frequently evolve because of a special opportunity or because "it seems like a good idea." Every single "good idea" need not be evaluated, but an organizational shift as notable as teaming must be examined both qualitatively and quantitatively for its effects on learning and student life. One of the wonderful dimensions of working with young adolescents is their candor when they believe they are in safe company. They are, therefore, excellent sources of sound data about how well program features are serving their needs. (See chapter 10.) Insights from formative evaluation that include student feedback constitute the most valuable basis for refining existing programs as well as for suggesting directions for further innovative work. Student-centered educational leaders make sure that student feedback is part of the school's evaluation process.

PLANNING GUIDELINES

1. *Become knowledgeable about young adolescents and teaming and help educate the faculty.*

   Read books and journal articles, watch videos, and attend conferences sponsored by professional organizations; visit schools with effective teams and engage in dialogue with professionals there. Then share your perceptions and encourage and enable faculty to do the same. Engage your students in conversation about what it is like to be their age; listen to them and include their insights in working with teachers. Establish a professional library in the faculty lounge and put copies of timely articles in faculty members' mailboxes. Give faculty members meeting time and schedule in-service around teaming issues of concern to colleagues. Develop your own personal expertise and draw others into learning about how teaming can work or be improved in your school.

2. *Ensure that the basic needs for teaming are provided.*

   A flexible master schedule, daily team planning time, control over grouping procedures, adequate adjoining physical spaces, a budget, and instructional resources are essential. Do everything possible to provide these basic supports, and if they cannot be provided for immediately, develop a plan and advocate for them with central administrators. Deliver, if possible, on requests that arise from team planning, such as transportation for field trips, technology resources, or attendance at professional meetings. It is rare that every need can be met, but promptly show your teacher colleagues your resolve to support them by doing whatever you can do. Seek grants to help finance legitimate needs and encourage teachers to do likewise.
3. *Help teams to develop and carry out their team plan.*

   Due to lack of background and experience, teachers often do not really know what teams need to do in order to function effectively. This is particularly true in large school systems that convert to middle schools. Faculty members are told simply to "become a team" without adequate orientation and preparation. In such situations, the principal must help teams develop goals and a team plan, focusing upon the issues addressed in this book. Helping faculty to use common planning time effectively is perhaps the best starting point. Sometimes principals offer teachers on a team the opportunity to "retreat" for a day of planning by providing substitute teachers and working with the students himself or herself as much as possible. One teacher wrote in a thank-you note that "the team retreat was *fantastic*—and having the librarian along awarded us another teammate who now looks at what we are trying to do in a new and much more positive light."
4. *Actively participate and give lots of encouragement.*

   Whether the principal is initiating team organization or maintaining teams already in place, the principal's visibility and active interest in school life are essential. As implied earlier, the principal must be aware of what teams are doing and what issues they face in order to help. Moreover, by working alongside teachers in planning sessions, by attending all-team meetings led by students, and by participating in evening events, the principal shows interest and support to three vital constituencies: teachers, students, and parents. Further, in spite of the plethora of administrative responsibilities that a principal must face, seek opportunities to participate and teach in a curriculum project, even if it is for only an hour here and there. In all of these contexts the most lasting contribution one can make is to encourage and recognize the people with whom you interact. Those individuals highly value their leader's affirmation.
5. *Give feedback: "strokes and suggestions."*

   Teachers, like most people, care a great deal about the affirmation that they receive from their supervisors. When teachers have gone an extra mile to accomplish a difficult or challenging task, such effort should never go unnoticed. It is important, therefore, that administrators take note of their colleagues' investment in their work. The platitude that "teachers aren't in teaching for the money" is especially true when they go beyond the ordinary as teaming necessitates. Suggestions are also valued representations of the principal's interest in a team or a teacher, especially if the suggestions are the result of consultation and reflection. A principal's perspective is always somewhat different from that of teachers, and teachers appreciate knowing that perspective when it is offered with earnest support for their initiative.

6. *Be vigilant about the overall school climate.*

   Stay well tuned to the school's interpersonal climate, doing all that you can to build a genuine sense of community. Get to know as many students as possible. Engage them in conversation and listen to their ideas and suggestions. Respect everyone and be firm wherever disrespect surfaces. Be wary of overcompetitiveness. Seek to develop all school themes and initiatives to which teams contribute. Many of the expectations and standards in a middle level school derive from the principal; make yourself in the image of what you expect from others.

7. *Work at achieving excellent communication.*

   Clear, accurate communication between principal and teachers is always a substantial consideration. Especially where large teams have been established, a leadership team composed of principal and team leaders can be a vital communication conduit. (See chapter 5.) When teachers are organized into teams, their meeting agenda includes daily planning times, all-team meetings with students, special events with parents, shared planning with off-team colleagues, joint curriculum projects, and so forth. Given this emphasis on communication, there emerge new opportunities for communication between them and the principal. Chapters 5, 8, and 10 emphasize the importance of teams' maintaining a daily log—a record of decisions and activities—that can be shared with the principal at regular intervals. The principal in turn responds promptly to issues identified in that log on an as-needed basis. Occasional scheduled participation in a team planning session further personalizes communication because it entails face-to-face discussion.

8. *Work with teams to establish an ongoing program for assessment/evaluation and staff development.*

   It will be necessary to collect information in order to assess progress, improve programs, and meet community expectations for accountability. Chapter 10 offers a number of suggestions for collecting quantitative and qualitative data from all school constituencies for these purposes. In addition to staff development programs already mentioned, orientation programs should be devised for new faculty members and parents if quality and understanding are to be maintained.

ADDITIONAL POSSIBILITIES

There are numerous ways that principals can prepare themselves to understand teaming more fully and to support teachers in building good teams. Some additional time-tested ways are:

- Form seminars with other middle level principals to discuss books and articles or specific issues.
- Create a principal's newsletter that frequently comments about team accomplishments.

- Build "back to school nights" around teams.
- Using the public address system or closed-circuit television to make announcements, convey messages about the community and the school or to tell occasional jokes or pose riddles.
- Recognize teachers and students at lunch time and in assemblies.
- Encourage periodic social get-togethers just for teachers and staff members.

CAVEATS

- Never be too busy to compliment people and to recognize their accomplishments.
- Don't be tolerant of or indifferent to any form of disrespect for others. People need to understand that, for their own sakes as well as for the sakes of their team and school, disrespect destroys community. Even our students are quick to say, "Don't dis me." Offenders need to be called to task, then helped to change their ways.
- Be especially wary of team competition. There is an irony that while one of the purposes of public education is to educate young people in the values of cooperation, sportsmanship, and teamwork, adults in a school sometimes find themselves pitted against each other. Young adolescents are perceptive about interpersonal relationships, and they "read" the adults around them through sharply focused lenses. It is highly important that principals, teachers, and staff recognize and even enjoy their individual differences and idiosyncrasies *without* letting them become overly competitive and/or divisive. Students will likely replicate what they perceive accepted relationships to be. To preserve a professional atmosphere of mutual respect for reasoned planning and cooperation, the principal must be ever vigilant for potentially destructive rivalries among students, teachers, and teams.

DEVELOPING A TEAM VISION

What do we believe about young adolescents?
About authentic education?
About teaching?
What is our guiding philosophy?
What values do we stand for?

Scenario 1

Mort and Larry, teachers at Edmunds Middle School in Burlington, Vermont, are sitting together over lunch in a pizza parlor following a provocative in-service session on experiential learning. They are excited about what they have just seen of young adolescent students learning from their community and from people beyond the school, of teachers and students jointly designing study projects, and about the possibilities for combining separate subjects into interdisciplinary projects. Without realizing the significance of what they are doing, these two teachers have begun discussing ideas, scribbling them on the backs of paper place mats. That conversation marks the birth of a two-teacher team.

A couple of days later Mort and Larry approach their principal with their ideas about teaming. He listens thoughtfully, asks a few questions, and begins to share their enthusiasm about their desire for a team of fifty seventh and eighth graders who would work with these two teachers for two years, engaging in experiential studies and studying journalism in addition to being accountable for the established curriculum. After a few days of detailed discussion the two teachers return to the principal with their draft of a plan. "Here's our idea of paradise." Scanning the document, the principal looks up smilingly and says, "Let's do it. I believe the school board will support such a clear vision."

Twenty years later the two teachers would reflect on that momentous day and how the paths they chose changed the direction of their professional lives. Ideas precipitated by that in-service program that flowed forth over a pizza lunch became a vision-defining experience. The Paradise Project, a team widely known and admired for its excellence in educating young adolescents, was the result. In addition to participating in a solid academic program, Paradise students have traveled an average of 40,000 miles per year, engaged in an extensive "achievement program" featuring practical skills and community service, and published journals about their travels. Without that original vision to sustain their planning in the beginning as well as in later years, such a program would never have survived much more than a semester, much less two decades.

Scenario 2

Visitor: *"Tell me about your team, Jimmy. What does it stand for?"*
Jimmy: *"What do you mean?"*
Visitor: *"What are your teachers trying to accomplish? What do you think is important about your team?"*
Jimmy: *"I dunno. Never thought about it."*

Scenario 3

Four teachers are gathered for their first planning meeting as a team. Bernice, the team leader, states, "I think it would be a good idea if we are as open as possible about what we want this team to be." As all nod in agreement, Kathy jumps in and says, "I'm not bashful; I'll start. I want us to really care about all our kids, to respect them, to listen to them, to give them real responsibilities. I want our curriculum to be exciting, to deal with important ideas, to help kids understand themselves and what's going on around them. I hope we will do a lot of interdisciplinary work. I also want us to discuss kids every week, to share what we know about their interests, learning styles, problems, and whatever so we can gear our efforts to their needs. To do all this, we've got to be serious and organized. I want us to meet every day, to be on time, to have an agenda, and make this the best team we know how. Now, what do you guys think we should be about?

Bernice takes a quick breath, then states, "Thanks for your openness, Kathy. I wonder if we might *list* the important things we want our team to stand for. After that, we could look for common ground to discuss."

Scenario 4

Ross and Nancy, experienced members of a two-teacher team at Shoreham-Wading River Middle School in Shoreham, New York, are in a planning meeting on a "workday" before school starts in the fall:

Ross: *"Even though we've talked a lot about what we want to emphasize with kids, we've never really spelled it out in a formal way. You know, qualities like responsibility, risk taking, trust—those sorts of things."*
Nancy: *"Agreed, good idea. Let's make a list. Let's see . . ."*
Both: *"There's respect . . . responsibility . . . cooperation . . . communication . . . acknowledgment . . . appreciation . . . trust . . . risk . . . individuality . . . compassion . . . contribution . . . commitment . . ."*
Ross: *"I count twelve in all. I'm sure we could add more, but that's probably enough. Maybe we should give them a more distinctive name. Hey, how about 'the Distinctions'?"*

Nancy: *"Great, but shouldn't we discuss all this with the kids, too? They'll probably have some ideas."*

Ross: *"Right. I guess we emphasize these characteristics in most everything we do, but I think it would be good to plan special activities to emphasize each 'distinction' throughout the year."*

Nancy: *"Sure. We could start by having kids write what they think each distinction means—maybe one they pull out of a hat, and one they choose. Then for 'appreciation,' they could write letters to someone who has meant a lot to them. And for 'trust,' we could have them . . ."*

Scenario 5

Pete, large for his age, has had difficulties in school from the beginning. He was a "late reader" and remains a very slow one to this day. His elementary and middle school report cards are peppered with *C*s and *D*s, along with numerous comments of "needs improvement" and "not working to his potential." Pete is frequently tardy and often comes to class without pencils, books, or assignments. Although he can be amiable at times, he has a flashing temper. He is especially sensitive to comments about his academic capabilities. He has been diagnostically tested for learning disabilities but was found to be not in need of special education services.

In discussing students for the first time in a Common Planning Time meeting in September, the newly formed Fantastics Team teachers, Sylvia, Jason, and Pam, become quite concerned about Pete. When no one is able to make helpful suggestions, Pam says, "Look, we agreed at the outset that every student on our team is going to be as successful as possible. Pete's biggest problem is that he has zero organization and doesn't get his work done. We've got to help him." Rolling up their sleeves, the Fantastics come up with four concrete options for helping Pete: allowing him extra time to take tests; planning a study skills minicourse for him and several other students; finding a college student to be a "big brother" to him; and placing him on a behavioral/academic contract that teachers sign off on daily, ensuring that each is aware of his progress and that staying in at recess and after school is required to finish any assignments not handed in. At the close of the discussion, Jason comments, "Pete's *not* going to fail." Sylvia smiles and adds, "Right. He's got a *team* behind him."

COMMENTARY

Where there is no vision, the people perish.

Proverbs 29:18

Look inside yourself, Simba.
You are much more than you have become.

The Lion King

We like to believe that others who teach at the middle level do so for the same basic motive that has drawn us into this vital work: commitment to the healthy development, learning, and success of young adolescent children.

We know from wide experience in schools that the most effective way of organizing people to support these youngsters and to address their needs is through well-organized, effectively functioning teams. We also know, however, that an overwhelming majority of people—teachers, students, and adults—think of school organization in terms of the conventional paradigm: a separate subject curriculum, forty-five-minute class periods, horizontal age grouping, and so on. Teaming is a passage to a newer but rapidly developing design. To access this passage, however, one must set aside much of the usual approach in order to focus the vision on young adolescent students, their transitions from younger childhood to adulthood, their unique needs and conditions, their accomplishments and capacity as learners, and the extraordinary promise they embody. Look at them in terms of potential to be nurtured and imagine what their schooling might look like if our overarching goal is to support their healthy development, growth, and learning. In so doing, we must also examine ourselves and the extent to which we have settled into comfortable routines that may or may not be in the best interest of the students we serve. If we were creating schools for the very first time, would we do it the conventional way? We must confront the ways our schools are organized and assess their functioning. Young adolescents embody far more potential than what conventional schooling has cultivated.

In developing their "vision of paradise" in Scenario 1, Larry and Mort were guided by several important beliefs. One was that students, given appropriate support, can take much greater initiative and responsibility for their own learning than they are usually afforded. Another belief central to their vision was that learning should be experiential, that is, students should frequently generate knowledge from firsthand experience, learning from people and events as well as from texts and other print resources. In so doing, students learn to connect "doing" and "thinking" and "feeling." Yet another key belief was that by having students for two years, Larry and Mort would be more able to cultivate leadership and citizenship responsibilities; older students would have responsibilities for younger ones by virtue of their additional year of experience in Paradise. They envisioned eighth graders helping to orient, lead, and teach their younger teammates.

Based upon those beliefs such a vision was well conceived and well placed. To some extent it reflected theory and philosophy associated with progressive education and middle level education in general. More significantly, it combined personal insights drawn from broad life experiences, teaching, and ideas acquired from others.

Larry and Mort's shared vision was put into practice some twenty years ago. Every year since, Paradise students perform extensive community service projects in their families and home community, travel thousands of miles annually in small groups with one of their teachers as they explore their region and the country, publish a literary magazine and journals about their travels as well as the school newspaper, and measure their individual progress through a Paradise Achievement Program that resembles the structure long used successfully by the Boy Scouts. (See Example 2.)

It is crucial to note that this particular team vision builds on the teachers' interests as well as on the students'. Both teachers enjoy travel, and both have literary interests. Larry is also a scoutmaster. The three rooms (two classrooms, one journalism room) that house Paradise reflect the "family spirit" of the inhabitants of that space as surely as a museum reflects its purposes or an ethnic restaurant reflects its heritage. There is an abundance of posted photographs and newspaper clippings; notes and letters from friends, contacts around the country, and former students; past and current issues of student publications; artifacts, maps, and photos connected with travels made over the years; promotional material and posters for distinctive Paradise events, such as the annual Paradise Auction; and award certificates and T-shirts bearing the team logo. Even two large teddy bears referred to as "travel bears" occupy a shelf, ready to go at a moment's notice. A bear always accompanies students on a trip; to them it represents the students and teachers back at school. The bear that remains at school represents those students who are traveling.

A key to comprehending the spirit of the Paradise Project is the approach that Larry and Mort take when planning curricular projects and trips. They state, "We begin by asking ourselves whether we are doing things for our students that they could do for themselves. If the answer is 'Yes,' we then ask ourselves, 'Why?'" Accordingly, students going on a particular trip plan every aspect of it; they teach one another the achievement program skills in a master-apprentice fashion; and the publications are almost entirely student directed.

Scenario 2 stands in stark contrast to Paradise. Jimmy's comments to a visitor mirror a situation far too common in many schools: Students really don't get it; they don't understand what their team is all about. When we work in schools we like to interview students, inviting them to "tell me about yourself . . . your team . . . what you are doing, learning." We find that young adolescents are usually very perceptive about what really matters. If Jimmy's team has a guiding philosophy, it isn't apparent to him. It seems reasonable to assume that he has little or no involvement in his team's direction. It is difficult to imagine his team having much of an intentional impact or satisfying his need to be an important part of a good thing. This scenario reflects a situation where the teachers, and perhaps the school or entire school system, are simply "going through the motions" of teaming. There has been no forethought, no planning, no vision. As someone has said, "It's hard to get there if you don't know where you are going."

When teachers meet for the first time as a team, it is imperative that all teachers openly state what their hopes and dreams are and to what they are willing to commit themselves. In Scenario 3, Kathy puts her cards on the table immediately. Although perhaps a bit overeager, she does have enthusiasm and commitment to her students and colleagues and is eager to get the team off on the right foot. Bernice, the team leader, wisely finds a way for new members to share their ideas more systematically. (Example 5 displays a Ven diagram that could have been used for this purpose: Team members individually list their values and key ideas and then discuss those that intersect.) It should be noted that openness by team members about their values and desires not only moves a team forward toward a shared vision, but also provides a referent when difficulties arise. For example, if team members are reluctant to discuss team interpersonal relations from time to time, it is appropriate for one of them to remind the group, "I thought we had agreed to honestly assess our group process from time to time." Usually it is easier to discuss sensitive issues in these circumstances than in circumstances in which no prior commitments have been made.

In Scenario 4, Ross and Nancy clearly illustrate the value grounding of their team. As accomplished, veteran teachers, they appreciated the importance of a well-developed team vision. Although they already knew what qualities and values they stood for, they had not yet involved their students in developing them in a systematic way. Thus they created activities that allowed students to talk and write about these values, giving feedback on the activities completed. (These activities are described in chapter 11, Scenario 2.) Thus the formulation of "the Distinctions" not only gave added direction for the team overall, but it also offered Ross and Nancy specific ways to put team values into practice.

Research indicates that teachers on "the very best teams" (George and Stevenson 1989) are committed to the belief that *all* of their students can be successful. Realizing that students learn in different ways and at different rates, they offer a variety of learning options and supports. They also recognize that the chief cause of school failure is students' not handing in assignments. (A few zeros averaged in with passing grades spell failure.) The prognosis for the Fantastics in Scenario 5 is excellent on at least two counts. First, their vision statement is more than words; they refuse to let Pete fail. They come up with various ways of helping him and are determined to make sure that he hands in his assignments. There are many so-called at-risk students like Pete in schools today. And the great majority of them could be significantly helped had they a team of teachers such as Sylvia, Jason, and Pam. Second, the Fantastics is a group whose members are pulling together. They seem to draw strength from one another and from their commitment. As Sylvia inferred, they are becoming a *team.*

PRINCIPLES

We offer some advice that is important for everyone but especially for teachers coming to teaming for the first time. We encourage you to think expansively, imagining the ideal, daring to dream in ways that are well beyond what actually exists in your current situation. However, you must also temper your imagining with what you believe is a prudent way to begin teaming in your particular situation. Successful teams such as the ones described in this book have evolved over time. Assume that you will do likewise. We have some concern that some readers might overreach in their first year. Think big, but plan more modestly for your first steps.

- **A team vision defines its ideals in writing**.

  Such a document should articulate the purposes and directions that guide teachers and students in their day-to-day lives, expressing team ideals. Thus there is coherence between those values and teaching and learning activities. The Paradise Project statement of philosophy (Example 1) includes statements about experiential learning that become coherent through the travel and writing components. Students need to see and to understand that what their team says it stands for becomes real in what the teachers and students do. Otherwise, vision statements are just so much lofty rhetoric. (See Examples 1–4 for philosophies of outstanding teams.)
- **Achieve vision through consensus.**

  Honest, candid give-and-take clarifies what everyone stands for. Find the common ground that will give your work shared purpose and direction. Although personal visions involve hopes and dreams, a team vision of necessity involves each other's personal aspirations and necessitates compromise. Voting has no place in the visioning process because split votes about fundamental issues inevitably lead to dissension. Bringing students' ideas and opinions into the agreement is especially important if students are to comprehend the intended coherence. Like adults, students will support what they help create and often ignore those things in which they have little stake.
- **Commitment to one's young adolescent students, to each other, and to the team plan is essential.**

  A vision is not simply "a collection of happy thoughts." It should never include ideas that sound good but that members have reservations about or have no intention of implementing. A vision expresses serious intentions that affect future actions and are an energizing source of meaning and purpose.
- **The developmental and academic needs of young adolescents are our primary concern**.

  Students are our clients. Their healthy growth and development comprise the *raison d'être* for schooling. In particular, it is important that the vision empowers students, ensuring that they have opportunities to learn about themselves and the world around them as they move toward ever-increasing self-sufficiency and active commitment to democratic citizenship.
- **Teachers need a sense of personal efficacy.**

  We need to believe that we are making significant differences in the lives of our students. In addition, some of our personal needs and interests must be met. Teachers who do not feel good about themselves or who are bored by their work are seldom able to meet kids' needs. Great teachers find their passions and pursue them.
- **A variety of team visions is to be expected in a single school**.

  As long as those programs complement the overall school philosophy, diversity should be expected and encouraged. Schools do not need to be like the military, with everyone doing things the same way. Teams are made up of individuals with distinct ideas, talents, skills, and interests. High-quality teams reflect the strengths of the teachers and students who comprise them.

- **Teaming is an evolutionary process.**
  Although there is a good bit of continuity from year to year, teachers' experiences and insights will also influence their vision. The vision statement should be periodically revisited to reflect the evolution.

PLANNING GUIDELINES

1. *Begin by dreaming.*
   In your mind's eye, envision what young adolescent students are like when they are at their best. What are they doing, saying, thinking, feeling? How do they relate to each other, to teachers, to others? What are teachers doing, saying, thinking, feeling? How are they relating? Be sure that everyone expresses his or her fondest hopes and desires and take notes on the discussion. The plan that you develop should reflect programs conceived to help students grow toward your common vision.
2. *Refine your ideas.*
   Which ideas are most important? Which are practical, and which are nice but seem remote or impossible at this time? What can be implemented right away, and what will take more time and experience? Are there things we must do and for which we have no choice? Are the elements needed for a team plan sufficiently addressed?
3. *Discuss your ideas with the students.*
   Challenge their thinking. Provoke their self-examination. Structure the discussion so that students can truly express their ideas. Ask them what kind of schooling would work best for them. A useful strategy is to put students into brainstorming groups with instructions to generate ideas about the various aspects of a team vision. Discuss the results as a whole group. Incorporate their ideas. If you have a large team, it might be more productive to do this first in advisor/advisee groups.
4. *Draft the vision statement.*
   Discuss, edit, and revise it until everyone commits to upholding it. (See the vision statements in Examples 1, 3, and 4.)
5. *Create concrete activities to achieve the vision's promise.*
   For example, "We believe in helping others; therefore, all team members will participate in a variety of community service activities over the year." The value message is clear; Involve students (and parents) in working out ways for students to provide service to others, and be sure that their activity is well communicated within and beyond the team. (See Example 2 for the "Paradise Project Achievement Program", and chapter 11, Scenario 2 for "the distinctions.")
6. *If necessary, solicit approval for your vision statement from authorities outside the team, such as the principal, superintendent, or school board.*
   This step can avoid difficulties down the road and can build support for your intentions. Keep an open mind, but be prepared to advocate vigorously for things you truly believe in.

7. *Translate the vision into a team plan.*

   The team vision will provide the philosophy that guides all the other elements of your team plan: governance, organization and procedures, identity and recognition, communication, curriculum, evaluation, and interpersonal relationships. Check to see that the vision provides guidance for these elements, and then begin to develop the full team plan.
8. *In particular, use your vision statement as a framework for evaluation.*

   Chapter 10 details the importance of taking stock of team development. Utilize elements of the vision statement as benchmarks for assessing how well you are doing.

ADDITIONAL POSSIBILITIES

- Elaborate the vision statement in a handbook that explains more fully how your team works. Parents will especially appreciate such a handbook.
- Use the vision statement at parent meetings to help parents understand your purposes and how you are organized and working to achieve them. For example, if your vision statement refers to literacy values associated with high levels of reading, be sure to convey this expectation to parents. Solicit their help in turning off the television and reading with their children.
- Show your vision statement to colleagues and visitors. Ask for their reactions and any evidence they may see of students' progress toward your goals.

CAVEATS

Team visions are initially generated more by teachers than by students because teachers must bring a sense of direction and focus prior to students' arrival in the fall. Also, teachers remain with a team over time, and if the team is to genuinely grow and develop, there must be considerable continuity of basic goals and values. However, teachers must solicit and incorporate student ideas if the vision is to be of any importance to students. Moreover, the *manner* in which good teams' goals and values are identified and implemented depends greatly on student ideas, initiatives, and ownership.

Be sure that your team vision is inclusive. Make sure that language, symbols, and philosophy are sensitive to race, gender, and other variables. A quick way to breed disharmony is to ignore students' unique backgrounds and characteristics.

Keep in mind that teaming is an evolutionary process. Think big, but move deliberately and consistently toward achievable goals, expanding as you see readiness on the part of students and team teachers. In developing a team plan, a timeline for implementing goals is helpful (e.g., "We will engage students in at least one interdisciplinary project by the spring semester of our first year together").

EXAMPLES

1. Paradise Project Statement of Philosophy
(Edmunds Middle School, Burlington, Vermont)

Our philosophy of education is one that has evolved through many years of observation, experience, and sharing with others. Our goal is the education of the "whole person," not just the intellectual person. Education must provide each of us with the skills to thrive in our world and the freedom to grow and to enjoy life to its fullest.

We will need the tools of reading, writing, communicating, and computing. We need a knowledge of . . . the universe in which we live . . . the physical nature and spirit of the being we call "man" . . . a practical working knowledge of a specific career skill to make our contribution to society and to "earn our keep."

And education must provide us with freedom . . . which makes it possible to enjoy and to thrive in the art of living. . . . Not external freedom [primarily] . . . rather, to work toward an internal freedom, an attitude that develops within one's self . . . the ability to think and to learn with an open mind, to free ourselves from being stifled by our own prejudice, bias, and limited experience . . . not to be smothered or limited by our feelings. And we must learn to . . . make decisions and to accept the consequences of our actions. . . .

To achieve this type of freedom, we must, ironically, give up a small amount of external freedom. Our classrooms must have a structured environment with definite goals and responsibilities, with a sound curriculum, controls on the use of our time, and expectations of behavior and performance that must be met. . . .

We try to develop a community within the project. A member is expected to accept responsibilities and show concern for the success of our community.

Our program of traveling throughout the country provides us with opportunities to meet and to share experiences with people in all walks of life. It exposes us to attitudes and beliefs that may be alien to those we hold dear. It gives us opportunities to have real-life, in-the-field study experiences, to broaden our horizons and to grow as persons through planning, group interaction, and follow-up. . . .

A student should grow as a person in all areas. . . . To aid us in determining some of the specific areas of growth and to monitor a student's progress toward these goals, we have developed the Achievement Program. . . . Writing and publishing the *Edmunds Examiner*, our school newspaper, and *Noun: People, Places and Things*, a magazine about our travels, help students learn many skills, meet deadlines, and assume much responsibility in producing something useful and real.

2. Paradise Project Achievement Program
(Edmunds Middle School, Burlington, Vermont)

The Paradise Project seeks to educate the "whole person," not just the "thinking person." As full participant in the Paradise Project, a member should be developing skills in many areas on a regular basis. A student should grow as a person. There should be growth in all areas—social, physical, intellectual, cultural, practical, emotional. To aid us in determining some of the specific areas of growth and to monitor a student's progress toward these goals, we have developed the Paradise Project Achievement Program.

We would expect that all members of the Project should be able to reach at least Level Three during their two years in the Project. Many will reach higher levels. A student reaching Level Six will have achieved the highest level of performance, will have made outstanding growth, and will be prepared to share with others the experiences and skills achieved.

When completed, the program should provide approximately fifty to sixty skills from which a student might choose when advancing. Some skills have two levels of achievement, Intern and Master, and are considered separate skills.

Although there will be a wide variety of skills from which to choose, we feel some skills are basic to growth within the Project and should be achieved by all. Therefore, some specific skills are required for advancement to the next level of achievement. A total of twenty-five skills must be achieved by Level Six.

All movement from one level to another will require review by an Achievement Committee. Levels One–Four will be reviewed by the teachers and Project members, Levels Five and Six by a committee of teachers, Project members, Project alumni, and parents.

- *Partial Skills List*

Community Service—Intern
Community Service—Master
School Service—Intern
School Service—Master
Public Speaking—Intern
Public Speaking—Master
Interviewing—Intern
Interviewing—Master
Trip Proposal Writing
Meal Preparation
Academic Achievement
Athletics—Intern
Athletics—Master
Emergencies
Slide-Tape Show—Intern
Slide-Tape Show—Master
Fund-Raising—Intern
Fund-Raising—Master
Contributor to a Publication—Intern
Contributor to a Publication—Master
Illustration—Intern
Illustration—Master
Writing for Publication—Intern
Writing for Publication—Master
Machinery
Typing—Intern
Typing—Master
Audiovisual
Photography—Intern
Photography—Master
8mm Filmmaking—Intern
8mm Filmmaking—Master
Reading
Communications

3. Alpha Team Philosophy

(Shelburne Community School, Shelburne, Vermont)

At the heart of the Alpha philosophy is our belief that each student is unique in his/her physical, social, and academic development. Instead of making an assumption about ability or maturity by grade level only, we provide a multiage environment where each student can grow accordingly. This multiage community provides the opportunity for students to learn from and with others during their three-year experience in Alpha. It fosters an environment where differing opinions are listened to and respected. As learners work together to consider the questions they have about themselves and their worlds, they develop skills for action and responsible participation in the world community.

We believe that students must be actively engaged in their learning for there to be a lasting influence. Therefore, we insist that topics be relevant to the student and that each student is involved in the choice and planning of individual learning.

The middle grades are an important time of transition. Students are developing lifelong learning skills and behaviors. We emphasize the development of self-respect and self-discipline. Students develop the essential skills to organize, plan, manage, and evaluate their learning. At this level, these skills along with creative problem solving and group process skills are more essential than any specific content.

The Alpha teachers are facilitators of learning. They are model learners who guide students in their exploration and share their enthusiasm for learning. Some of the key characteristics of Alpha are:

- A multiage community
- Individualized planning and assessment
- Integrated curriculum
- Student-teacher partnerships
- Collaborative problem solving
- Reflective learning
- Demonstrated application of skills
- Teacher as facilitator and model learner

4. Watershed Team Philosophical Foundations

(Radnor, Pennsylvania, Middle School)

The ultimate goal of the WATERSHED program is to promote the students' abilities to gather, retain, interrelate, apply, and communicate firsthand information; and to foster within each student a positive sense of responsibility for and pride in the improvement of those abilities.

The materials, methods, and procedures employed in the program to achieve this ultimate goal all stem directly from the following philosophical tenets underlying the WATERSHED program.

1. Primary learning skills are processes, not sets of facts. These processes, which are used to handle information, are more important than any particular set of facts.
2. Integrated learning methods more closely match natural learning styles because they focus the learner's attention directly onto relationships, higher level thinking skills, and processes of applications.

3. Methods involving hands-on and firsthand learning through self-motivated discovery and a reliance on primary resource materials are more effective than secondhand methods.
4. Successful learning is directly tied to the students' senses of self-investment and self-discipline, their commitment, and their willingness to accept responsibility.
5. The characteristics listed in number four above are most readily achieved when students are permitted the opportunity to practice them within a supportive atmosphere of encouragement teamed with high expectations.
6. Traditional letter grade systems cannot adequately reflect the WATERSHED program's emphasis on processes. Furthermore, such grades too often become an end in themselves without concern for the learning that is the true aim of education. Therefore, we use written comments on a weekly basis to describe the students' ongoing development and achievement. These comments provide useful information that specifically recognizes and praises the students' accomplishments while delineating areas that need further attention and improvement.

- WATERSHED Basic Objectives

1. To create a learning environment in which the students accept responsibility for their learning.
2. To provide students with an awareness of the relevance of learning and of their personal connections with the materials covered, and to demonstrate the interrelatedness of all learning.
3. To emphasize the importance of fundamental thinking and communication skills, and to encourage learning from primary rather than secondary (e.g., textbook) sources.
4. To create a learning environment that promotes cooperative rather than competitive learning.
5. To illustrate that education is best achieved when it is a cooperative venture shared by teachers, students, and parents; and, to that end, to maximize the parental involvement in the learning process.
6. To demonstrate that effective learning is a lifelong pursuit that transcends the limits of the school's walls.
7. To emphasize the ecological, historical, economic, political, and cultural importance of watersheds.

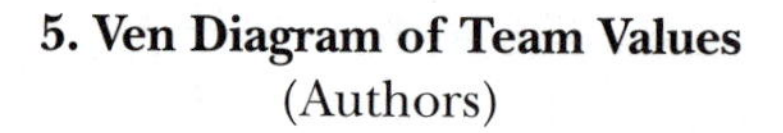

5. Ven Diagram of Team Values
(Authors)

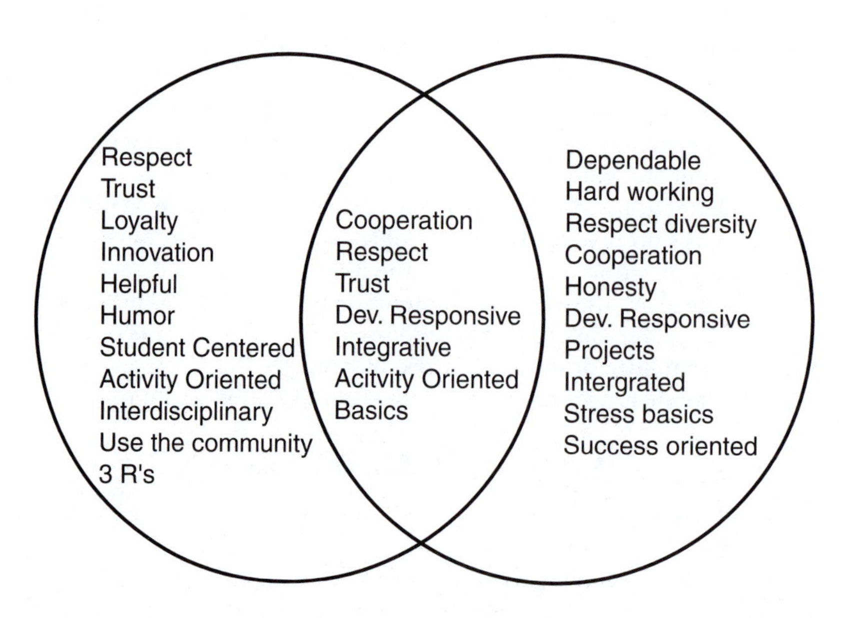

GOVERNANCE

Who will do what?
What will be the team leader's role?
How will we make decisions? Reach agreement?
What will students decide?
How will we handle discipline? Rules?
How can we be sure that we will all stick together?

Scenario 1

The five teachers on the Adventure team have assembled for their daily planning meeting. Jeff, the team leader, opens the meeting with a description of his plan for Back to School Night for the parents of their students. The program will begin with parents rotating among their children's teachers according to their individual schedules, followed by a general meeting and refreshments. He speculates that the whole program can be completed in an hour and a half. He further designates four tasks that need to be carried out by his colleagues: advertising and promotion, food, scheduling, and program. He will act as emcee, and the other teachers will need to prepare a ten-minute overview of their curriculum. Jeff then asks for volunteers for the four planning tasks he has designated.

Scenario 2

Dennis Walters has been a continuing challenge for students and teachers alike on the High Flyers team. The Flyers' number one team rule, arrived at after several team discussions, is their own spin on the Golden Rule: "Treat others as you want them to treat you." Whereas Dennis enjoys roughhousing, the overwhelming majority of his classmates do not. In fact, they increasingly avoid contact with him. His restlessness and reckless conduct around the classroom and hallways often result in shoving or sucker-punching others, especially boys. Occasionally such incidents have escalated into wrestling matches that have to be broken up by teachers. Although Dennis insists that he is sorry and is trying to control his impulses better, his classmates are wearying of his lapses. Dennis's failures have reached the point that some kind of action to protect everyone's interests must be taken.

At one All-Team Meeting where several students complain openly about Dennis, the High Flyers' teachers, Curt and Sam, propose that the team decide on conditions that Dennis must meet if he is to be allowed to continue to be a part of their team. Seven of the forty-nine team members volunteer to serve on such a committee to draft a proposal for the team, and Sam agrees to meet with them. Their eventual recommendation is that a vote be taken to place Dennis on probation with the stipulation that the next time he violates a team rule, he will have to spend the following day at their school's time-out room, losing the right to be part of whatever the High Flyers are doing for that day. If he fails a second time, the same consequences will apply. A third failure during a school term will result in a team request that the principal suspend him from school for one day. With Dennis in attendance, a firm, focused, but compassionate discussion ensues. Ultimately the High Flyers adopt the proposal by a 45-to-2 margin with two abstentions. Afterward several students offer encouragement to Dennis, saying, "C'mon, you can do it."

Scenario 3

The sixty-six students and three teachers on the Eagles team begin their Friday morning meeting with reports from two student committees that have been investigating potential sites for the team's annual trip that brings closure to the school year. Andy, the spokesperson for the State Parks Committee, gives a brief overview of what his committee has learned about the availability, costs, and regulations for school use of state parks. Each of the three parks being considered is described by a different member. Their report concludes with an estimation of total expenses for each site. Next, Marty and her three committee members report on what they have learned about two privately owned summer camps that would suit their needs for the team trip. All students are then invited to ask any questions they have about any of the sites. When their questions have been answered, Joe, the head teacher, organizes a secret ballot vote.

Scenario 4

Louis, the thirteen-year-old Unity team moderator for the month of March, reports at the team meeting that Earline has found anonymous hate notes in her locker on three occasions. He reads the notes aloud, especially the most recent one threatening that her long, blond hair is going to be cut. The students sit in stony silence. Earline, near tears, says that she doesn't have any idea who is responsible for the notes. One by one, students express their indignation. One student challenges his classmates to live up to the team name of "Unity." Another asks, "Are we going to let one screwed-up person ruin our team?" Carol, another teacher, says that it is very easy to become confused and angry during adolescence and that all students should look at themselves and resolve to be fair toward others in all their social interactions. Louis brings the discussion to a close by observing that "relationships can't be controlled by rules. We need to work at this—Let's get with it!" Although the meeting closes with a somewhat vexing ambience, several students make a point of going over to reassure Earline.

Scenario 5

Pioneers teachers Meg, Mark, and Nat are meeting in May to finalize their team budget proposal for the coming year. Nat, a superior geography teacher, is very excited about an expensive new geography text. Meg, an equally accomplished specialist in science and technology, wants additional computers and software for teaching a year-long meteorological theme. Mark, the Pioneers' math specialist, wants to set aside funds for a series of local field trips that will show students how mathematics is incorporated into so many professional careers. After more than an hour of discussion, the Pioneers teachers face the fact that they simply do not have the resources to finance all of these expenses.

Their solution is an inevitable compromise: Nat proposes that they purchase just ten copies of the geography text to be shared by students. Meg figures that if they invest only in the software, they can work with the computers they already have access to. Both Nat and Meg pledge to work with Mark to line up parent drivers for small group outings to observe applications of mathematics in the adult career world.

Scenario 6

At the nine hundred-student Shenandoah Middle School, twelve core team leaders, two unified arts team leaders, the principal, and two assistant principals assemble after school for their biweekly leadership team forum. Their focus today is curriculum. A few of the teams have developed special activity-oriented projects that have captured the imagination of the students and the attention of the parents. On other teams, a few students are occasionally doing engaging work; but most teams have yet to move from square one. In a freewheeling conversation, it emerges that:

- Some teachers seem jealous about what other teams are doing.
- Special subject teachers feel left out; only a few so-called good teams have asked for their input and help.
- Several teachers have a real knack for inventing curriculum to which the students respond.
- Some teachers are extremely reluctant to digress from their textbooks and what they perceive to be the expectations of high school teachers.
- A few team leaders feel that they lack the expertise to lead curriculum reform on their teams.

After over an hour of spirited discussion and exchanges of anecdotes, the group recognizes its school's need for an in-service emphasis on active curriculum. Members also suggest that the principal consider requiring each team to carry out at least one significant activity-oriented project per team for the coming year and providing in-service support in anticipation of that requirement. They also discuss procedures for teachers visiting one another's classrooms.

COMMENTARY

We are our choices.
Jean-Paul Sartre

Democratic governance is the most fundamental principle of our American culture, and schools must provide the very best possible opportunities for youth to learn about their various freedoms and the dimensions of personal responsibility that comprise our complex culture. Having a say over both one's current and future living and working circumstances is fundamental to developing responsible citizenship. This basic truth of human nature applies to adults as well as to young adolescent students. School groups, clubs, and other youth organizations function best when the adults and youth who are involved get to make many of the decisions that ultimately affect them.

The Adventure team described in Scenario 1 has vested a good bit of authority and responsibility in Jeff, its team leader, and he appears to be functioning in the rather independent, autocratic way that has become all too familiar in schools. After being designated "the leader," he has proceeded independently to plan an upcoming event in considerable detail. To teachers who appreciate such a colleague's take-charge style, membership on the Adventure team might seem ideal. Many teachers value colleagues who expedite matters. To the more democratic reader, however, such an arrangement would constitute at best a difficult working condition. The Adventure team's day-to-day functioning appears to be built around a particularly strong role for the team leader. Our experience has taught that a fully functioning team at its best is a synergistic partnership in which every team member leads from time to time and both gives and receives energy from shared commitment and energy. Although it must be remembered that there is not any single way for all teams to accomplish good governance, we urge that teachers approach their work with an expectation and spirit of equal partnership.

Just as adults should work toward equal responsibility, so must their students. Democracy in its purest rendering is simply talk by committed people about a common issue. In Scenario 2 Dennis's behavior is the issue; teachers Curt and Sam provided a format for the High Flyers to confront and to try to resolve a matter that was eating away at their community. Furthermore, their proposal constituted a fair and reasonable opportunity for Dennis to take responsibility for himself. It also protected everyone else's interests. And perhaps most importantly, the process modeled how civilized people in a free democracy can go about dealing equitably and morally with each other. A distinct advantage of working with young adolescents has too often been overlooked, namely, that they want to resolve differences fairly and are capable of reasoning to just conclusions. Further, their inclination toward forgiveness and support for the underdog is a precious and increasingly endangered virtue.

There must be a correlate that as authentic opportunity for responsibility increases, so does genuine ownership. The Eagles teachers in Scenario 3 understand the capabilities and governance needs of their young adolescent students, and they have taught them how to systematically go about the process of defining a problem, investigating resources, gathering pertinent data, and making recommendations—no small matter for young people making their way in our increasingly complex culture. The students' handling of the problem of selecting a site for their team's culminating trip stands as solid evidence of learning a fundamental problem-solving process and enjoying the sense of personal efficacy that derives from having exercised real initiative and responsibility.

The challenges for students in developing a positive personal identity will frequently lead to kids making familiar human mistakes. Earline, the victim of the hate notes described in Scenario 4, was understandably hurt by the experience. Her teammates needed to confront this situation directly in order to gain greater understanding of their time of life, each other and themselves, and their needs. The realization that the team's values and name, "Unity," have been contradicted by the incident is a vital reference point for discussion. Teacher Carol showed important restraint and maturity in the perspective she brought. The key things about this scenario are the credibility of the team meeting and its affirming atmosphere. Although an unfortunate and hurtful incident has occurred, such incidents have occurred throughout human history, and they are probably inevitable. What is most hopeful about this situation is the way in which it has been confronted by kids whose concerns are both supported and guided by similarly concerned and affirming, optimistic adults.

School budgets have traditionally been organized around the needs of academic departments. In Scenario 5, the Pioneers are fortunate because their school budget expenses are determined according to the school's teams. Meg, Mark, and Nat have identified some legitimate needs, but their projected costs outstrip their resources—a familiar circumstance for most of us. They must make decisions about team expenditures based on a comprehensive overview of the Pioneer educational goals and program they have created. Given this shared ownership, they willingly compromise and support each other's priorities. Our experience shows that teachers are frugal about both spending money and anticipating future contingencies.

Scenario 6 illustrates the fact that effective team leaders can play important roles in helping both their own teams and those of an entire school. Through the Leadership Team Forum, Team Leaders and their principals address problems common to all teams. By hearing all sides of an issue, strengths and weaknesses can be identified, and decisions can be made that improve the functioning of all teams. In this particular scenario, curriculum was the issue, but team policies, climate, evaluation, or virtually any topic could be focused upon. In large schools, leadership teams are especially important because faculty meetings are often unwieldy forums for decision making about important concerns. Generally, team leaders bring issues raised in their own teams to the leadership team meeting. They then return to their own teams to discuss the leadership team's thoughts and possible actions. In this manner, teams can communicate effectively with administrators, and the continual improvement of teams can be at the forefront of the all-school agenda.

A frequent question about teaming is: How are students disciplined? There are numerous theories about student behavior, systems for classroom management, and strategies for disciplining students. Individual schools sometimes adopt a particular approach to ensure consistency. School rules handed down by administrators and/or faculty are common. And in spite of dubious evidence about their effectiveness, detention halls and in-school suspension programs seem to be almost institutions in themselves in schools serving adolescents.

Although there are advocates of a variety of approaches to getting students to conduct themselves responsibly, our experience has taught that a reliable indicator of an effective, successful team is the diminution of behavioral incidents and disciplinary referrals to the school office. Often teams negotiate some team rules with students. (See Example 2.) An important mark of success in achieving authentic team governance is evident when students conform their behavior to the standards that they have helped to create. Interpersonal conflict usually diminishes drastically, often disappearing altogether, when young adolescents and their teachers work out behavioral expectations, standards, and consequences among themselves. Many young adolescents will reject outright rules and regulations handed down by adults, but they will ultimately end up with similar standards when they are authentically engaged in constructing a process for themselves. However behavior rules are developed, it is essential that they be based upon treating others with respect. Also, they should be few in number, reflect broad principles, and be stated positively.

Each of the scenarios portrays a governance process that has been created by teachers who have agreed about some educational goals and developed a procedure for making decisions. What stands out is that although differing definitions of "democratic process" are in evidence, a requisite of successful teaming is that teachers work out a team governance plan. Not all of us are equally disposed toward sharing authority for decision making with students, so we must begin in a place that is manageable for us. Wolfgang and Glickman (1990) are a particularly helpful resource, offering a range of discipline approaches geared to students' levels of development. The ideal we seek, however, must be a setting in which young people grow into taking responsibility for governing themselves effectively and morally. Nothing less will do if we are to successfully address the challenges of preparing youngsters to live responsibly in the present as well as in the more complex worlds of high school, higher education, work, and adult life.

The Role of the Team Leader

The role of Team Leader requires additional elaboration. As Scenario 6 indicates, large schools with multiple teams of several teachers each often find that designated team leaders are necessary to accomplish many of the school's administrative functions. Often smaller teams also designate one teacher as the team leader. The important issue is that one or more persons accept responsibility for seeing that particular tasks are accomplished. Specific duties vary according to the priorities of a given team.

Sometimes team leaders receive extra compensation for carrying out specific duties not expected of other teachers. In other cases, teachers on a single team will simply rotate the role and responsibilities each year, ensuring that each teacher has the benefit of the distinct perspective of that leadership role.

Team Leader roles vary from one school or team to another, but in general the team leader is responsible for:

1. Leading and monitoring development of a team vision.

   The vision and plan of a team are the product of a collaboration of every team member's ideas. The Team Leader assures that it is a collective vision and that that vision guides development and implementation of the team's educational program.
2. Leading team meetings.

   On a day-to-day basis the Team Leader usually prepares an agenda and conducts Common Planning Time meetings, seeing to it that everyone shares in team responsibilities and discussions. It is also commonly the responsibility of the team leader to see that accurate team records are kept on a daily basis so that the team log is complete and up to date.
3. Communicating with administrators, other teams, and parents.

   Principals of large schools often schedule regular meetings of team leaders to assure efficient and comprehensive communication. Team Leaders report their team's major activities, learn about other teams, discuss issues, and works with other team leaders to improve teaming throughout the school. In addition, they coordinate team-parent conferences and other means of communicating with parents.
4. Coordinating curriculum planning and teaching.

   As explained earlier, a distinct advantage of teaming is that teachers can plan and coordinate curriculum more effectively when they work closely on a team. It is sometimes the Team Leader's responsibility to see that such coordination occurs and that time schedules, grouping arrangements, and resources are used effectively.
5. Monitoring student and team progress.

   Although every teacher shares this important responsibility, the Team Leader sees to it that *all* students, not just those who command attention, are discussed and accommodated in an equitable manner. In addition, the Team Leader ensures that student assessment is carried out in a thoughtful and comprehensive manner and that the team systematically reviews its overall progress.
6. Preserving a safe, protective climate.

   In order to gain the most from every team member, it is important that every teacher participate and contribute to team business. In conducting team planning meetings, the Team Leader is able to involve all team members. Where there is disagreement or conflict, it is the Team Leader's job to move toward resolution.

If the conflict is beyond the skill of the Team Leader, the matter goes forward to the principal. Building consensus is vitally important to team unity.

It is important to note that a leader is not someone who does everything, but rather is someone who sees to it that everything gets done. Moreover, all team members, including students, assume various leadership roles over time. Characteristics of team leaders expected by team members as reported by Larson and LaFasto (1989, 123) include the following:

1. Avoid(s) compromising team objectives with political issues.
2. Exhibits a personal commitment to the team's goals.
3. Does not dilute the team's effort with too many priorities.
4. Is fair and impartial toward all team members.
5. Is willing to confront and resolve issues associated with inadequate performance by team members.
6. Is open to new ideas and information from team members.

Leadership in a changing contemporary school is no small order, to be sure. There are countless pressures from outside and inside a middle level school. It is often a challenge just to remain focused on the directions that one has chosen. So much depends on the full participation and loyalty of every teacher that leading change is at the very least daunting. Sarah Johnson, a thirteen-year-old student in a middle school, has benefited from learning how to be a leader by having firsthand experience and by observing the excellent models that her teachers are. She speaks particularly eloquently about what good leaders do:

> "One thing I've learned is how to be a good leader, which is not dominating the group but leading the group in a way so that everybody adds ideas and makes input in an organized way. That's the way we get the job done."

PRINCIPLES

By *governance* we refer to the provision for making decisions on and about how the team will function. Some decisions must be made only by teachers in consultation with the principal. Others may be made after consultation with specialists and parents. However, by far the most important decisions on effective teams are made by the teachers in consultation with each other and by teachers and students in collaboration. It is through this process of deciding that teaming has the greatest potential for helping young adolescents grow as active, optimistic, loyal citizens in a democratic society. In our experience, after students have sampled a democratic way of life, they'll continue to choose it over all alternatives.

- **Teachers must concur about their decision-making process.**
  Just as teachers must come to a consensus about vision (chapter 4), they must also find common ground about how they will work together and the ways in which students can be involved in decisions about the team. The eventual plan

should not be decided by a majority rule, however. Everyone needs to concur about something as important as this aspect of planning. Although the eventual plan may allow for voting on particular matters, the tone should be amicable.

- **Teacher roles and responsibilities must be defined.**

  Teaming entails a great deal of shared responsibility. For the sake of orderliness and understanding, roles and responsibilities should be anticipated and spelled out. They may be filled by volunteering, by lottery, or by assignment, according to the preference of the team.

- **Students must have a say in their team governance.**

  If students are to take the team seriously, they must become involved in ways that hold meaning for them. Although teachers will likely choose the team name and define the team vision, student decisions about items such as colors, logos, and special activities will initially help them develop connections with the team. Engaging students in significant decisions about rules and curriculum holds the greatest potential for their development. When the processes are authentic for them, such things as rituals and traditions will emerge as a kind of glue holding it all together. Teachers must continuously ask themselves, "What voice do students have? How is the team good for them?"

- **The governance process, including the plan for discipline, should be publicly stated.**

  After there is agreement about how decisions are going to be made, what teacher and student roles have been defined, and how the process can be amended—publish these decisions. Include information relevant to students and parents in a team handbook so that they will understand their status and what is expected of everyone. Decisions about strictly professional processes need not be included, of course.

- **Common planning meetings and all-team meetings must be regularly scheduled and conducted in an effective, purposeful manner.**

  These meetings, discussed in chapter 6, are the governance vehicle.

PLANNING GUIDELINES

1. *Agree upon a decision-making process.*

   Team members usually aspire to make decisions by consensus, and that spirit bodes well for building interpersonal solidarity. However, gaining consensus is sometimes extremely time consuming. Many teams require consensus only where vital issues are at stake. For less vital issues, they may choose to vote. For routine issues, if team members cannot reach consensus, they may have members take turns making the decision or even draw straws or flip a coin. What is most important is that no decision must be allowed to become divisive. Teachers' interpersonal loyalty is *crucial.*

2. *Brainstorm a list of things that students can do for themselves but are done for them by teachers.*

   This list may include simple items such as taking attendance or dismissing class at the end of a period, or complex items such as helping design a curriculum project, tutoring a peer or leading an All-Team Meeting. Consider these items as you develop rules and procedures.

3. *Identify teacher roles and responsibilities that need to be filled.*

   Identify teacher roles that need to be filled: Team Leader, secretary or scribe, newsletter editor, parent liaison, timekeeper, service project coordinator, and so on. Solicit volunteers for the roles that you deem appropriate. Consider expertise, desire, and overall workload in assigning responsibilities; be sure to allow students to assume responsibility whenever feasible. The only essential role for all teams—even two-person partner teams—is Team Leader. Someone must consistently take responsibility for coordinating team affairs.
4. *Establish a schedule and governance procedure for common planning time (CPT) and all-team meetings (ATM).*

   What will be the "rules of the meeting"? For CPT, be certain that everyone concerned understands clearly the time, place, agenda, and expectations for the meeting. For ATM, be certain that issues of concern to students are included in the agenda, addressed, and decided upon in a democratic fashion, as described in Scenario 2. The format for CPT and ATM is discussed in chapter 6.
5. *Develop rules for discipline and behavior that are simple, positive, and based upon broad principles of respect.* (See Examples 1–3.)

   Be sure to involve students in the rule-making process and work to gain their commitment to these guidelines. Scenario 2 illustrates a problem-focused, organic process of dealing with the need for a rule.

ADDITIONAL POSSIBILITIES

- Members of long-standing teams evolve well beyond merely perfunctory ways of working together. In some cases teachers smile knowingly and say, "We've worked together so long, and we know each other so well that we can complete each other's sentences." Such cases are remarkable, to be sure, and that quality of understanding is a goal worth pursuing. Teams don't reach that point, however, unless they've built a substantial process for successful collaboration.
- An additional dimension of governance that often serves teams well is a parent advisory group. At the outset there will be enough issues needing attention to justify postponing establishment of such an advisory group. However, after a comfortable routine has been established, such a group that meets with the teachers several times a year can become a source of both general advocacy and constructive help on initiatives such as material resources, chaperones for trips, sponsors for service projects, and so forth.
- Encourage students to discuss governance issues through the curriculum. Literature for adolescents such as *Lord of the Flies* is often a good place to concentrate these discussions because adolescents' decision making is a notable theme. Social studies units often include excellent governance and decision-making elements.
- The ultimate evidence of effective governance lies in the ways that students go about living and working with each other. It is in *their manifestation* of strategies for planning studies or projects, dealing with interpersonal disputes, and reflecting on their growth and learning that teachers can recognize the effects of teachers'

efforts. When students freely draw upon the strategies that teachers have modeled in their own transactions, there is certain evidence of learning and growth.

CAVEATS

Assume that your governance processes and your comfort with them will evolve as you gain experience in making decisions more collaboratively. Do not permit expediency to overwhelm democratic procedures. Autocratic decisions may be faster and more efficient, but they also send mixed messages about where rights and authority are vested.

Be patient with each other and stick together! There will be lots of unanticipated developments. Protect and preserve your relationships with each other. With shared commitment and trust, everything is possible; without them, it is unlikely that you will be successful or satisfied.

EXAMPLES

1. Team Constitution

(Marquette Middle School, Madison, Wisconsin)

We, the class of Rooms 201/202 [sic team] at Marquette Middle School, in order to form the best class possible, pledge to live by the following statements:

- We appreciate our individual differences. We recognize that each person is unique.
- All individuals will be treated with respect and dignity. There is no room for put-downs in our room.
- We will be honest with one another in order to build trust.
- We will learn to resolve conflicts, which may involve learning to live with nonresolution.
- Each person will truly listen to every other person.
- We will cooperate and collaborate with one another.
- Learning will be meaningful.
- We recognize that people learn in different ways.

We agree to abide by these truths to the best of our abilities, both as unique individuals and as a cooperative and collaborative community.
(Brodhagen 1995, 83)

2. Discipline Plan Procedure

(Authors)

1. Develop basic rules and their rationale with students. Limit them to a small number—5 or 6 at most—and state them in a positive manner. Post them and/or put them in the team handbook.

2. Develop positive consequences (teacher acknowledgment and appreciation, privileges, rewards, etc.).
3. Establish negative consequences for disobeying rules; these increase for repeated offenders.
4. Plan for extreme cases.
5. Plan for involving parents and guidance. Send a copy home.
6. Share with the principal.

3. Team Rules

(a) B. B. Team (Better than Best) Community Code
(Winooski, Vermont, Middle School)

- Respect learning. It's the reason we're here.
- Be kind and peaceful at all times.
- Everyone has the right to speak and be heard.
- Treat all our possessions with care.
- School should be fun and full of celebration.

• *(b) Troika Team Rules [sign hanging from ceiling]*
(Jackie Robinson Middle School, New Haven, Connecticut)

Welcome to Troika—Pod for Progress

Rules to Follow:

• be here by 8:05 • ~~talk loudly~~ •
~~chew gum~~ • work quietly •
use a pass when leaving •
~~throw stuff on the floor~~ •
respect others • put things away •
smile • do homework • ~~argue~~ •
~~waste time~~ • ask questions •
~~lie~~ • love • be happy • ~~cheat~~ •
~~steal~~ • relax • ~~smoke~~ • ~~eat~~ •
~~curse~~ •

ORGANIZATION AND PROCEDURES

How will we function day to day? Week to week?
How will we structure time and tasks?
What roles will teachers and students fulfill?

Scenario 1

Jimmy: *I've got two tests and a big project due tomorrow. I'll never be able to do well on all of that. It's too much. What's more, I've got to stay after school today. Ol' Mr. Harris is making me stay just because I was talking to Gerry during a writing assignment. That's not fair; I wasn't bothering anyone. Some of my other teachers let us talk . . .*

Lewis: *Huh, that's a downer. On my team, we never have more than one test a day. Each teacher has a different "test day" reserved if they want to use it. And if a big project is due, there never are tests on that day. The teachers work it out. . . . All of them have the same rules, too. We helped make the rules. It's hard to get away with stuff, but it's fair . . .*

Scenario 2

The Dolphin Team planning period begins ten minutes late because Frank has had to talk with the repair shop about his car and because Ellen has been talking with the counselor about a student. Shortly after the meeting begins, Mary states that she is frustrated by planning meetings because they are not conducted in a businesslike manner. Because everyone does a lot of talking, team members don't manage to discuss and take action relative to many issues that need attention. She urges that they develop a written agenda for each meeting and stick to it. Regina, the team leader, agrees and in addition suggests that they devise a weekly structure for their planning meetings. Mary and Frank concur. Frank suggests that they devote one day to discussing students. Mary urges spending a day to plan advisory activities. She suggests Friday so that they can review the past week's events and plan for the week ahead. She further suggests that one day weekly be set aside to discuss and develop curriculum. Gradually, a weekly plan emerges.

Finally, Regina points out how much of team planning time is being devoted to parent conferences that all three teachers attend. After much discussion, they decide that unless there are compelling circumstances, only the student's advisor—and the student, when feasible—will attend.

Scenario 3

The Skyscrapers Team at Calhoun Middle School in New York City is meeting, as it does every Monday, to discuss students. Team members are joined for a portion of the meeting by a physical education teacher, who has a close relationship with one of the students. (An assistant principal temporarily covers his class.) Because the six students who are "next" on the alphabetical student team listing are known in advance, team members have given forethought to them. The team is careful to talk about students' learning styles, interests, and overall development as well as their academic work and behavior, with the advisor keeping notes. As always, unless there is an emergency, discussion is limited to "five plus" minutes for each student, time being kept by an egg timer with a bell. When closure on a particular student is not gained in this time period, the team exercises its self-imposed option to extend conversation for a maximum of two minutes. When team members fail to come to a consensus through extended discussion, it signals that there is "a lot going on" and that the student's advisor needs to have a conference with the student or parents or both. Conversely, when the team can talk for only thirty seconds about a student, teachers realize that the student is getting lost in the shuffle and that a conference again is indicated.

All six students are discussed before the forty-five-minute common planning period ends. In the few minutes remaining, the teachers talk about students who will need special consideration in a forthcoming meeting with the school psychologist.

Scenario 4

One of the important tasks during a Flyers Team meeting prior to the start of school is to divvy up responsibilities. After brainstorming and prioritizing the various tasks that will need to be done, each member chooses a number of them for which he or she agrees to take primary responsibility. For example, Ed volunteers to coordinate the community service program; Georgianne, the Back to School Night team activities for parents; Molly, the fall camping trip at the YMCA Camp Cheerio; Sally, the team minicourse program slated for February. The team members also agree that student coordinators for many activities will be decided upon during appropriate all-team meetings. Because the team orientation program on the first day interfaces with the all-school orientation, the team asks Georgianne, the Team Leader, to head this activity. When taking and distributing team minutes are brought up, there is silence—no one volunteers. Because no one *wants* to do the job but it is one that definitely needs doing, members decide to rotate the role of recorder on a weekly basis. The recorder is to use a minutes-taking form that the Flyers developed last year, placing one copy in each teacher's mailbox, including that of the specialist teacher affiliated with the team, and one copy in the team log.

Scenario 5

Eight students from the Paradise Project (see chapter 4, Scenario 1) and one of the teachers, Mort, are on a trip to visit the Foxfire Program in Rabin Gap, Georgia. They are staying with a host family (sleeping bags in the family room and living room) with whom Emily, the eighth-grade trip leader, has made arrangements. Before supper, two students announce to the hosts, "We are 'bull cooks.' How can we help with the meal?" After supper, two other students clear the table and do the dishes. Emily then calls a trip meeting at which the day's events are discussed, plans for the evening and next day are outlined, and Brad, the trip treasurer, gives a financial update. After an hour or so of homework and journal writing, the eight students engage in jokes, games, and storytelling with their hosts and their hosts' children. Before bedtime the "trip mommy," Dennis, checks to make sure that no one is homesick.

The next morning, students again help with breakfast chores. The "van maintenance supervisor" reports to Mort, "We are a quart low on oil, and the front left tire needs three pounds of air." After the students have cleaned up and packed, they hug/thank the hosts, present them with Paradise Project T-shirts and a certificate of appreciation, and set out "on the road."

Scenario 6

Students and teachers of the Wizards Team are sitting on the floor in the multipurpose room for an all-team meeting. Marty, the student leader, opens the meeting with a pun that brings predictable groans from the Wizards. This introduces the "joke of the day," told by Alice, another student. Jim, a teacher and the team's resident riddle-puzzler-mystery man, poses another of his brain twisters: "If a brick weighs seven pounds and a half brick, how much does a brick and a half weigh?" Although numerous answers are called out, Lauren, not known for her problem-solving prowess, is the only student to solve the problem within the two-minute time limit. When asked how she got the answer, she explains, "Simple. I just drew a balance beam, put a brick on one side and a half brick and seven pounds on the other side. So a whole brick must weigh fourteen pounds, and a brick and a half weighs twenty-one pounds. It's easy." Completion of the joke and puzzler rituals signal that the Wizards have come to order.

Next, two students present aspects of independent study projects in which they have been engaged. Randy tells of his research into the former Negro Baseball League, conveying to his teammates his admiration for the skill of players such as Josh Gibson and Satchel Paige, and his moral indignation that they were not afforded the opportunity to play in the major leagues until after World War II.

Joyce then presents her study of comic book superheroes, explaining their admirable qualities and superhuman powers and commenting on the lack of real-life heroes that students have today. She also shares a cartoon strip about X-Man, her favorite superhero, which she has designed.

Lastly, the team members enter into a "town meeting" to discuss a recurring problem: snowballing. Some students are angry because they are being hit by randomly thrown snowballs during after-lunch recess. They want the school rule prohibiting snowballing to be enforced. Other students says that snowball battles are fun and that they should not be prohibited because of a few "accidents." After much deliberation, the students, assisted by their teachers, agree upon a plan to take to the school's leadership team for consideration. Students who wish to engage in snowballing may do so in a clearly marked area that has a ten-yard-wide "neutral zone" in the middle so that no "close-up" throws can be made. Those students who do not wish to be involved are to stay clear of the area. Further snowballing is to be allowed only on days that the snow has not become icy.

COMMENTARY

This time, like all times, is a very good one if we but know what to do with it.

Ralph Waldo Emerson

There are many procedures that teams can develop to make schooling more comprehensible, consistent, purposeful, and hassle free, both for students and for teachers. These procedures include important policies about scheduling, testing, projects, homework, assessment and discipline, as well as less important policies about headings on papers, coordination of audiovisual equipment, field trips, guest speakers, and a host of other items. Getting organized and developing sensible patterns of operation are two of the first tasks that teams should undertake. The absence of these procedures leads to bickering, confusion, and wasted time; the presence of these procedures leads to a flow and enjoyment of team life.

In Scenario 1, Lewis's team seems to understand the significance of thoughtful policies; Jimmy's team does not. Like many middle school students, Jimmy has a hard time planning ahead and tends to study only when an assignment is due. When multiple assignments are due the same day, he feels overwhelmed. By having set days for assignments and spreading them prudently, Freddy's team helps him structure his time, greatly increasing his chances of being successful.

Young adolescents need to operate within a structure that is consistent and just. Jimmy perceives his team as capricious, with teachers having different rules and enforcing them in different ways. Lewis, on the other hand, knows what to expect. The rules that he had a hand in developing are consistently enforced by each of his teachers.

As Scenario 2 indicates, teaming requires much collaboration and careful planning. Therefore, effective use of common planning time is a must. Teams that do not use their planning time wisely not only will fail to realize their potential, but also are likely, over time, to have this time taken away from them. Team meetings should not be run like corporate board meetings; it is very important that they involve personal sharing and good-natured give-and-take. However, they must be purposeful. Although developing appropriate procedures will not guarantee focused planning, it will greatly enhance the possibility.

The Dolphin Team teachers in Scenario 2 have been floundering in a manner typical of many inexperienced teams: They are a bit lax, and their discussions meander and frequently don't lead to action. However, they are beginning to get on track. Agreeing to be on time for meetings, to work from an agenda, and to follow a weekly structure that ensures systematic discussions about students, curricular matters, and advisory activities is a key procedure in facilitating effective team planning.

As noted in chapters 1 and 2, knowledge of one's students is critical to effective team functioning. A very important way of gaining such knowledge is to discuss students during common planning time, when teachers can share insights and concerns. Too often, however, discussion of students is confined to comparison of grades or repeated conversation about the few students who are "acting out" and driving teachers wild. The Skyscraper Team in Scenario 3, however, has developed a highly significant way of sharing information about students. The team's procedures focus discussion while ensuring that *every* student will be considered several times a semester in a way that looks at the student's full growth and development. It is especially important that every student is discussed because it is the quiet child, rather than the acting-out child, who may have the most serious problems. Moreover, unless items other than behavior are discussed, insights about how students learn and about which teaching/learning strategies may be appropriate for them may not be available to teachers. Skyscraper procedures also provide for immediate follow-up when needed and provide for input from special subject teachers on occasion.

There are many, many tasks for teams to do. Well-functioning teams prioritize these tasks, determine how many they can reasonably handle, and then assign responsibilities for organizing and developing strategies to accomplish their tasks. In Scenario 4, the equitable manner in which the Flyers team assigns responsibilities is noteworthy. Some coordinating responsibilities are chosen by teachers because of interest; sometimes a particular team member with special expertise or experience is suggested by a teammate. When no one volunteers for the task as recorder, responsibility for it is rotated on a weekly basis. (For other tasks, drawing lots might be appropriate.) Significantly, certain responsibilities are shared with students.

In chapter 4, we noted that Mort and Larry, the Paradise Project teachers, state, "We begin our teaching with the question, 'Are we doing something that students could do for themselves, and if so, why?'" Scenario 5 in this chapter illustrates the power of this statement because it shows the extent to which students can in fact assume responsibilities. Virtually every detail of their nine-day trip, and a procedure for carrying it out, was planned by the students, and their jobs while on the road were carried out like clockwork. Being so well organized not only lightened the load for Mort and made things flow smoothly, it more importantly empowered students, enabling them to learn a great number of academic, social, and real-world skills and values. It should also be noted that numerous procedures were in place for the forty-two students who remained at the school to enable them to assume increased responsibility for their learning while there with only one teacher.

The All-Team Meeting (ATM) is the one time when all teachers and students meet together. As such, it is of prime importance in building team spirit and identity, recognizing student accomplishments, handling governance issues, communicating, and generally relating to one another. In Scenario 6, we see that the Wizards have certain rituals for their meetings, offer opportunities for students to share their schoolwork, and provide a forum for discussion and decision making. Moreover, the meeting is led by a student, assisted by the team leader. The format that meetings take will vary from team to team, but if teams are to thrive, regularly scheduled ATMs are a must. In other chapters, scenarios that take place in ATMs elaborate and reinforce the importance of these meetings.

PRINCIPLES

- **Thoughtful team organization and procedures are essential to effective team functioning and the well-being of team members.**
  In their absence, confusion and ineffectiveness are likely to reign. Team goals and tasks must be carefully analyzed to see which structures and procedures best facilitate them. These structures and procedures should be prioritized, with the greatest time and effort devoted to developing and sustaining those that are most important.
- **Responsibility for coordinating and carrying out team policies and procedures should be evenly and equitably divided.**
  Many policies and procedures will of necessity be the purview of teachers; however, students should be given the opportunity to take initiative and responsibility wherever feasible.
- **Daily Common Planning Time (CPT) for teachers is essential.**
  If a team is to function successfully, the core teachers must be in continuing communication. It is unrealistic to expect people to accomplish a collaborative process such as teaming without time and opportunity to communicate about their process. Sometimes successful teams will meet formally during the school day fewer than five times a week, but those meetings are augmented by more informal after-school conversations. Occasionally a successful team will have only two or three formal meetings a week, but those meetings are of sufficient duration (e.g., ninety minutes) to accomplish team business.
- **Scheduling and grouping must be planned by teachers.**
  Although the administration must arrange the master schedule, including lunch and special subjects, day-to-day scheduling should be accomplished by teachers in accordance with their curricular goals. This arrangement provides them with the flexibility to manage time and to group students in a way that can best meet student needs.
- **All-Team Meetings must occur regularly, at least weekly.**
  Sometimes an All-Team Meeting (ATM) of teachers and students is the format for beginning and ending each school day. More often, however, ATMs are a less

frequent occurrence. Because this meeting serves as the primary context for many team functions, it should occur regularly, not less than weekly. Ideally, students learn from adult models how to successfully lead and participate in these meetings.

- **To emphasize their importance and to ensure that all persons concerned are aware of them, policies and procedures should be written down and made readily available to team teachers, students, parents, administrators, and other faculty.**

  In addition, those persons designated to carry out team responsibilities should be identified to all concerned.

PLANNING GUIDELINES

1. *After reviewing team goals, determine and prioritize areas where policies and procedures are needed.*

   Some of the major areas concern planning meetings, all-team meetings, curriculum, grading homework, acceptance of late work, offering re-tests, parent conferences, student behavior and relationships, parents, other faculty, and administration. (See Example 1.) Hold an all-team meeting at the beginning of school to discuss these issues and allow time at subsequent meetings for student input. Give special attention to academic procedures and to those that pertain to students and faculty members treating one another in a just and respectful manner. Focus on the quality of relationships, not simply on rules and procedures.
2. *Review responsibilities for carrying out team policies in a reasoned and fair manner.*

   These are discussed in guideline 2, chapter 5.
3. *Devote careful attention to the manner in which Common Planning Meetings are held.*

   Establish a regular meeting place, and have it equipped with a file cabinet with information about students, parents, and advisory activities; a team calendar; office supplies; a coffee pot; and hopefully a phone and computer.

   Develop a format (see Example 2) and clarify expectations about punctuality, agendas, record keeping, decision making, and the role of the team leader. It is especially important that a structure be developed to provide weekly time for a systematic way to discuss students (see Example 3), discuss and develop curriculum, and plan advisory activities. Assess your CPT meeting process frequently, especially in the early stages of your team. Look for what is working well as well as for ways to improve. Remember that like other aspects of teaming, these processes should evolve over time.
4. *Maintain good records.*

   Exemplary teams document their work, just as physicians, scientists, and other professionals do. Carefully written records of decisions are recorded and maintained in a team book, usually a three-ring binder that can be lent at regular intervals to the administration in order to be informative about the team's activity.

Minutes should also be placed in the mailbox of any special subject teachers affiliated with the team. Most teams rotate responsibility for record keeping. A form for such recording, such as the one in Example 4, is often helpful.

5. *Work out procedures for flexing the schedule.*

   Where teams have a block schedule (see Example 5) and sufficient autonomy, students can be grouped in a highly effective manner. The entire core block can be used for a single activity such as a field trip; regular periods (if they are initially set up) can be condensed to create an "extra period" to accommodate all-team meetings, speakers, films, minicourses, remediation, and so forth; double periods can be created for science labs or lengthy projects. Example 6 illustrates some of these possibilities.

6. *Work out procedures for grouping students.*

   In most instances, heterogeneous grouping is advisable. If school policies require ability grouping for one subject (most often math), make sure this does not result in all subjects being ability grouped. Because teachers control grouping, classes can periodically be regrouped to accommodate student needs or to provide a better mesh of personalities and learning styles. Also, students can be regrouped for special interest or skill development courses that teams may add to the schedule.

7. *Plan All-Team Meetings thoughtfully.*

   They need to include at least three elements: (1) having fun (jokes, music, skits, puzzlers, group singing, etc.), (2) presenting student work, and (3) responding to student issues or problems. Teachers will need to convene and lead initial ATMs, but the goal should be to involve students as early as possible. Plan for students to make presentations. As students gain understanding of how to lead or moderate these meetings, draw them into leadership roles until the teachers become primarily bystanders.

8. *Develop and circulate a team handbook in which team policies and procedures that pertain to students are clearly stated.*

   Those policies and procedures that pertain to common planning functions should be kept in a special booklet or in the team log.

9. *Periodically assess and discuss the effectiveness of team procedures.*

   Example 7 provides a type of survey that team members may use for this purpose.

ADDITIONAL POSSIBILITIES

A few teams that have daily ATMs invite students to help document team activities by summarizing each day's activities in a student-maintained team book. The book is a large bound volume of blank pages. Each day different students take responsibility for recording the day's events, sometimes augmenting them with sketches and/or photographs. Patterns of activity and spirit become evident in just a few weeks of such documentation. This kind of record keeping also provides further data about the effectiveness of the team. (See chapter 10.)

CAVEATS

- Don't underestimate the importance of being organized; it can make or break you.
- Be sure to use common planning time thoughtfully. It is virtually impossible to have a well-functioning team unless this is done. Moreover, unless this time is used effectively, it is likely to be eliminated from the schedule. This is especially true in schools where teachers are granted both individual and team planning time on a daily basis. It's a case of "use it or lose it."
- Be continually sensitive to ways in which students can develop initiative and responsibility. Doing for students what they can do for themselves robs them of the opportunity to learn many skills, to mature, and to become increasingly independent.

EXAMPLES

1. Common Procedures

(Authors)

Homework
Test schedule
Parent conferences
Field trips
Audiovisual coordination
Grading
Special projects
Heading on papers
Guest speakers

2. Sample Weekly Structure for Common Planning Meetings

(Authors)

- Monday—Discuss students systematically
- Tuesday—Instructional issues
- Wednesday—Student issues (at-risk students, student recognition, etc.)
- Thursday—As needed (progress reports, parent conferences, phone calls, school business, etc.)
- Friday—Plan advisory activities for next week

3. Team Discussion of Students

(Calhoun Middle School, New York City)

- Devote at least one common planning meeting per week to discussion of individual students.
- Make known in advance students to be discussed.
- Arrange for crucial special teachers to attend.
- Have advisors keep notes.
- Discuss all students systematically.
- Unless there is an emergency, limit discussion to five minutes per student. The team may elect to continue a discussion a maximum of two minutes longer.
- Advisor follows up with student/parent conference when no closure can be attained or when no one concerned knows the student very well.

- Discuss student interests, learning style, social development, and so forth, as well as grades and behavior.

4. Team Meeting Log
(Authors)

Comet Team Meeting Log

Members Present:

Date ____________________

Items discussed	Decisions

Action items	Person responsible

Comments:

5. Chrysalis Team Schedule
(Mt. Abraham Union Junior/Senior High School, Bristol, Vermont)

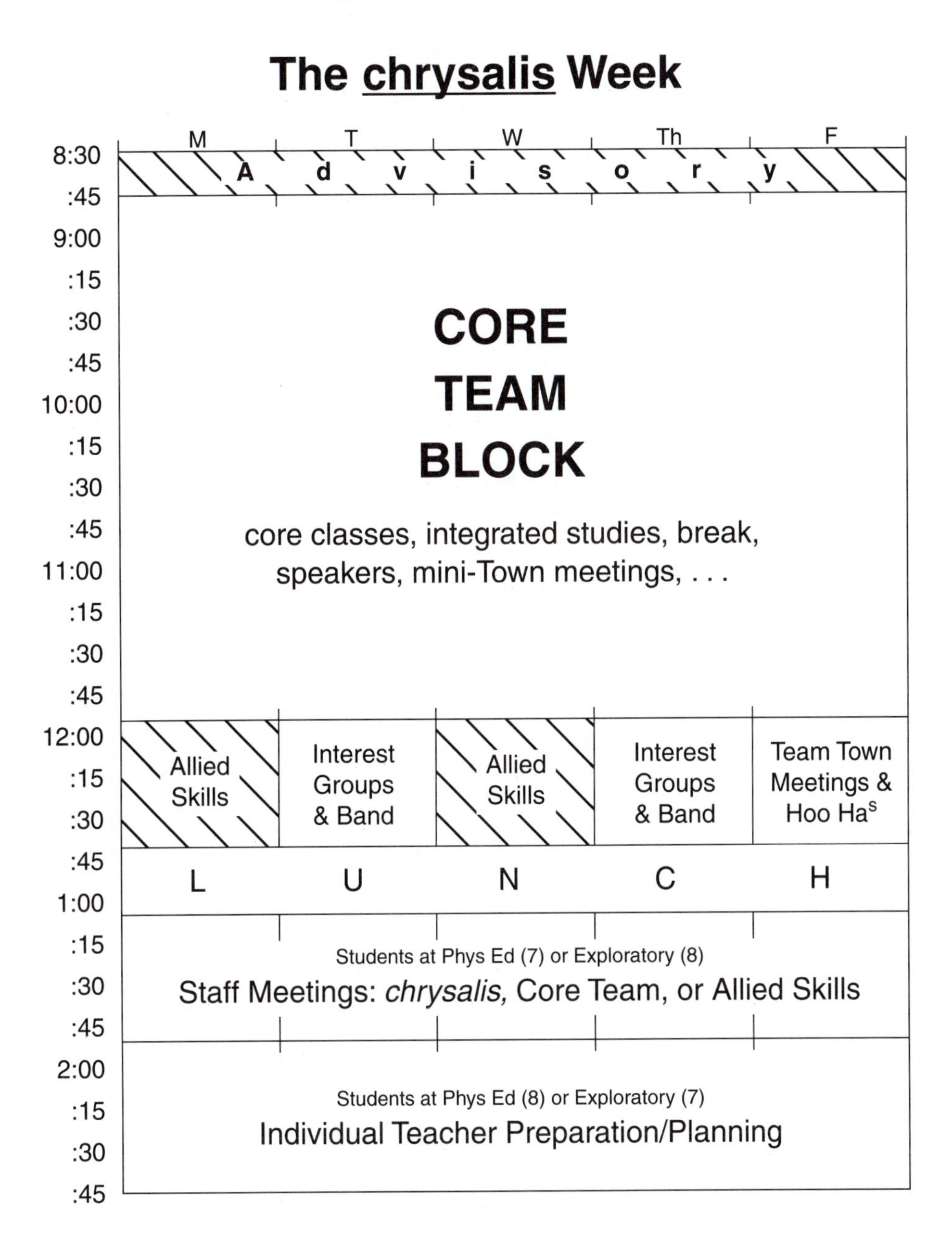

6. Some Ways to Flex a Schedule
(Authors)

(a) REGULAR BLOCK OF CLASSES
(Letters stand for groups)

Period	SCI	SS	LA	MA
1	A	B	C	D
2	B	A	D	C
3	C	D	A	B
4	D	C	B	A

(b) MAKE TIME FOR A FIELD TRIP

FIELD TRIP

(c) CREATE AN "EXTRA" PERIOD

Period	SCI	SS	LA	MA
1	gr. A	gr. B	C	D
2	B	A	D	C
3	C	D	A	B
4	D	C	B	A
SPEAKER, FILM, MEETING, MINICOURSE, SKILL SESSIONS, ETC.				

(d) CREATE A DOUBLE PERIOD

<table>
<tr><th>Period</th><th>SCI</th><th>SS</th><th>LA</th><th>MA</th></tr>
<tr><td rowspan="2">1+2</td><td rowspan="2">A
LAB</td><td rowspan="2">B
PROJECT</td><td>C</td><td>D</td></tr>
<tr><td>D</td><td>C</td></tr>
<tr><td>3</td><td>C</td><td>D</td><td>A</td><td>B</td></tr>
<tr><td>4</td><td>D</td><td>C</td><td>B</td><td>A</td></tr>
</table>

Monday/Tuesday: groups A&B have a double period—one day for science, the next for social studies.
Wednesday/Thursday: groups C&D have a double period—one day for science, the next for social studies.
Friday—All groups have their regular schedule.

7. Team Procedures Evaluation
(Source Unknown)

Please answer each question by circling your response on the following basis: 1 never, 2 seldom, 3 sometimes, 4 often, and 5 always.

My team:

1. meets at a regularly scheduled time	1	2	3	4	5
2. members are punctual	1	2	3	4	5
3. meets in a place that provides for privacy	1	2	3	4	5
4. uses an agenda	1	2	3	4	5
5. sets a time limit for meetings	1	2	3	4	5
6. meetings are formal and to the point	1	2	3	4	5
7. stays on task during the meeting	1	2	3	4	5
8. uses democratic procedures	1	2	3	4	5
9. uses responsibility for making decisions	1	2	3	4	5
10. has been effective in solving student discipline	1	2	3	4	5
11. searches for alternatives when making decisions	1	2	3	4	5
12. decisions are followed through by all members	1	2	3	4	5
13. keeps a record of team decisions	1	2	3	4	5
14. gives each member an equal opportunity to participate	1	2	3	4	5
15. delegates responsibility to all members	1	2	3	4	5
16. capitalizes on each member's strengths	1	2	3	4	5
17. members share ideas and materials	1	2	3	4	5
18. plans for and meets with parents as necessary	1	2	3	4	5
19. uses interdisciplinary units as part of the curriculum	1	2	3	4	5
20. utilizes flexible scheduling	1	2	3	4	5
21. members do their fair share	1	2	3	4	5
22. groups students for heightened effectiveness	1	2	3	4	5

CREATING IDENTITY AND RECOGNITION

Who are we?
What do we stand for?
How do we represent ourselves?
How do we acknowledge and celebrate?

Scenario 1

A three-foot-tall, green, papier-mache alligator rearing on its hind legs atop a table greets visitors to the hall of the Gator Team at Brewster Middle School at Camp Lejeune, North Carolina. Lining both sides of the corridor are cutouts of camouflage-colored alligators, each displaying a picture and biographical information about a student Gator. A vanity license plate proclaims, "I love my Gators." Posters and banners remind Gators that "Life takes team effort" and admonishes them to "Put your heart into school and school into your heart." We learn that "Gators say, 'No' to drugs, alcohol, and tobacco." Scattered signs, posters, and other decorations—some in the hall and some in classrooms—recognize individual student accomplishments. Students recognized include "Gator of the Week" for each academic subject, members of the Gator honor roll, students who have participated in the Mathketeers contest, and those who have read five or more books during the past grading period. In addition, every Gator's birthday is listed to be celebrated in due course. Farther down the hall, a large, freestanding alligator cutout stands with a suggestion box and a sign soliciting ideas about "how to improve the Swamp." One cannot miss the many messages about what it means to be a Gator.

Scenario 2

Bobbi and Reginald, veteran teachers on the sixth-grade Harmony Team, have a knack for working successfully with kids labeled "problem students." As a result, they are always assigned a good number of students who are having difficulties in school. They relish the opportunity. The two teachers and fifty students learn together in one big room that is set up in learning centers. Posters of various heroes—especially those who have been peacemakers, such as Gandhi, Martin Luther King Jr., and Mother Teresa—are prominent. There is a cooling-off chair in one corner of the room. In another area there is a punching bag. In the drama area, students frequently "invent plays." Sammy, a rather heavy boy, is a frequent user of this area, engaging others in improvisations that he writes about pregnant mothers. Bobbi and Reginald learn that Sammy is one of eleven children!

The first order of business every year for the Harmony Team is to work on building community spirit. Every morning All-Team Meetings are held and include a lot of discussions about why people do the things they do, how they feel when others hurt them, and ways to get along together. Students who are having particular interpersonal difficulties are given a lot of individual time, and there are phone calls home to report positive actions and accomplishments. The Harmony team, whose logo is a rainbow, always develops a number of rituals and in-house jokes that punctuate its day.

One October, just as the students were coming together as a team, five consecutive days of standardized testing were mandated by the school system. On the first day of testing, one student cried a great deal and lay on the floor under a desk. The second day, a student squeezed a gerbil to death. The third day, one student gouged another with a pair of scissors. Bobbi and Reginald, mightily concerned, drafted a letter to the superintendent to describe the effect that the testing was having on their team. They ended the letter with the statement, "Everyone is always talking about teachers being accountable. We have decided it is time for us to be accountable. We refuse to give these tests any longer." Two days later, the superintendent called them in and heard details of their testing experience. He responded, "We need more teachers like you. You don't have to continue the tests!"

During every year, there are several weekly recognitions for students' accomplishments and improvements. Students in pairs bake cupcakes so that every student's birthday is acknowledged. Those students with summer birthdays are recognized on designated Fridays. When the team members have recess after lunch, the teachers frequently play games with them.

In kickball games, a favorite, whenever a student makes an error, the teachers clap their hands and say, "That's okay, you'll do better next time." They also declare it an "out" for the offending side if a student criticizes a teammate for making an error. This is followed by discussions about the effectiveness of criticizing others whom you want to improve. Slowly, students begin to encourage each other when they make mistakes, and the team's overall relationships improve.

On the last day of the school year, the Harmony Team holds a picnic in a nearby park and invites parents. Again working in pairs, students make trophies for one another out of aluminum foil, coat hangers, and paper cups. Every student is recognized for at least one accomplishment. "Funniest," "Best Kickballer," and "Biggest Blusher" are among the many citations given. Amid laughter, tears, and hugs, the students say good-bye and leave for the summer.

Scenario 3

As students and their parents finish their covered-dish supper, two members of the Pioneers team introduce their team's just-completed interdisciplinary, integrated study of Cameron Park—the first planned community in Raleigh, North Carolina, designed and built in the early 1900s. Student-made drawings, maps, photographs, and papers decorate the walls. Three-dimensional models of homes built to scale by pairs of students reproduce a three-block area of Cameron Park. This evening's gathering provides students with the opportunity to show their parents their scholarship and to teach them what they learned; the gathering also culminates this formal study for the three teachers and seventy-five seventh and eighth graders who comprise the Pioneers.

Opening the formal part of the evening's program, Amanda and Sarah explain how the study was decided upon, the questions that students and teachers brainstormed, a list of their research activities, and how responsibilities and a timeline were developed. Neil, Tommy, and Henry then give an overview of the history of Cameron Park, showing maps they had drawn on overhead transparencies and slides they had taken of selected streets and buildings. They explain that streets had been purposely designed narrow and winding to slow traffic and that the back alley garages, which replace on-street parking, led to distinctive communication patterns among residents. Their overview is followed by a series of small group presentations: human interest stories gleaned from oral history interviews; graphed survey data about residents' satisfaction with living in Cameron Park; flora and fauna of the area; another photographic essay depicting changes over time but especially since World War II; changes in zoning laws and real estate values; and environmental factors affecting the area. In closing, the Pioneers sing an original composition written in conjunction with the music teacher. No one could fail to be impressed by the quality of these students' commitment to their work and this solid evidence of their growth as twelve-year-old scholars.

Following the formal presentations, students more than hold their own in a spirited, informative question-and-answer period. One parent asks (with tongue in cheek) what skills students think they have learned in the study. Another asks how the project ties in with state curriculum requirements. A third asks how students think Cameron Park compares with more recent developments built in the suburbs of Raleigh. Yet another adult guest, a resident of Cameron Park, wants to know where she can get additional information on its history.

The following day, thanks to the presence of a newspaper reporter who had been invited by students, the local newspaper runs a feature story on the Pioneers' Cameron Park project, complete with two photographs and selected quotations from students.

Scenario 4

The Swanton Central School in Vermont serves a small mixed community of Anglo and Native American (Abenaki) families. Linda Pearo and Joan Lumbra see in this mix a special opportunity to combine elements of both cultures in a multiage team of fifth and sixth graders—a team they named the Songadeewin Family. In a week of student orientation and workshops designed to shape the team its first year, students and teachers create a Songadeewin Family Creed, a statement of beliefs:

> We believe that we belong to a safe, caring community; we are "Keepers of the Earth." We are Songadeewin Family; we are strong in heart, mind, and spirit.

- Heart—We believe we are healers; we resolve our differences fairly and peacefully.
- Mind—We believe we are pathfinders; we travel many roads to knowledge.
- Spirit—We believe in celebrating the good fortune of the earth and its people.

Our mission is to foster a love of and respect for the earth, its inhabitants, and their knowledge. Our goal is to give service to the earth for the many gifts the earth has given us.

The students also set forth "Nine Ways of Knowing," which embrace specific team commitments:

1. We work toward a safe, caring community.
2. We care for our earth.
3. We reflect and value the contributions of Native Americans.
4. We respect and value families.
5. We are peacemakers.
6. We seek knowledge and better ways.
7. We celebrate.
8. We give service.
9. We share our gifts and strengths.

On Fridays the team holds a Songadeewin Family Recognition Ceremony at which group and individual accomplishments of team members are acknowledged. Teachers and students take turns identifying specific examples of what students have done in accomplishing the values embodied in the "Creed" and the "Nine Ways." These standards also serve as an ongoing basis for team evaluation and planning. (See chapter 10, Scenario 5.) From time to time parents, other adults, and high school students may be invited to participate and be recognized for their community contributions that reflect Songadeewin Family values.

COMMENTARY

A thing is what it does.

Alfred North Whitehead

As the first chapter strongly emphasizes, young adolescents have profound needs for belonging, for being part of a caring community, and for being recognized for their accomplishments. Indeed, sociologists indicate that a prime reason why some young people turn to gangs is to satisfy these very needs. Creating a climate where the desire to belong to a good thing can be met is a primary goal of teaming. Where that climate is lacking, students' academic, social, and at times moral development can be thwarted. A positive climate does not come about by good intentions, of course. It comes about by careful planning followed by action. The creation of meaningful symbols, rituals, ceremonies, acknowledgments, and special events bonds students and teachers and makes explicit a team's beliefs and values.

In Scenario 1, the mobility of military families accentuates young adolescents' developmental need to assimilate quickly into new groups and form interpersonal bonds within their middle level schools. Cognizant of military family life and sensitive to their students' needs, teachers at Brewster Middle School pay special attention to developing a strong sense of team identity. They work hard to create a spirit of belonging by ensuring recognition for every team member. All five teams—Gators, Bears, Rabbits, Frogs, Owls—define themselves as clearly and vividly as possible, emphasizing who they are and what they stand for in ways that complement those same qualities in the military context that is so much a part of their students' family lives. Each team is represented through a mascot, logo, slogan, and team colors; each team engages students in unique events and traditions; and each team provides numerous ways of recognizing students for their academic and personal accomplishments. These team identities have been achieved so successfully at Brewster that they have remained relatively unchanged over the years. Students don't want the names to change, and younger children in the elementary school look forward to eventually being on the same teams that their older siblings or neighbors were on.

Bobbi and Reginald, the extraordinarily talented Harmony Team teachers in Scenario 2, surely understand that students have a great need to belong, to have a meaningful identity with a group. Their teaching strategies and their relationships with students are grounded in this understanding. It is very evident that they care deeply about their students, understand them, and find numerous ways to help them understand themselves, relate better to one another, and become successful in school. The two teachers also understand the importance of recognition. None of this happens by chance. These two teachers are quite clear about their own identity, as witnessed by their courage in refusing to continue giving standardized tests because of the tests' debilitating effects upon their students. As the superintendent said, "We need more teachers like you."

Progress in taking increased responsibility for themselves and their own intellectual and academic growth is urgent and essential if young adolescents are to fulfill their potential as learners and citizens. It is likewise very important that they be honestly and appropriately recognized for their progress, both as individuals and as members of a community. One of the best and most natural ways to achieve such recognition comes at the culmination of a significant project, when families come to look at their children's work and learn from their experience. In the Cameron Park account (Scenario 3) a number of factors made that evening worthwhile. The presentation was held in conjunction with a covered-dish meal, a setting that by its very nature fosters sharing, communication, and community building. The program dealt with a substantive academic and intellectual project in which students had invested a great deal of thought and effort. Family members were drawn into their children's project as concrete details and explanations flowed. The study reflected several types of learning that illustrated the multiple ways that learners demonstrate knowledge. As the evening drew to a conclusion, there was also an opportunity for parents and other guests to interact with students and give them feedback. Although teachers had guided the structure of the evening, they had also wisely made sure that the students were the true hosts and presenters. It was, after all, their accomplishment that drew the parents in the first place. The additional astute touch of inviting a reporter brought wider recognition for their good work, which in turn enhanced the public's understanding of the quality of the team and the school.

An aphorism goes something like this, "If you don't know what you stand for, you'll stand for anything." The Songadeewin Family is at no risk of such apathy. Through their "Creed" and "Nine Ways of Knowing" the two teachers and their students have made it exceptionally clear just who they are and what they stand for. In daily expressions of their Creed, students come to understand "values" in general as principles for living one's life, and through membership on their particular team they naturally identify with those values. For many generations scouting has responded to young adolescents' identity needs in similar ways, and like scouting, Songadeewin's values are acceptable to virtually everyone. A team such as this one has potential for considerably more impact that scouting, however, for students spend six or seven hours a day five days a week in a living context that they help shape and by which they assess themselves and each other. Team identity becomes very real through their weekly celebration of team members' accomplishments in the Recognition Ceremony. There is no question just where this remarkable team stands, and because students are recognized for their citizenship in relation to its values, Songadeewin Family constitutes a powerful educational influence for the two years that students are members of the team.

PRINCIPLES

- **Team identity and recognition stem directly from the team vision.**

  A philosophy that advocates cooperation leads to rituals, mottoes, creeds, and activities that stress the process of working constructively together to achieve shared goals. Where student initiative and responsibility are envisioned, these behaviors are readily acknowledged to spotlight the connections between stated values and actual accomplishments. Whenever particular student behaviors are sought and valued, we must continuously call attention to them and recognize them when they are manifested.

- **All students have an essential need to belong, to be part of something that they recognize as worthwhile.**

  For this need to be met, adults need to demonstrate unmistakably their respect for students who are in a critical period of growth, and they must show that respect in how they interact with students. True student respect for teachers in contemporary times, however, has to be earned. A sense of belonging and identification with a team are especially enhanced when students are empowered to participate in the team's governance: formulating and interpreting rules as needed, assuming leadership, and making some of the decisions related to their own education. Teachers must also demonstrate respect for each other.

- **All students, as individuals and as members of groups, have a basic human need to be recognized for their accomplishments and contributions to others, the efforts they put forth, the initiatives they take, the responsibilities they assume, and the positive attitudes and citizenship they display.**

  Often a compliment, a smile, or a knowing wink will suffice. Whatever the method, such acknowledgments say, "I notice you. I am aware of what you are doing. I value what you do. You are a worthwhile person." All human beings need and value such messages; however, they are especially needed by young adolescents who are seeking to establish themselves and to put into perspective the competencies, strengths, and needs that define them.

- **Recognition should come from students as well as from teachers.**

  As young adolescents seek to establish themselves more independently from their parents, recognition and approval from peers may become even more valued than that from teachers. An environment in which recognizing others is seen as not just legitimate and desirable but also expected can be shaped by teachers whose own style of relating to others reflects those same values. Through team rituals, meeting structures, and personal guidance, effective team teachers actively promote systematic recognition for students, encouraging them to recognize one another. When such an ethos is established, students frequently begin to acknowledge teachers, staff, parents, and those beyond the school community.

- **Recognition must be authentic, consistent, and equitable.**

  Students and teachers must see the actions and attitudes that are acknowledged as genuinely praiseworthy. Recognition for trivial deeds and frivolous attitudes shows disrespect for students and will shortly become counterproductive. On the other hand, all students need the personal affirmation that derives from being recognized. Further, recognition should extend to all students and not be reserved for the same students over and over again. Where teachers and students are sensitive and aware of the many types of contributions that others can make, widespread yet authentic recognition can be accomplished.

- **Team identity and recognition are fostered through a variety of visual representations.**

  Logos, aphorisms, banners, signs, mascots, bulletin boards, certificates of appreciation, and a host of other visual displays announce to the school community and remind students of what the team values and is seeking to accomplish. They reinforce individual and team expectations and remind students that they are part of a group that stands for distinct values. Should anyone doubt the power of such representations or consider them childish, simply attend a college or professional team sports event. There you may see adults with painted faces howling like wolves in support of their favorite team. Given the meaning that such symbols have to adults, imagine how much influence they have for ten to fourteen year olds longing to be part of and associated with a particular group.

- **Special team activities, rituals, and celebrations help define a team as a family or community.**

  A team newsletter, camping trips, covered-dish dinners, fairs, holiday observances, and the like not only promote community spirit but also ensure opportunities for students to demonstrate initiative and to take responsibility. Such activities will also involve students in significant learning as they undertake the planning, organization, and arrangements that such events require. Furthermore, events such as culminating activities for an extensive curriculum project, a play or a show, birthdays, and problem-solving contests also celebrate individual or group accomplishments. As teams mature over time, certain activities take on special meaning and become team traditions. Such traditions might be simple things such as patterns of humor in team meetings, games, or annual events, such as a "Great Paper Airplane" contest. A more solemn example is the "naming ceremony" of the Songadeewin Family (Scenario 4), a team in a school that serves children of both Native American and Anglo-American origin.

- **Parents and the wider community need to be included in certain identity and recognition activities.**

  The culminating activity of the Pioneers' study of Cameron Park (Scenario 3) is an excellent example of an important way that adults may be brought into the process of recognizing young adolescent students for their accomplishments and contributions. Because parents and family members are usually the most important people in students' lives, prudent teachers include them and sometimes others from the community in events at which students are able to demonstrate their achievements. When activities such as service learning or "family learning" projects involve adults directly, they should always participate in recognition events. Informing the media about team activities can lead to increased recognition for students and the school, generating support from building and central office administrators as well as from school boards.

- **Team identity should reflect loyalty and pride in the entire school.**

  Much like pride in one's ethnicity should be a complement to one's identity as an American, healthy attitudes toward other teams and the school itself ensure a spirited school climate. In our sports-oriented culture, it is easy for unhealthy competitiveness to arise between teams. When this happens, everyone loses. Effective administrators and team leaders work together in a highly professional way, coordinating activities and understanding that much of the school's mission is carried out through teams. Adults must be models for their students. "We are all in this together" must be everyone's maxim.

PLANNING GUIDELINES

1. *Review your team philosophy/vision statement.*

   Assess its implications for team identity and recognition strategies. What is the essence of your beliefs about kids and learning that you wish to symbolize and translate into activities? Develop an overall plan for implementing your decisions.

2. *Seek to establish a clear identity and sense of community from the outset.*

   Send a letter of welcome to students and parents before school opens, explaining team goals and opportunities. (See Example 1.) Hold a picnic or other informal gathering early in the fall so that students, parents, and teachers become acquainted with one another better and learn about the team's educational plans for the year.

3. *Plan a team orientation for the first day of school.*

   It is vital that students feel from the outset that their team is a special group that will help them be successful and more fully enjoy their school. If possible, coordinate general orientation activities through team advisory groups, and be sure to hold an inspiriting, welcoming all-team meeting this first day. At that meeting relate team goals to school goals and plan to introduce administrators, exploratory teachers, counselors, and other staff. New students may have little idea of what a team is, and they will need to experience the whole team directly.

4. *Choose a team name, motto, logo, and so forth that convey positive values and lend themselves easily to visual representation.*

   One preference is for names directly related to the team mission: Paradise, Excellence, Explorers, Adventurers. Some schools have a schoolwide theme for team names such as animal names, colors, or names related to school location, for example, Whales, Dolphins, and Starfish near the sea coast. Acronyms such as PRIDE, YES, or SPIRIT form another category of names. Teams' mottoes may derive from the teams' names and should be considered in the naming process: Discoverers—"Learning about Ourselves and the World," Carpenters—"Building Our Future Now," and YES—"Youth Experiencing Success." Next, create a team logo or devise activities through which students may design a logo which can go on letterheads, buttons, T-shirts, book covers, bulletin boards, and numerous other places. (See Example 2.) After these various representations have been established, a variety of other identifying characteristics can be developed. (See Example 3.) Sometimes this work can be done in advisories, or special team activity times may be designated for these purposes. In getting a new team established, students will benefit from participating in the processes of choosing and creating their new team's identity. It is also appropriate for teachers to make these choices in advance in order to give the team some degree of definition from the beginning.

5. *Plan ways of recognizing individuals as the team gets started.*

   Student of the Week award(s) can be given for academic, artistic, citizenship or athletic accomplishment or improvement. Exceptional effort recognition is always possible. Acts of kindness, courage, perseverance, good humor, service to school or community, and a host of other qualities invite early and continuous recognition. Students may further benefit from participating in designating awards and criteria for them. Awards may also be accompanied by a team certificate of recognition of appreciation (Example 4) or a bulletin board display. In some instances redeemable coupons from local merchants are used to convey the seriousness of recognizing citizenship and individual accomplishment. Another important way to recognize students is through brief telephone calls or notes to parents about their child's progress. One way to acknowledge birthdays is to draw names from a hat and to have two or three students prepare treats for an individual's birthday.

Summer birthdays and holiday birthdays may be celebrated on designated days or as surprise events. Additional recognition suggestions are listed in Example 5.

6. *Plan all-team meetings at least once each week but more frequently if possible and needed.*

   These community meetings are the nucleus of democratic experience, and they are crucial for affirming students' conscious affiliation with the team. It is customary for two teacher teams to hold one or more daily team meetings, but larger teams may find it difficult to meet more frequently than once a week. In addition to discussing upcoming events, attending to team business, engaging in fun activities, and recognizing students, it is also important to provide time for students and teachers to express any concerns that they may have about the quality of life on the team. Discussions may center around rules, expectations, interpersonal relationships, or other issues. Often these issues can be the subject of advisory group discussions.

7. *Make concerted efforts to establish positive connections between the team and the students' parents.*

   Back to School nights or other special parent events provide valuable orientation for parents to the teaming concept and to their child's specific team goals and procedures. (See Example 6.) Remember that your students' parents attended schools that were not organized into teams; they will need your help to understand your intentions, values, expectations, and procedures. Do all that you can to see that they understand and support your initiative. Team award ceremonies, culminating events, special days, and musical or dramatic productions are obvious times to involve parents. Some teams find effective ways to involve parents directly in joint curricular investigations and community service programs. Adults from the community who may teach minicourses or sponsor various types of community projects may also become involved. In one instance, all participants—parents, siblings, students, and teachers—attended a team breakfast where they read poetry and prose that they had written in a project focusing on family roots.

8. *Make it a point to periodically assess the degree to which team identity and recognition efforts are having the intended effects.*

   The most certain way to augment teachers' impressions is to ask the students for feedback. How are we getting along with each other? With kids from other teams? With other teams? Are group cohesion and team spirit increasing? Are we learning? Is there an atmosphere of mutual respect? Are students satisfied that rules and policies are being administered justly? Is humor an integral part of our day-to-day functioning? Are there many ways for students to participate in team efforts? Are they sharing responsibility for planning and carrying out activities? Is a wide range of students being recognized appropriately? Are students encouraged to "be the best that they can be"?

CAVEATS

Don't undervalue the importance of articulating and reinforcing team values through representations, events, and assessment. Some of us may be personally uncomfortable with certain accoutrements of teaming such as names, colors, aphorisms, and the like. It is natural for young adolescents to associate themselves with such trappings, however, and if we are to address their needs as they are, we must overcome our own reluctance. In the vernacular of a contemporary ad popular across age groups: *Just do it!*

Engage students in building identity. How much to define the team prior to students' involvement is a judgment call. But for the team to become a meaningful association for young adolescents, they must have considerable say in how the team evolves, what it does, and how they figure in it. Some students will inevitably take greater interest than others. If the team is to become trusted and accepted by all, however, students must participate in its expansion and in elaboration of the teachers' initial planning.

Teach democracy as lessons in authentic participation. The All-Team Meeting described in chapter 5 is a perfect venue for going well beyond mere rhetoric about democracy and American values of self-determination and free speech by giving developing children clear models of how to actually live and work together cooperatively and respectfully while preserving individual rights and responsibilities. Invite students to develop a "Bill of Rights for Students" and a "Bill of Responsibilities for Students." Anyone who doubts young adolescent perceptiveness about basic rights and their suspicions about external manipulations should read Zlata Filipovic's (1994) journal about her life and reflections on her chaotic, war-torn community of Sarajevo in the 1990s.

Be extremely wary of competition among teams. Friendly competition can be enjoyable and productive for some, but it can also easily become excessive and get out of hand. An overemphasis upon competition is poisonous. Student recognition, for example, can become something to compete for rather than to celebrate unless it is widespread and equitable, and students who are seldom recognized may become alienated and resentful. Any type of contest can become destructive to a team's spirit of community when a "winning is everything" attitude emerges. There is also risk that team identity can lead to excessive competition with other teams. When "being number one" rather than "being the best we can be" becomes the goal, destructive attitudes and behaviors toward other teams will easily evolve. We must also remember that we teachers are not immune to this type of competition and that when it runs rampant, faculty morale suffers greatly. We must never lose sight of the fact that we are role models for our students, and as such we must be particularly conscious of our example relative to competition.

Don't underestimate students' capacity for taking greater responsibility for themselves, for learning how to set individual and team goals, and for working toward their accomplishment. Students are interested in forming partnerships with their teachers, and they know that they are not yet ready to go it alone. Yet, motivated, goal-driven, well-supported young adolescents can achieve remarkable accomplishments. Avoid expecting too little of them in these terms.

EXAMPLES

1. Jungle Gem Team Brochure to Students

(Griffin Middle School, High Point, NC)

TEAM TEACHERS

The Jungle Gem Team is a two teacher team. That means that two teachers teach all of the core subjects.

Ms Rittenhouse is the math and science teacher on the team. She enjoys reading, playing tennis, and watching TV in her spare time.

Mrs. Hinkle is the social studies and communication skills teacher on the team. She enjoys reading, playing tennis, and spending time at the lake.

Mr. Knox works with this team as an advisor. Many of you may also have him for art. He is a talented artist.

IN THE JUNGLE . . .

We're very excited to have you on the Jungle Gem Team. We have a great year planned that will include many wonderful opportunities to have fun, to learn, and to get to know the members of your team. Many of our activities are not yet confirmed, but in the past we've enjoyed the following:

-field trips to Wake Forest Museum of Anthropology, the N.C. Zoo, the Piedmont Environmental Center, the Chinese Acrobats, a touring theater production, a Chinese restaurant, and many others
-quarterly team auctions with lots of pizza and other goodies available for purchase with Jungle Jack
-Knowledge Bowl competitions
-service projects
-monthly team meetings
-guest speakers
-Citizens of the Month lunches

WELCOME TO THE JUNGLE GEM TEAM

*Mailed to students just before opening of school.

HH

The Jungle Gem Team is one of two teams in the seventh grade house. Our house is called The Habitat House. That's our symbol at the top of the page. We hope that this year The Habitat House will become your "home for learning".

We don't have just one symbol for our team. We use lots of symbols, but you'll recognize them because they're all related to the jungle. Our team colors are blue and green. One thing that makes this team unique is our token economy system. You will have chances to earn Jungle Jack almost every day.

This Jungle Jack will be used to assess fines for breaking rules, but you will also be able to use it to purchase several items and/or privileges.

SUPPLY LIST

-3 ring binder
-tabbed dividers
-notebook paper
-pencils, pens
-small package of colored pencils
-pencil pouch
-1 spiral notebook

PLANNERS WILL BE PROVIDED

SCHEDULE

8:30–9:00 Home base
9:00–10:45-1st block
10:45–11:45- lunch/reading
11:45–1:35-2ndblock
1:35–3:25-encore

All academic classes meet on Monday. Math and communication skills classes meet on Tuesday and Thursday. Science and social studies classes meet on Wednesday and Friday. All encore classes meet daily.

LAWS OF THE JUNGLE

Be prepared
-materials
-time
-attitude

Show respect
-for others
-for self
-for property

Failure to follow the laws of the jungle will result in the following:
-warning
-time out
-student/parent conference
-lunch detention
-after school detention
-fines (Jungle Jack)
-behavior contracts
-parent contact
-office referral

Jungle Jack fines will be assessed for minor violations.

2. Sample Letter to Parents
(Authors)

August 8, 1995

Dear New Venture Students and Parents,

Welcome to the Venture Team! This will be the fourth year that the four of us have worked together with seventh and eighth graders as a small community of learners within our middle school, and we think our team has achieved a terrific record in academics, extracurricular activities, and citizenship. It is exciting to have you joining us, and we look forward to getting to know you and work with you.

At 5:30 P.M. on Friday, August 25, our eighth graders will be hosting a cookout at Lakeside Park, Pavilion 6 for everyone associated with Venture. There will be a cookout, games, and a brief presentation and question-and-answer session about our team. We hope every new Venture student and parents or guardians will be present for this important get-together. We expect to finish by 8 o'clock, but because it is still light for another hour, anyone who wants to play volleyball or soccer is welcome to stay longer. You are not required to bring anything, but if you want to help out, please call Sam Austin (658–2239) or Clare Modigliani (658–4772).

We're looking forward to meeting you and to having a great year!

Sincerely,

Wally Bean   Jane Martin   Annetta Tasker   Phil White

3. Team Motto/Creed

- ***(a) PRIDE Team***
(Winooski Middle School, Winooski, Vermont)

P Personal responsibility
R Respect for all
I Interact with what's going on in class
D Determine to make this the best year ever
E Excellence in all we do and say

- ***(b) Constellation Community Middle School Team***
(Long Beach, California)

Recited every morning:
"Anything that hurts another person is wrong.
We are each other's keepers.
I am responsible for my own actions.
I take pride in myself.
Leave it better than you found it."

4. Team Logos

• *(a) Kingdom of Well*
Rutland Town School, (Vermont)

• *(b) Alpha Team*
Shelburne Community School, (Vermont)

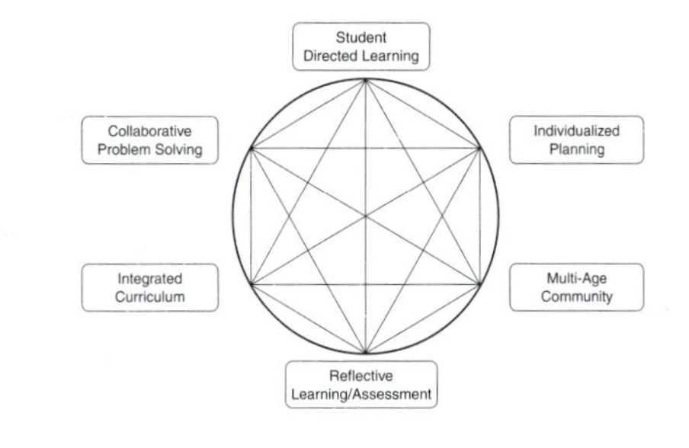

• *(c) Paradise Project*
Edmunds Middle School,
Burlington, Vermont

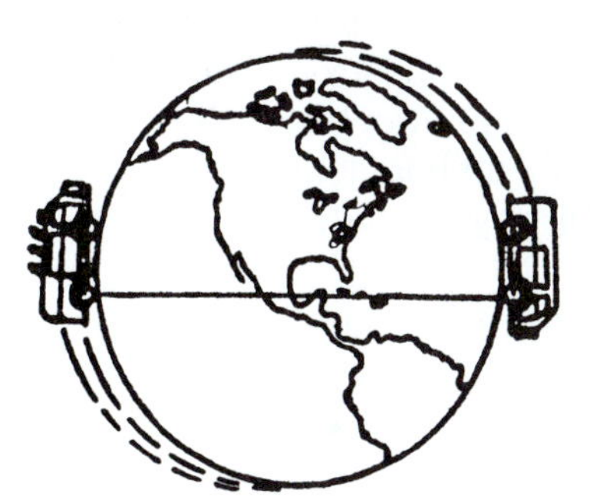

• *(d) PRIDE Team*
Camel's Hump Middle School, (Vermont)

• *(e) Challenger Team*
E.A. Gibson Middle School,
Danville, VA

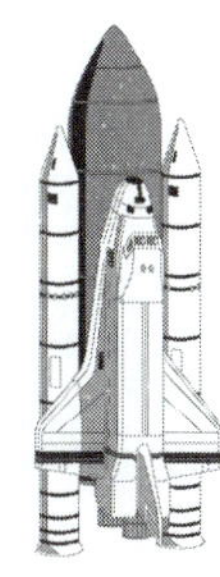

• *(f) Jungle Gem Team*
Griffin Middle School,
High Point, NC

• ***(g) Futuristics Team***
Bonner Middle School,
Danville, VA

5. Visual Representations of Team Identity
(Authors)

Team name
Motto
Colors
Logo
Mascot
Creed
T-shirt, cap
Buttons, pins, stickers
Pencil, pen, book covers
Coats of arms
Banners
Signs and posters
Decorations—room, door, hall
Team photos/biographies
Bulletin board messages
Displays of student work

6. Paradise Project Certificate of Recognition
(Edmunds Middle School, Burlington, Vermont)

Paradise Project

CERTIFICATE OF APPRECIATION

The Paradise Project wishes to express its appreciation and gratitude to Chris Stevenson for your support.

signature   June 22nd 1989 date

7. Team Recognition Activities/Events
(Authors)

- Student(s) of Week or Month awards
- Academic accomplishment
- Academic improvement
- Athletic accomplishment
- Athletic improvement
- Service to school and community
- Leadership
- Exemplary attitude
- Acts of kindness or courage
- Unusual effort
- Birthdays
- Displays of student work
- Recognition ceremonies in conjunction with special events
- Recognition in conjunction with distinguished person's birthday, for example, Washington's Birthday Award for leadership and Jimmy Carter Award for Peacemaking
- Certificate/ceremony of recognition for supportive persons outside the team, such as parents, adults from the community, other teachers, principal, superintendent, school board members

8. Special Team Activities and Events
(Authors)

Fall orientation day, picnic (see Example 1), or retreat
Community service projects
Interdisciplinary/integrated units
Minicourses
Intramurals
Field trips
Camping trips
Academic competitions
Problem-solving contests
Annual play or musical
Assembly programs
Field days
Simulations
Career Day
Clubs
Writers groups
Book reading groups
Parents nights
Art show/fair
Backwards Day
Caroling
Contests
Dress Up Day
Geo bee
Spelling bee
Green Up Day
Halloween carnival
Hat Day
Hobbies fair
Lip sync contest
Literary magazine
Parents appreciation events
Pizza party
Privilege cards
Recycling project
Science fair
Short story competition

Newsletters
Picnics
Parents breakfast, covered-dish meals
Holiday observances
Fairs
Skit night
Talent show
Team photo/video
Wadee

COMMUNICATION

What kinds of information do people need?
How can we keep everyone informed?
What responsibilities can the students assume?

Scenario 1

Bonnie McMahon, a Team Leader at College Park Middle School in Hickory, North Carolina, has long been a lover of challenges and the outdoors. When it occurs to her that an Outward Bound experience would be a wonderful way to build community within her eighth-grade Tiger Team, she broaches the idea at an all-team meeting. Students and teachers are excited about the possibility but wonder, "Where can we get the money?" Bonnie then goes to her principal, Martha Hill, who says, "Great idea. This is a good issue for the Leadership Team [the principals plus team leaders] to tackle." This team has several suggestions for obtaining funding and encourages the Tigers to move forward, considering their endeavor as a pilot project that other teams might want to pursue in the future. Remarkably, through a series of well-publicized fund-raisers and donations from businesses and parents, sufficient money is raised to send 105 eighth-grade students and their teachers on an Outward Bound trip in the spring. It is a rousing success; students come away energized, they listen to each other better, and they show more of a "can do" attitude.

That summer, a group of teachers participates in the Active Learning Seminar at Harvard University, a program that helps teachers to engage students in experiential learning. They are galvanized by the seminar and return to school determined to make outdoor challenge experiences part of a comprehensive team program for service learning. The Leadership Team sets the wheels into motion, and the whole school enthusiastically endorses the plans.

From these beginnings, College Park's Service Inside-Out program is developed throughout the school. Sixth graders concentrate on "Service to Self," participating in a one-day ropes course challenge; peace-building initiatives through exchange activities with Japanese students; making collections for the Salvation Army soup kitchen; and tutoring nearby kindergarten students. Seventh graders focus upon "Service to School," producing a weekly program on the school's closed-circuit TV; creating a cafeteria program to honor student "citizens of the week"; establishing a pep club to build school spirit and raise money; beautifying school grounds; and raising money for the homeless. Eighth graders emphasize "Service to Community," with each team adopting a nonprofit organization, preparing meals, collecting donations, and working with the elderly. They also sponsor and facilitate the work of the Bloodmobile. Each eighth grader keeps track of service hours donated, the total having reached 1,495 hours the previous year. Students who contribute ten or more hours attend a five-day wilderness experience at the North Carolina Outward Bound School. All students in each grade document and reflect on their service efforts through journals, essays, and discussions with peers and teachers.

Today Service Inside-Out is supported by the entire community, attracting grants, ideas, and commendations. Now in its fifth year, it is increasingly student-centered and integrated within the full school program. Its success is substantiated by the fact that the other middle and high schools in the system now have service learning programs modeled after it.

Scenario 2

At Bergan Middle School, staff development days are often devoted to team planning so that the special subject teachers affiliated with the team for advisory purposes can participate. During a Shakers and Movers team meeting, Danika, an art teacher, says, "I feel left out. I know it's not your fault, but I never get to meet with you or know what's going on because the kids are with me during your common planning time. I believe I could contribute a lot if I had the opportunity." Rosemary, the team's curriculum guru, immediately responds, "I'm sure you could. I've seen how turned on the kids are by your classes, and I'll bet there is a ton of ways we would work together." Curtis chimes in, "Well, we've talking a lot about learning styles, multiple intelligences, and all that jazz; let's *do* something." Meredith, the team leader, says, "Great. Let's get going. What are some ways we can communicate better? What are some projects we can do jointly?" Out of this discussion emerges a plan that ensures that: team minutes will be placed in Danika's mailbox daily; the "extended team" will meet biweekly after school and will go to a play or movie on occasion; and core teachers will visit art classes periodically during individual planning time. Also, the group lays the groundwork for a "rites of passage" interdisciplinary unit that incorporates Danika's African mask project, and the team muses about the possibility of a series of minicourses in the final three weeks of school that involve much creating, making, and doing. At the end of the meeting, Danika smiles and says, "I should have spoken up sooner!"

Scenario 3

The Protostar Team approaches parent conferences in a rather unique way: Students plan and lead conferences with their parents and one of their team teachers. Because students are members of this team for three years (sixth through eighth grades), they learn from experience and the guidance from teachers and peers how to plan a conference agenda and present evidence of their schoolwork. In conducting the conference, Protostar students summarize the learning goals that they have set and the progress they have made. Selected examples of work from their portfolios illustrate this self-assessment. Teachers engage younger students in small group lessons and individual conferences to guide their assessment plan and to provide reassurance. Eighth graders who have become especially adept in this process also advise younger and less confident classmates in preparing for this important exchange of information between students, parents, and teachers about the students' growth, learning, and needs.

Scenario 4

Three times a year at six- to eight-week intervals, Willy and Chris, partner teachers on a fifty-member multigrade team at Fayerweather Street School in Cambridge, Massachusetts, hold Parent Nights. The expressed purpose of these sessions is to ensure communication between parents and teachers. Teachers describe the team's collective work and growth and solicit impressions, ideas, and questions from students' parents. This program has emerged from the teachers' realization that parents are their most influential allies, so they have actively worked to build partnerships with them. Students prepare a folder of their recent work and written guidelines for their parents to review, but it is understood that this particular evening does not include individual parent conferences. Available dates for conference sign-ups are posted, however. A typical Parent Night consists of a commentary on the core academic skills program, a videotape or slide show of curricular projects (such as the unit's week-long, on-site study of Block Island), and an overview of upcoming units of study. Parents are also recruited to volunteer time and other resources to help achieve the team's goals and programs.

Scenario 5

Once a month a dozen or so Wildcat Team students remain several hours after school engaged in the familiar activities associated with meeting a press deadline. They comprise the editorial staff of *Pawprint,* the team's newsletter. Because this multiage team includes both seventh and eighth graders, the lead editorial tasks are carried out by older students, who simultaneously teach the ropes to their younger counterparts. The newsletter is published nine times each year, with every student working as an editor at least once. This four- to six-page newsletter contains summaries of curricular projects, reports of team activities, a calendar of upcoming school events, and a variety of feature articles. Virtually all of the articles are written by students (occasionally a teacher or parent provides a byline), and layout is accomplished through a computer software program that carries the team name and logo. Photocopies are collated, stapled, and distributed by each issue's editorial staff. In addition to this regular publication, the eighth graders produce *Tracks,* an annual literary publication.

Scenario 6

Connie and Walt, who have been teaming together for six years, are thoroughly committed to engaging students in extensive, community-based learning that usually culminates with a publication. In years past their students have published a county history, a collection of regional folklore, a calendar with each day annotating an event in local history, a teen recreational guide to their town, and a book of interview-based biographies of eminent people in their state.

When Connie learns that, due to lack of space, the local library is planning to throw out all of its copies of the *Daily News* from 1920 to 1960, Connie shouts, "Walt, this is it! Let's get these newspapers and use them to do a project on World War II." Walt responds, "Super. There must be all kinds of ways to get the kids involved." After borrowing a truck, the team hauls all the papers from 1936 to 1948 to a rental space provided by a friend who is a history buff.

In looking over articles brought into the classroom, students are intrigued by the daily accounts of the war and what occurred on the home front. They are especially taken with stories about people from their community, and they express a desire to interview some of them. A contingent of students accompanied by their teachers subsequently persuades the editor of the *Daily News* to print an article about their proposed project, wherein they solicit people who lived through the war to be interviewed. Some 150 citizens respond, about half of them veterans. After developing a questionnaire and honing their interview skills, pairs of students conduct sixty interviews. They learn of death, fear, loneliness, bravery, camaraderie, romance, and hardship. A highlight of the interviews is an hour-long session with a survivor of the Battle of Monte Casino. Some five hundred soldiers, freezing and near starvation, stormed a mountain to capture an abbey inhabited by Italian troops. Only twenty-five soldiers returned from the mission. The entire team is enraptured as students listen to the account of one of these survivors.

After transcribing and editing their interview tapes, students fashion the interviews into stories, some of which the *Daily News* runs in a two-week series. Given this exposure, the team is easily able to sell the five hundred copies of the booklet that contains all of the stories, thus meeting its expenses.

COMMENTARY

If we maximize communication, we can minimize coercion.

Edgar Dale

It is clear from both formal research and exemplary practice that when teachers, administrators, parents, and community members share understandings effectively, team goals and activities gain support, and students perform better as learners and as responsible citizens. Without clear communication, misunderstandings, suspicion, and outright rejection of team initiatives can occur. With clear communication, sometimes remarkable things can happen, as evidenced by some of these scenarios. Communication strategies that promote understanding and build confidence in the educational program, especially those that engage students in significant ways, should be a primary goal of every team plan from the beginning.

The evolution of the Service Inside-Out program in Scenario 1 graphically demonstrates the importance of communication within the school. In gaining support for the original Outward Bound experience, Bonnie communicated effectively with her students, teammates, fellow team leaders, and principal. And by including others in the school, the initial idea was transformed over time from an isolated event to an ongoing, communitywide program, acclaimed for meeting some of young adolescents' deepest needs. Two other points are noteworthy. The school has an effective communication network, including common planning and all-team meetings, a leadership team, and a tuned-in, caring principal. Additionally, by using this network and including those outside the team, competition between teams was nonexistent, and school spirit flourished.

Scenario 2 portrays another aspect of in-house communication, namely between teams and special subject teachers. Unfortunately, this is one of the thorniest issues in middle level education. Often one of these teachers is affiliated with a team but is unable to meet with it. The source of the problem is that for core teachers to have common planning time, their students have to be somewhere, and that somewhere is invariably with the specialists. The problem is compounded by the fact that society does not deem important the areas that these subjects represent and thus does not provide enough money to hire a sufficient number of teachers. It is little wonder then that special subject teachers often feel unappreciated, overworked and left out. Yet they have potentially an enormous amount to contribute. Frequently they have unique insights about particular students and well-developed problem-solving skills and offer numerous opportunities for hands-on learning that can lift teams beyond the pale of pencil, paper, and book activities. Indeed, Charity James (1975), the great British educator, commented after an extensive study of teams in the United States, "Rarely did I see a team doing truly innovative work that did not substantially involve the arts."

In this scenario, Danika is experiencing some of the isolation that many special subject teachers feel. But fortunately she is a person who speaks up and is on a team that understands what her genuine involvement can bring to everyone. It is commendable that the Shakers and Movers made a commitment to communicate regularly with Danika and to collaborate with her on curricular endeavors and that she made a reciprocal commitment. The future bodes well for the Shakers and Movers because they are open to new understandings and have a powerful new resource in providing a stimulating education for their students.

Communicating with parents, especially about their children's academic progress and social development, must be a high priority for teams. Young adolescents largely understand that they need to become successful learners and contributing citizens to the school community. They are also quite capable of learning how to assess their efforts and accomplishments. With guidance and support, they can also learn how to present themselves to others as learners, workers, and citizens, especially their parents, who obviously have a vested interest in the matter. As illustrated in Scenario 3, the Protostar teachers have acted on this realization by creating a student process for organizing three-way conferences. The teachers also contribute an evaluation of the students' learning and suggestions for further work. Parents may also provide input. After teaching their first wave of students how to conduct and present a self-assessment of their progress, teachers engage these more experienced students in helping younger classmates with the process. Student accountability becomes a much more real element in evaluation when youngsters have these responsibilities. Parents also get a much fuller understanding of their children's activities and growth.

Although parents are responsive to teachers' invitations to school events when their children are in the primary grades, unfortunately, it is often a challenge to get them to turn out when their children reach middle school. In Scenario 4, Willy and Chris managed to get beyond that apparent indifference by creating incentives for parents to attend: a special preparation by their children, a professional assessment of the whole team, and some previews of coming activities with an opportunity for parents to take part. Willy and Chris's well-attended sessions testify to the *potential* that exists to cultivate parent support and participation. Although a school often hosts some version of a Back to School night, thoughtful teams will seek opportunities to build a positive, supportive parent constituency with more frequent and personalized occasions, such as this example of Parent Night.

Periodic team publications provide a way for a team to communicate with all of its constituents. Realizing this fact and agreeing upon the importance of every student becoming meaningfully engaged in writing, the Wildcat teachers in Scenario 5 wisely created a journalistic theme for their language arts program. They appreciated the value of all students seeing their names in print as editors and writers. The availability of contemporary technology facilitates both the team's annual and monthly publications with modest cost. The literary magazine includes "best pieces" from the eighth graders' two years on the team, illustrating the variety of student voices and the quality of the literature they produce. The monthly newsletter stands as tangible evidence of the team's commitment to writing and communication. Together, the publications provide information about the Wildcats' activities, insights, and hopes. They also exemplify a responsible work ethic.

In addition to depicting imaginative ways for students to engage in substantive writing and to take control over their own learning, Scenario 6 powerfully portrays the value of communication and involvement with the community at large. Connie and Walt are wise in focusing students' writing on local events because these are of natural interest to students and townspeople alike. By directly communicating with the latter, they gain all manner of support: access to old newspapers and a place to store them, an entrée to World War II veterans and home front folks to interview, recognition for their outstanding work, and publicity that enables them easily to sell their books. Further, each of their projects builds additional support. Because the team efforts have been so well communicated, the team now receives small innovative project grants from the school system and has community sponsors for its publications.

As the scenarios and commentary indicate, this chapter focuses primarily on the information-giving and information-receiving aspects of communication. The interpersonal aspects will be discussed more fully in chapter 11. Still other communication issues are raised in chapter 5.

PRINCIPLES

- **Communication is *vitally important.***

  When people do not know what is being done and why, misunderstandings can easily occur. People can neither support nor honor team efforts if they are unaware of them. Further, good communication builds trust within the community, provides access to new ideas, and opens doors to constructive assessment.
- **Communication with parents depends greatly upon teachers' personal knowledge of their children.**

  Paul Schwarz (1997), co-director of Central Park Secondary School in East Harlem, New York, whose remarkable school has virtually 100% attendance for parent conferences, states the case well: "Parents don't want to come to school meetings where teachers and administrators talk at them about fundraisers, district guidelines, minutes of the last meeting and the like. But they are interested in their children, and will make a special effort to attend conferences where teachers know their children well and where they can talk meaningfully about their hopes, dreams, and concerns about their kids." As stressed throughout this book, teaming enables teachers to know students much more personally. Successful teams translate this closeness into significant communication with parents.
- **All constituents need to be informed.**

  "Constituents" include students, core team members, affiliated specialist teachers, administrators and supervisors, parents, and certain community members. Each has an interest in the team; each can contribute to it.
- **Communication mechanisms need to be established.**

  Common planning meetings and all-team meetings are especially important times for clear and effective communication within the team. These meetings steer the day-to-day operation of a team. All aspects of team operations depend on teachers and students understanding one another as well as team goals and procedures. In addition, team leader meetings with the principal and systematic communication patterns with parents greatly facilitate outside the immediate team operations.
- **Student involvement in communication efforts is essential.**

  Students' participation not only provides a significant vehicle for their initiative and responsibility while building communication skills, but it is also a practical necessity if a comprehensive approach to communication is to be accomplished. Teachers simply do not have the time to write newsletters, direct video productions, and so forth.

PLANNING GUIDELINES

Communication within the Team

1. *If special subject teachers are affiliated with your team, make every effort to communicate regularly with them and include them in team activities as much as possible.*

Placing team minutes in the special subject teachers' mailboxes, visiting their classes from time to time, socializing, sharing curriculum plans, and numerous other strategies listed in Example 2 can enhance communication.

2. *Review purposes and routines for all-team meetings (ATMs).*

   As chapter 6 indicates, these meetings should be regularly scheduled at least once a week. A teacher, perhaps the team leader, who is an effective model for conducting meetings should be in charge for the first several meetings. Students should be recruited to handle announcements, share their work, or lead singing or other activities prior to each meeting to be sure that students get involved. The educational goal is to turn over responsibility for planning and conducting ATMs to students as quickly as they can manage them sucessfully.

3. *Solicit student suggestions for team activities, curriculum projects, collaborations with other teams, and parent activities.*

   An anonymous suggestion box may become an effective way to get this kind of communication under way. Do not be dismayed if you receive some flippant suggestions at first. Over time students will use this mechanism effectively if they believe that their ideas are given earnest due consideration.

4. *Publish a team newsletter, so that it is managed and produced by students.*

   Be sure that over a term there is a role for every team member and that every student's name and writing appear at least once. (See Example 1.)

Communication within the School

1. *Keep the principal up to date on team activities.*

   The principal's support of team activities is essential, and he or she must be well informed if that support is going to be active. Sharing the team log (see chapter 5) on a regular basis is one way of conveying detailed information, but also invite the principal to visit CPT meetings, ATMs, curriculum events, parent nights, and other activities that will further ensure continuing communication. Consult the principal in advance about planned activities that need administrative support.

2. *Keep off-team colleagues informed about team activities.*

   A teamed school is likely to have regularly scheduled meetings of team leaders with the principal to coordinate school events and to see that everyone is as aware as possible of everyone else's team activities. Go further, however, by planning events that involve other teams in noncompetitive ways. For example, invite other teams to join selected activities such as plays/skits, concerts, and culminating curriculum events. Be sure to distribute team newsletters and other publications to special subject teachers and other staff as well as to central office personnel and school board members. Invite these colleagues and other faculty to participate in the team evaluation. (See chapter 10.)

3. *Develop good communication with guidance counselors, special educators and part-time consultants such as psychologists and social workers. Become as fully aware of their skills and services as possible, and keep them informed of team acitivities. They can be of enormous help to both teachers and students.*

Communication with Parents

1. *Publish a team handbook.*

   Even a sketchy first edition of a handbook will help students, parents, and others understand what the team stands for and what its social and academic goals are. Although the initial version will be written entirely by teachers, revisions and expansions using student input will occur as the team's programs evolve. (See Example 3.) Send a handbook to every student and parent prior to the beginning of the year. Include in it a calendar of as many important events in the coming year as are possible to determine at the time.
2. *Arrange a schedule of meetings during the year to report the team's work, accomplishments, and future plans.*

   These meetings may include segments of Back to School night, picnics or potluck dinners, culminating events of curriculum projects, and so forth.
3. *Each day call two or three parents whose children are on your team to identify yourself, give feedback about the children, inform parents about team activities, and urge them to participate in events you have planned for them.*

   Positive messages about their children are especially appreciated. In far too many instances, parents hear from teachers only when there is a problem concerning their children.
4. *Acknowledge every note or message that comes directly from a parent, and send a thank-you note every time a parent helps with team activities.*

   This is simply common courtesy that over time will build trust, appreciation, and support for the team.
5. *Identify the students' advisors as the first person to contact in communicating with the team.*

   In elementary school, parents routinely contact the teacher when they need to communicate. In conventional intermediate schools, however, parents frequently call the principal or assistant principal because no one knows their children well. In a well-designed middle school, the advisor, the students' advocate and friend, is in the best position to serve as a bridge between home and school.

Communication beyond the School

1. *Create a volunteer communications committee within the team whose responsibility is to communicate team projects and activities of public interest to local media, especially community newspapers, which are often eager to receive copy from the school.*

   This is good experience for students. Depending upon the nature and scope of the endeavor, parents also can provide much help.
2. *Contact businesses, friends of education, and others who may be able to help with apprenticeships, minicourse leaders, and so forth (see chapter 9), or who may be able to provide funding or services for special projects.*

   Again, students and parents can be effective here. If extensive programs are developed, a competent parent coordinator can be invaluable.

ADDITIONAL POSSIBILITIES

- Sound communication procedures will provide valuable returns for any team. At the very least, provisions must be made to ensure accurate, efficient communication among the teachers on the team and among them and the students. However, building communications with other constituencies is a task that should not be long delayed. After a solid foundation has been established, additional initiatives may be appropriate. From the virtually limitless ways of communicating with constituents, consider these examples:
  - A two- to three-day team retreat at the beginning of each year.
  - A column written by parents in the team newsletter.
  - A parent advisory council that meets with teachers several times a year to serve as a sounding board and to provide feedback from other parents.
  - A parent procurement committee to help locate resources needed to support curriculum initiatives.
  - A parent booklet that emphasizes things that parents should understand about young adolescents and ways that parents can help their children and the team.
  - A video about the team or team curriculum activities to be shown on the local cable public access channel.
- For parent conferences, consider asking the parent or parents to list the three things that they are most pleased with concerning their child and the three things that they are most concerned about. The teacher does the same. All parties compare lists. The results may surprise you.

CAVEATS

Teach students the processes that will enable them to publish their own work, then see that their efforts are disseminated to interested others.

Unless there is an emergency, or an unusually complicated situation requiring all teachers' input, do not have all team members attend parent conferences. Such conferences consume huge amounts of common planning time that is needed for other matters. Normally the student's advisor should handle a conference. Explain this policy to students and parents from the beginning. A form for recording parent conferences is included in Example 4.

In communicating with parents, remember that it is just as important to gain information as to give it. Listening is highly important.

Cultivate the understanding and support of parents for your educational program and advocate for their children.

EXAMPLES

1. Sample Newsletters

***(a) Kingdom of Well Team's* KOW Bell**
(Rutland Town School, Vermont)

"What We Have Here Is a
Failure to Communicate"
Cool Hand Luke—1967

Learning through the grapevine that some sixth-grade parents have concerns about math grouping and the pace of instruction, we reasonably wonder how and when we would have been made aware of these concerns. The question is this: **How shall the concerns of parents and teachers be communicated to each other?**

Let there be no mistake about the feelings of Randy, Tina, and Dutch: We need to be made aware of your concerns when they arise so we can take appropriate action if necessary. You need not feel uneasy about approaching us with concerns; we are trying to meet the needs of fifty-four individual kids and over a hundred parents, and surely we will not, perhaps cannot, satisfy everyone, but it is our job to try. Your suggestions, comments, even criticisms, may help us improve instruction. And it's only fair that we hear from you.

Maybe practicing writing or saying the following comments will get you loosened up: "Hey, Dutch, when are you going to do something exciting in math? My kid is bored." Or

"Is my kid EVER going to get a locker, Mr. Dewey? That's the main reason he came to the sixth grade." Or

"Mrs. Ryan, is my daughter going to be challenged in reading?" Or

"My kid missed her math assignment because she was at a band lesson. Don't you write assignments on the board?"

So where do we go from here? We said in the first *KOW Bell* that we would use this newsletter as a means of communication, and we meant it! We will rededicate ourselves to that idea, here and now. Please answer the following few questions as candidly as possible. We will tally the results, consider your comments, make adjustments if possible, and revisit this whole thing in the next *KOW Bell.* Promise.

– Should parents and teachers share concerns? Yes No

– Do you have concerns you would like to share but haven't? Yes No

– Why? (if applicable)

– Do you feel comfortable sharing your concerns with the sixth-grade team? Yes No

– Why not? (if applicable)

– Can the *KOW Bell* be helpful as a communication link between parents and teachers? Yes No

– Do you have concerns about math? Yes No

– What are they? (if applicable)

• *(b) All-Star Team Newsletter (Alexander Graham Middle School, Charlotte, North Carolina)*

ALL-STAR ACHIEVEMENTS RECOGNIZED AT TEAM PICNIC

The All-Stars enjoyed a picnic on May 16. The students on the team brought bag lunches, and beverages were provided by the team teachers. The picnic was held from 12:50 to 1:40. The celebration began with awards being given to some of the All-Stars.

Chip Lewis was recognized for his second place finish in the CMS writing contest.

Ann Chaplin received an award for being the district winner in the Optimist Oratorical Contest held in Southern Pines. This is the first time Alexander Graham has taken top honors by both school representatives. In addition to the plaque, Ann also received a $1,500 scholarship from the Optimist organization. Congratulations, Ann, on this tremendous accomplishment.

Another outstanding accomplishment by Greg Skidmore was recognized at the picnic. Greg placed eighth in a high school math competition. No other Alexander Graham student has ever placed as high as Greg in this competition. Congratulations, Greg!

Courtney Horn was recognized for her accomplishment in track. She broke the school record for the 800 meters. She will also be recognized at the school sports cook-out.

Bulldog Pride winners were also announced on May 16. Winners were Lauren Schneider, Jim Martin, P. J. Thompson, and Stewart Tonnisen.

A final individual award was presented to Shameika Marshall. She was recognized for her outstanding concern for the welfare of another All-Star. We certainly appreciate all her good efforts this year.

Finally, all All-Stars were congratulated on making our school goal on the state writing test. This is an accomplishment in which we can all be proud. Way to go, All- Stars!

2. Ways to Communicate with Special Subject Teachers (SSTs)

(Adapted from Garvin [1989] and Korinek and Walther-Thomas [1994])

1. Assign SSTs to teams.
2. Assign team advisees to SSTs.
3. Send team minutes to SSTs.
4. Share curriculum plans in each discipline with SSTs and vice versa.
5. Plan out-of-school social events for all team members.
6. Visit SST classes during team planning period.
7. Have core teacher substitute for SST who attends team meeting.
8. Have administrators or paraprofessionals sub for SST to visit core classes and/or team meeting.
9. Recruit retired teachers to substitute for SSTs to attend team meetings.
10. Use PTA funds or grants to hire a "floating" substitute for SSTs.

11. Plan with SSTs during lunch with dessert provided by the school.
12. Build in all-team meetings during in-service days.
13. Occasionally meet together before or after school. Or plan a "zero period" when all faculty, but not students, are required to be at school.
14. Plan joint field trips.
15. Plan interdisciplinary units—team, house, all-school.
16. Plan "correlated" activities (e.g., stress certain skills, vocabulary, etc.).
17. Possibly schedule an exploratory course four days a week. On the fifth day, the SST has team planning, and the students go to another special, once-a-week exploratory.
18. Possibly have an SST teach one team's students for nine weeks and thus share a common schedule and planning time. (SST moves to another team each nine weeks.)

3. Excerpts from Alpha Team Handbook
(Shelburne Community School, Vermont)

Alpha is an educational collaboration between students, teachers, and parents. A positive relationship between school and home is essential to the success of the students.

- ***Schoolwork/Homework***

The Alpha student's homework is a natural outgrowth of schoolwork. Students are expected to determine how they will meet their goals each week by planning their time at school and at home. Homework is not assigned in the traditional sense, although an Alpha teacher will help a student determine what work needs to be accomplished at home in order to meet a goal. Often students will choose to do their individual work at home in order to leave school time for group projects. We encourage parents to stay informed of their child's progress by supporting work at home, reviewing the week's schedule and goals, showing an interest in current projects, and asking for details about the day when the student comes home.

- ***Progress Portfolios***

Progress portfolios are sent home at the end of each trimester. These portfolios include samples of student work, reflections, and teacher evaluations. They are supplemented by interim reports at the six-week interval that address the progress and quality of student work and behavior. In addition, Alpha teachers frequently send reports home to evaluate a project, summarize a unit of work, address a problem, or applaud success.

- ***Parent Conferences***

It is essential for Alpha parents and teachers to maintain close contact, and we encourage regular conferences during the school year. In addition to teacher-initiated conferences, parents may arrange a conference at any time by scheduling an appointment through the school guidance office.

- ***Parent Participation***

Coming into the classroom to help share an interest, or simply to observe and ask questions are wonderful ways to become involved and learn firsthand what Alpha is all about. Accompanying us on a field trip is also an excellent way to get to know Alpha better. Getting involved in the questioning and learning between students can be an enlightening experience.

4. Team Parent Conference Form

(Nancy Doda)

STUDENT'S NAME: ______________________ DATE: __________

REASON FOR CONFERENCE: ______________________

____

____

PARENT CONCERNS: ______________________

____

____

____

TEAM CONCERNS: ______________________

____

____

____

STUDENT CONCERNS: ______________________

____

____

____

PLAN: (1) ______________________

(2) ______________________

(3) ______________________

SIGNATURES:

____

TEAM REPRESENTATIVE OR ADVISOR

____

PARENT

____

STUDENT

NEXT CONFERENCE OR FOLLOW-UP: ______________________

CURRICULUM

What will our students learn?
How will we organize curriculum and instruction?
How do we develop initiative and responsibility?
How do we make sense of ourselves and our world?

Scenario 1

Kathy McAvoy and Dennis Carr teach as partners with sixth graders at Mt. Jefferson, Maine, Junior High School. When they began discussing the possibility of involving their students in choosing topics for integrated curriculum studies, they encountered some skeptical adults. "Kids would just want to do sports and rock music and TV." Undeterred by doubters, they invite their students to join them in a brainstorming session to identify topics or themes that students would like to learn more about. It soon becomes abundantly self-evident that eleven-year-olds are very interested in complex issues of substantial academic content. The list of topics that the kids want to study includes:

Careers and the Economy
Pollution
The Future
Government
Education
War and Peace
Crime
Shelter
Health, Survival, Death
Energy

Buttressed by these responses, Kathy and Dennis discuss with students the choice of a single topic for a teamwide study. After a good bit of contemplation, they choose to study crime. Their subsequent work includes generating lots of questions to guide their inquiries into the topic. It also involves collecting, organizing, and describing information obtained from interviews, periodicals, and electronic sources. Students write formal letters and use the telephone to track down answers and additional resources. They learn concepts about the psychology of crime and gather data about criminals and types of crime. They find out about recent technological and scientific advances in crime prevention. To show their parents and other adults the range and depth of their investigation, they hold an open house. Some students even begin to contemplate career possibilities in crime detection and prevention.

The adult skeptics are compelled to reconsider their doubts about the seriousness of sixth graders' ideas and interests. They also have to reconsider young adolescents' capabilities for doing more adultlike investigations. And these students give them ample evidence of the high standards of their academic and intellectual accomplishment. Perhaps most telling, though, are their testimonies about their learning:

> Some people . . . thought we weren't learning anything. WRONG!! We had to find all the information on what we were studying. We were the ones who did the projects . . . vocabulary logs . . . read . . . design inventions . . . do lots of writing . . . learn about computers, and whatever else you or your group planned. We had to study the past to predict the future or if there was going to be a future.
>
> (Alexander 53)

Scenario 2

The Alpha team of Shelburne, Vermont, Community School has spent several weeks in an integrated study of Africa. The fifty-five sixth-, seventh-, and eighth-grade students, led by their teachers, Carol and Than, have planned virtually every aspect of their study. Groups are formed to explore different regions of the continent (e.g., northern Africa, central Africa, etc.), and each group gathers information about the history, geography, economics, politics, culture, arts, and foods of its particular region. Books, magazines, films, documents, guest speakers, and information from various African embassies are used to gather the information. As the culminating event of the study, the students plan an evening at the "Market Place" for parents and families.

Arriving guests are given a program and invited to purchase "Alphites"— stage money that can be exchanged for samples of African foods. Then guests circulate among seven large booths devoted to the regions of Africa. At each booth are students dressed in native costumes that they made with help from parents and the home economics teacher. In exchange for Alphites students offer several food samples they have prepared that are indigenous to the region that they have studied. Around the booths are large, colorful student-made maps labeled with names of regions, towns, geological features, agricultural products, and natural resources. Paintings, photographs, masks, shields, animal carvings, statues, pottery, and a variety of other artifacts complete the booths. Three-ring notebooks containing graphs, illustrations, and an abundance of basic information about the region are available for browsing. Students explain their key findings and respond to guests' questions.

Guests are then asked to gather for an African drum concert—entertainment to be presented by ten students who constructed drums and learned to play them with help from their music teacher. Then all of the members of the Alpha team come together to perform dances that had been taught by a parent helper who had professional training as a dancer. A most powerful moment comes with the singing of the South African national anthem. The students learned it in the native language. Words are provided for parents and other guests.

During the following question-and-answer session, parents learn more details of the project and how it was developed. In one significant interchange, a parent asks a twelve-year-old if she knows all about those regions that her group has not studied. Pausing momentarily, she replies, "No, we don't. Do you? There's so much to learn I don't think any of us can know all of it. But what's important is that we know how to find out." Smiles of understanding and a smattering of applause follow. Carol and Than close the evening by acknowledging parents and others who helped with the study, and they thank everyone for attending.

Scenario 3

With the Thanksgiving holiday just a few days away the seventh- and eighth-grade Voyageurs are putting finishing touches on "Roots"—an integrated curriculum project conducted with family members. Utilizing oral history interviews, especially with parents and grandparents, and correspondence and telephone contact with other relatives, students have collected and transcribed a wide array of family stories. They have also interviewed family members about their recollection of events such as the bombing of Pearl Harbor, V-E and V-J days, the assassinations of President Kennedy and Dr. Martin Luther King Jr., and humankind's landing on the moon. Several students have made videotapes of their interviews to ensure that the experience can be preserved as a permanent family record.

Parents had learned of the project at the Voyageurs' opening family picnic in September. Teachers explained their goals and pointed out some important ways that parents and other relatives could be part of this home-school curriculum unit. In turn parents have helped their children document selected household artifacts that have been passed down through their families such as furniture, china, pictures, tools, and official documents. Each artifact has been photographed and described in writing for posterity. Parents have also written about some of their own favorite recollections from childhood and adolescence.

The Voyageurs' rooms contain numerous displays of these collected writings, photographs, and drawings. A potluck supper consisting of favorite family recipes is scheduled for the Tuesday night before Thanksgiving, and students are busy completing decorations and the presentations they will make. All students and their family members in the area or visiting for the holidays will come together for the supper and a student presentation about family values to culminate the study.

Scenario 4

Ronnie, an eighth grader at Sidwell Friends Middle School in Washington, D.C., is participating in the Troika team's apprentice program. The program allows students to explore interests and possible careers as they work three hours daily with adults in the community. Ronnie has chosen to work with Dr. Burns, a veterinarian. A week into the program, Ronnie arrives for his work a half-hour late. Dr.

Burns meets him at the front door, hands on hips, visibly annoyed by Ronnie's tardiness.

Dr. Burns: *"Ronnie, it's 1:30. Where have you been?"*
Ronnie: *"I, uh, uhf, stopped in some stores on the way here."*
Dr. Burns: *"Look, Ronnie. I have a schedule to keep. If you can't get here on time and have the animals cleaned and ready for treatment, I don't have any time for you. Is that clear?"*
Ronnie: *"Yes. Yes, sir. It's clear."*

(Note: Ronnie was punctual every day for the balance of his apprenticeship.)

Scenario 5

Steve has just attended a holiday chorus program at Triad Nursing Center, where a number of the students on his Cougar Team at Fernwood Middle School have performed for the residents. As he is leaving, he hears one of the students tell another, "Man, was I scared—you know, all that stuff you hear about Alzheimer's disease and other problems. But those folks were great. Hey, I could be like that someday, and I sure wouldn't want someone to be afraid to take care of me."

An idea flashes across Steve's mind. He searches out Vicki, the music teacher and chorus director, to relate the conversation he has just overheard and says, "Vicki, what would you think about working with our Cougar Team to develop an ongoing service project with the nursing center?" Delighted by the proposal, Vicki quickly replies, "Sure. When can we start? I've got a lot of ideas."

Over the next few weeks, Vicki meets several times with the Cougar teachers and once with the entire team. Before long, a plan is in place. Mr. Harkins, the director of the Triad Nursing Center, sets up training sessions to inform students about the needs of the elderly and to sensitize them to what they are going to experience. The team decides to incorporate the sessions into an interdisciplinary study of the aging process. Students will go to the center at least once a week for an hour or so to talk or play games with residents, read to them, write letters, and do simple chores for them. The general idea is simply to be a friend. Because each student will adopt a particular resident, the students name their endeavor the "Adopt-a-Friend Project." Parents and teachers are enlisted to help with carpooling students to the nursing center.

The kids quickly become involved—some of them deeply so. Alicia is paired with Carl, a severely depressed man whose wife had recently died. At their first meeting, Carl states that he wants a boy to adopt him. When she leaves, he says, "Good riddance." Surprisingly, Alicia persists, and after several visits, Carl's hard shell begins to crack. As she leaves after the fourth visit, he stuffs a heart-shaped pillow—a bingo prize he had won—into her hands. "Thought you might like this," he whispers. Soon Alicia's parents become involved, eventually "adopting" Carl as a family member. They visit frequently, take him on family outings, do his laundry, and encourage him to stop smoking.

During a snowstorm, many nurses and aides can't make it to the Triad Center. Cougar students within walking distance fill the breach. Two students work the entire weekend, sleeping on couches in an activity room.

Soon other projects emerge. In a Christmas musical that Vicki directs, students and their adopted friends perform together. A ninety-four-year-old man plays a village carpenter; an eighty-year-old woman portrays a bag lady. Students and parents plant a garden. Videotapes and photographic essays are created. A spirit akin to that of a loving, extended family sweeps through the Triad Center community, and a sixty-year age gap steadily dissolves.

Scenario 6

In response to student interests, the Dream Builders team has initiated orbital studies—independent projects that "orbit" the regular curriculum but that require development of the planning, organization, and presentation skills that are central to the Dream Builders' stated educational mission. Wally, one of the new members of this multiage team, nervously awaits presentation of his first orbital study about rusts—fungi that grow on vegetation in the woods around his house. His preparation has been thorough, beginning with collecting samples and researching them through books with Jack, one of his teachers, and Marla, the librarian. Wally has also visited an agricultural extension agent assigned to the area and has met with a plant physiology graduate student at the nearby university. He has made a chart to portray three rusts common to the area, and he has outlined his presentation notes on index cards. Although he has prepared very well, he is still apprehensive. After all, it is sometimes hard to talk with older kids, much less presume to teach them.

Five students are making presentations on their orbital studies simultaneously in various places. Six classmates come to Wally's presentation. In seven minutes he has told them and shown them everything he has learned about rusts and fungi. They seem genuinely interested in the subject, and Wally encourages them to handle the samples. He is asked several questions such as whether or not any of the samples are poisonous and whether or not they can attach themselves to people. When the student questions are exhausted, each guest fills out a brief evaluation form about the study and the presentation. Wally is thrilled by the six "excellents" he receives. As he puts his materials away he explains to Jack, the teacher who had helped him, "I could have told them a lot more if I'd had more time."

COMMENTARY

The most important question about schooling is,
How can we make schooling more like living?

Charity James

Somehow schooling in this century has gotten educators (and the general public) away from concentrating on how our children learn best, on how they most naturally go about learning concepts and becoming skilled, and on how we can understand more accurately just what and how they have learned. We seem to be increasingly concentrating on making proclamations about what children need to cover and then applying various measurement devices that are believed to tell whether or not they know it. Further, many of us appear to have ended up with the mind-set that what young adolescents need to know and be able to do is accurately represented in content- and skill-driven textbooks and curriculum guides.

We need to take another look. Although it is understandable that we regard such guides and scope and sequence charts as resources for worthwhile subjects to *cover*, experienced child-centered middle level educators understand that the correlation between *covering* and *learning* is dubious at best. Fortunately, there are teachers such as those in the preceding scenarios who understand how young adolescents go about learning and what their learning looks like. Furthermore, growing numbers of middle level teachers are gaining faith that their young adolescent partners are themselves the key to sound curriculum experience and developmentally appropriate pedagogy.

Middle level curriculum must become much more integrative if young adolescents are to fully develop their potential as learners (Beane 1993). By *integrative* we mean curriculum that focuses on issues and topics that are grounded in students' ideas, interests, questions, and connected with pertinent disciplines and subject matter. Where such balance exists, students are always learning in ways that are authentic to them. There are many excellent examples of integrative curriculum that should be very useful to teams exploring curriculum innovations (Arnold 1990, Stevenson and Carr 1992).

However, few people understand curriculum integration as just described, whereas virtually everyone recognizes the traditional model of separate subjects and electives. Consequently, it would be immoderate for teachers inexperienced with integration to completely abandon the separate subjects, at least at the beginning of teaming. Besides, it is also necessary that teachers are able to preserve some portion of their program in ways that are familiar and comfortable to them. Yet, movement toward making connections between students' interests and priorities and their studies must begin and be nourished from the outset. One experienced middle level team teacher wisely suggests that teachers be very attentive to students' progress in the core skill areas while keeping an abiding focus on integrative learning. It may be true that the greatest single challenge to teachers making a transition from departmental organization to teaming is a felt conflict between separate subjects and curriculum integration.

It is good to keep in mind that moving from a "coverage of single subject" approach to integrated curriculum does not imply abandoning state and local curricular guidelines. In most instances, these are set forth as skills and concepts, sometimes with broad areas of content to be addressed; in no case is a particular methodology designated. Required skills and concepts can thus be incorporated into student-centered, integrative studies. Consider the Alpha team's African study, for example, as a means of studying the regions of that continent. Moreover, the content of a textbook is never synonymous with individual state curriculum mandates. A state-"adopted" textbook is but one resource for helping students meet guidelines or standards. Hence, teachers, even those in rigid environments, have more leeway in developing curriculum than they may realize. (See Examples 3–6 for integrative curriculum ideas.)

Scenario 1 is an explicit example of this contest of faith about curriculum. Two teachers who were teamed believed that, given supporting conditions, their sixth graders would make choices and commitments to learning that would in turn honor the teachers' trust. And so it happened, causing others who didn't share the teachers' vision to reconsider the responsibility and judgment of young adolescent learners. Although the quality of the work that the students produced and the learning that they demonstrated to adult audiences removed all skepticism about the academic quality of their work, what was especially assuring were the children's voices about their personal empowerment through the study. In this anecdote there is surely a fundamentally important message about the urgency of teachers' taking greater confidence in their students and their potential. We all must be wary of expecting too little of our young adolescent students.

Alpha's African "Market Place" in Scenario 2 depicts the culmination of a very substantive curriculum project that accommodated a generous range of students' learning styles and modes of expression. Students engaged in an enormous amount of collaboration in small groups, learning how to work together toward shared goals. One student commented that he had learned through that project that "leadership is getting everybody to contribute to the goal without letting your own ideas be in control."

Alpha students were effectively becoming self-directed learners: formulating questions, gathering information, making decisions, organizing displays, researching recipes and preparing unfamiliar foods, creating costumes, and learning dances. They also fully appreciated the importance of being able to draw upon parents and community resources and to utilize available technology. The "Market Place" culminating event illustrates the extent to which students become invested in an integrated study that encourages and supports individual initiative and the opportunity to work together in small groups.

Of special significance is the fact that students were completely involved in planning and developing their study from the outset. Africa constitutes a rich and fascinating corpus of knowledge through which young adolescents can develop as skilled learners by planning, organizing, and deciding. The students decided initially which region of the continent they would investigate and how they would organize their study. They negotiated important choices about divisions of responsibilities, research strategies, human resources and materials to be utilized, apportionment of limited time, and ways to demonstrate to teachers and other adults what they had learned. Throughout the process their teachers were listening, questioning, responding to students' questions, making suggestions, and helping them structure and assess *their* progress. Indeed, the Alpha teachers fulfilled their self-description as "facilitators and models of learning" (see also chapter 4, Example 3).

Family studies and "me units" have long been taught in the primary grades. Children's dominant social unit has been their family, so it is logical that teachers build curriculum upon that background as well as help affirm their young students. Given the change processes of early adolescence, however, there is an equally compelling case for exploring one's family background and connections in much greater depth in adolescence. So much of the value content on which decisions and choices are made rests on family values as they are perceived. Further, a home-school study brings parents and adolescents together in a working relationship that benefits both generations.

The Voyageurs teachers in Scenario 3 were astute to present their plans for the unit to parents in the early fall, explaining their rationale, answering questions, and soliciting help. Also, they were wise to bring the unit to closure at a peak time for family gatherings—Thanksgiving. The freshness of the students' work and the opportunity to share it with relatives whom they may not see very often augur well for further promoting the intrafamily connections and dialogue that the teachers saw as particularly important for their students. Such a curriculum unit comes together relatively efficiently and easily for team teachers who interact daily with each other and the same students.

Team organization is also uniquely structured to meet students' individual needs. When curriculum is truly integrated, students exercise their personal abilities and interests in concert with their classmates. No longer must everyone do and learn exactly the same things at the same time in the same ways. The distinct abilities of particularly advanced learners can be accommodated without having to resort to pullout programs or class groupings which are likely to foment tensions associated with discrimination and elitist divisions. Students with special talents can develop at their own pace, contributing their unique perspectives to team studies. Likewise, academically and physically challenged learners can be supported by individualized arrangements that enable them to focus on their needs alongside their classmates. An effective democratic team foundation builds upon curriculum that is integrated so that every student is challenged and rewarded according to his or her abilities and aspirations. The next three scenarios illustrate strategies for facilitating students' individual interests.

In Scenario 4, the Troika team's apprenticeship program that Ronnie chose to join awakened him to some realities of the adult world, namely the importance of meeting others' reasonable expectations of him. In lieu of a physical education class and an activity period, he opted to work with a veterinarian within walking distance of his school for three hours each school day over a three-month period. The apprenticeship enabled him to extend his considerable interest in animals while learning skills and providing useful service.

Perhaps most significantly, though, it gave him the opportunity to learn responsibility in a way that counted. As Ronnie entered a real-world situation with real-world expectations and consequences, Dr. Burns became a clear teacher. He unhesitatingly let Ronnie know what he expected, and Ronnie got the message. Fortunately, he also rose to Dr. Burns's challenge.

The great majority of young adolescents are idealistic and positive about life, especially when their educational context affirms their worth, invites their participation, and complements their interests and abilities. Students growing up and learning in such circumstances want to contribute to others, to make the world a better place. Service learning projects like "Adopt-a-Friend" in Scenario 5 are ideal channels for giving wings to these attitudes and desires. But again, the key to truly meaningful experience is that those who perform the services have choices about what they take on.

While providing highly useful service, Cougar students are also learning a great deal about the elderly, themselves, interpersonal and intergenerational relationships, responsibility, and commitment. The nursing home experience invited them all—students and teachers—to look to the future, especially as it pertains to their families and themselves. It is also noteworthy that Alicia, who befriended Carl, is now in college pursuing a career in health care.

Although service learning projects can be established by individual teachers or done on a whole-school basis, teams provide the most efficient and coherent structure for facilitating them. Service can usually be easily tied to the core values upon which the team is founded, and youngsters are experienced enough to be able to see connections between what the team says it values and what its members actually do. Teaming also provides a context in which academic study and reflection can readily be integrated into service projects—something that research indicates is crucial if these experiences are to maximize students' potential for learning.

It is incumbent upon team teachers to initiate and sustain collaborations with special subject teachers. Steve, for example, also modeled the kind of collaboration that he expected of his students by seeking out Vicki, a music teacher, for information and advice. Savvy team teachers pursue close collaborations with artists, librarians, and all other special subject teachers available to them, recognizing their potential support and the value of their expertise.

Middle level teachers recognize the importance that young adolescent students place on having personal expertise. Anyone who listens to their conversations quickly recognizes their need to be able to tell others "the real deal." The unit teachers in Scenario 6 created a curricular opportunity for their students to develop individual expertise, and Wally's initial project about rusts illustrates a kind of research and presentation experience that is perfectly appropriate to his age. Whether or not he ever faces a standardized test item about rusts, he has taken a big step toward becoming a more self-directed and self-sufficient scholar. The process began with his noticing something in his immediate environment that he did not understand and progressed over a couple of weeks to his having developed adequate understanding to make a presentation to classmates, some of whom were a year or more older than he. And beyond his most portentous goal of successfully presenting his work, the affirmation that he received via his peers' evaluations should propel him even further toward future scholarly experiences.

It is not possible to overstate the importance of teaming as an organizational format that lends itself to matching students' abilities and interests with developmentally appropriate curriculum and pedagogy. In fact, this very connection is rationale enough for team organization. And even if a new team begins with a traditional framework of core subjects and electives, as long as teachers are visibly (to the students) moving toward more fully integrated studies, the prognosis will be good. Young adolescents of the looming new century are in so many ways a breed apart from the adolescents of the childhood of most of their teachers that old ways must be transformed to accommodate their awareness and readiness. The scenarios in this chapter illustrate the meaning of the middle school dictum that "curriculum must be based on the nature and needs of young adolescent learners."

PRINCIPLES

- **Every student must develop personal efficacy as a learner.**
  We have never met a young adolescent who didn't care about being competent. Although areas of competence may or may not match very well with conventional educational values, a desire for competence is always present. Likewise, so much of young adolescents' sense of self-worth is tied to "what I can do" that curriculum must always be grounded in the assumption that students can be successful learners and contributors. Given today's unprecedented expansion of information and technology for accessing it, it is more crucial than ever that students develop an attitude of inquiry, a confident disposition about finding solutions, and personal resourcefulness in learning to find and analyze the information they need. The change process of early adolescence is a rich opportunity for teachers to focus on helping students learn how to grow as learners. It is also a crucial time for developing the skills and disposition of a genuine learner because their future schooling will not likely address such personal needs. When curriculum is developmentally appropriate, students learn how to learn. Absolutely nothing useful or desirable is gained when youngsters fail over and over at tasks set by teachers. An attitude of "separating the sheep from the goats" has no place in schooling at the middle level.
- **Curriculum is developmentally responsive to the needs, interests, and abilities of young adolescents.**
  Developmental responsiveness is the bedrock of middle level curriculum. It focuses curriculum upon fostering students' intellectual, physical, social, emotional, and moral growth, taking into account the societal forces that affect their growth. Such curriculum deals with students' own questions, is geared to their levels of understanding, and provides variable degrees of structure; it engages them in active, hands-on, experiential learning in which they frequently collaborate with others. The subsequent principles elaborate additional characteristics of developmentally responsive curriculum.
- **Curricular mandates are balanced by student interests.**
  Teachers are obviously held accountable for state and local curricular requirements and obviously must meet them if they are to have credibility. Although the rigidity with which mandates are applied varies greatly among schools, developmentally responsive teachers find ways to incorporate student concerns while teaching required skills and concepts.

- **Curriculum deals with substantive concepts, issues, skills, and values.**

  Where curriculum focuses on "covering material" and content that students find to be irrelevant or even trivial, boredom is certain to result. Given the enormity of student interests and a wide variety of curriculum possibilities, teachers must help students engage in activities that deal with important ideas and must genuinely promote the development of scholarly habits and standards. The major criteria for judging curriculum are: Does it help young adolescents make sense of themselves and their world, and does it open doors to additional and more complex learning?
- **Young adolescent students find their curriculum personally empowering.**

  Young adolescents, although profoundly in need of nurturance and support, want to grow up—to achieve their own identity, to become increasingly more independent and self-sufficient. As teachers become more confident and proficient, they increasingly involve students in planning and assessing their work, engaging them in significant decisions about and responsibility for personal goals, curricular content, methods, materials, and timelines. In so doing, teachers provide numerous opportunities for student collaboration, role taking, and leadership.
- **Making connections is paramount.**

  Although at times there may be emphasis upon specific disciplines or skills, the emphasis is on helping students to see the "big picture," to see the interrelationships and connections among ideas as they seek to construct meaning. This is seldom accomplished where separate subjects taught in fifty-minute periods are the daily fare. Example 1 presents a continuum of integrative possibilities through which teachers and students might progress over time. It is especially important to blend the unified arts and other traditional "exploratory" subject matter into team curriculum (see Example 1, chapter 8).
- **A wide variety of teaching/learning strategies is utilized to accommodate differences in student learning styles, intellectual abilities, backgrounds, and idiosyncrasies.**

  Given the developmental variability of young adolescents, pedagogy must also be responsive in the same ways as options for curriculum studies. Some of the time a single instructional method is necessary, but in order to help all students be successful, multiple approaches are also essential. Although there are times when students need to be "stretched" by teaching approaches that may not be familiar or easy, it is usually best to rely upon and return to their strengths and preferred modes of learning. Varying teaching/learning strategies applies not only to the ways that students develop skills and ideas, but also to the choices they have in demonstrating their understanding. (See Examples 5 and 6 for extensive description lists of these options.) It is further important that teaching/learning strategies match the goals and nature of the task. For example, if the goal is to convey a distinct concept such as the water cycle, direct teaching is efficient and most likely the most appropriate method. On the other hand, if the goal is to stimulate inquiry, having students develop questions and procedures is needed. Further, be sure to provide significant opportunities for students to explore content relative to their cultural and personal backgrounds.

- **Curriculum makes effective use of community personnel, resources, and activities, both within and outside the school walls.**

  Numerous adults in any community have a great deal of value to share, and many of them would like very much to do so. Opportunities to involve the community include service learning projects, integrative studies of the community, apprenticeships, internships, oral history interviews, surveys, guest presenters and demonstrations, minicourses, and job fairs. Community-based learning provides opportunities to do socially useful tasks, to explore adult issues that relate to youth, to take on new roles, and to connect students with potential role models. Example 1 identifies some additional possibilities.
- **High expectations for all students are a given.**

  When young adolescents are provided with appropriate opportunity, challenge, and support, they are usually capable of far more than they are given credit for. Teachers' expectations tend to become self-fulfilling prophecies; thus, high expectations promote positive attitudes and behaviors and motivate students to achieve. Low expectations and indifference breed apathy and lack of effort. When high expectations are thoughtfully implemented, rigorous and high standards of scholarship come naturally.

PLANNING GUIDELINES

1. *Schedule specific planning times on your team calendar, at no more than two-week intervals, to discuss and plan curriculum.*

   If you don't schedule time, momentary issues will get in the way of curriculum planning. Assume that from time to time an entire meeting will need to be devoted to curriculum. Include exploratory teachers in the planning to the extent possible, setting up special times to meet with them if necessary. (See Example 1, chapter 8.)
2. *Although you may initially choose to organize curriculum according to separate subject areas, gradually move toward integrated studies as the primary focus.*

   Example 1 illustrates a continuum of integrated curriculum possibilities, whereas Example 2 shows how an integrated unit might be structured.
3. *Periodically review your team goals and philosophy along with state and local curricular mandates to guide your planning.*
4. *Engage students to as great a degree as feasible in planning major studies.*

   Begin by surveying their interests and concerns; create webs of their existing knowledge and questions. Never forget that an integrative study is built upon students' questions and concerns; therefore, students must be fully engaged in planning. (See Example 3.)
5. *Develop a general curriculum plan that stresses developmental responsiveness and that balances student and teacher interests with curricular mandates.*

   Develop a timeline for the year and spread out the major activities that require the highest levels of collaboration.

6. *In developing any particular topic, be guided by the following questions:*
   - What are the really important issues/ideas/concepts/principles? What major values/ethical issues are involved?
   - How does this topic relate to students' lives here and now, and how can those relationships be enriched and extended? Which topics and activities stimulate inquiry and promote active learning that takes into account the previous questions? Example 4 lists potential sources of topics for integrated studies.
7. *Use an assortment of teaching/learning strategies, providing balance of whole-group, small-group, and individual activities.*

   See Example 5 for an extensive listing of strategies and Example 6 for alternative ways that students can demonstrate knowledge of a topic.
8. *Engage students in personal goal setting and assessment relative to their learning.*

   In developing individual goals, you may wish to have a student contract to do some required activities—some that are chosen from a restricted list and some that are free choice.
9. *Pay special attention to advanced learners and exceptional or underachieving students.*

   Develop peer tutoring and other helping programs and provide opportunities for independent work such as orbital studies. Don't let any students "fall through the cracks." Provide swift follow-up for students who don't meet their responsibilities by a telephone call home or a note to parents, by staying after school, or by other means appropriate to the team plan.
10. *Assume that your team's curricular program will evolve as you gain experience.*

    Build on your most successful experiences and explore new opportunities to engage your students in learning as you think they are feasible. Where team members determine to learn one or two new teaching/learning strategies annually and share them with one another, significant progress can occur over time. In particular, constantly strive to make your efforts increasingly integrative, personalized, and empowering of young adolescents. Beginning teams should develop at least one interdisciplinary project in their first year and then build toward integrated projects from this experience.

ADDITIONAL POSSIBILITIES

As teams grow and learn from experience, curricular efforts invariably become increasingly learner-centered. Thus:

- Teachers become less reliant on outside authorities and more confident in their own abilities and those of their students.
- Students make more choices and assume greater responsibilities, becoming increasingly responsible in carrying out planning and assessment.
- Teachers take more risks in trying new ideas.
- Teaching/learning strategies become more diversified.
- Learning becomes more holistic and substantive.

- Students achieve at higher levels, become more confident learners, and enjoy learning more.
- Teachers and students enjoy increasing personal efficacy.

CAVEATS

Don't underestimate what your students are capable of doing. Although substantive curricular change may not come as quickly as you or they would prefer, when students and teachers trusting each other and the process, remarkable things can happen. Because of prior schooling or deficient personal backgrounds, some students will have had little preparation for assuming more responsibility for their own learning. It may take additional time and individual planning to build their momentum. If necessary, break tasks down into smaller manageable units to exercise discrete skills and to cultivate confidence. Provide structure according to your best estimates of students' needs. Remember that young adolescents are capable of astonishing accomplishments under the right circumstances.

Don't lose faith in colleagues. We *all* are engaged in reconceptualizing our roles as teachers in teams and with integrative curriculum. Build on successes, design plans that will enable your team to evolve gradually, be quick to praise and slow to criticize, and keep moving forward.

Pay attention to your system's curricular mandates but don't become totally bound by them. In most instances teachers are responsible for teaching specific skills and concepts, but we generally have considerable leeway in how we teach them. Be clear in your own understanding that a textbook is not an appropriate curriculum for young adolescent learners. At best it is one resource among many for the kind of learning that empowers our students.

There is obviously far more to know and to do than we can begin to master. Therefore, select important, useful, and interesting issues to explore and tasks to learn and as much as possible engage your students in setting priorities for team study. Avoid the compulsion to simply "cover material." It is far better to achieve substantial depth in a few significant studies of importance to your students than to settle for "covering" an array of topics that students have little or no say in choosing. It would be wise for us as teachers to think of them more as our customers than as our wards.

EXAMPLES

1. A Continuum of Curriculum Integration

(Adapted from Brazee and Capelluti, 1994)

The following is a way of conceptualizing and defining various approaches to curriculum integration along a continuum:

—— 1 ———— 2 ———— 3 ———— 4 ———— 5 ———— 6 ——
Conventional Correlated Interdisciplinary Integrated Integrative Empowering

1. Conventional (separate subjects—no integration)
2. Correlated (teachers teach the same skills, vocabulary, and concepts in different disciplines—example: "We'll all talk about ratios this week")
3. Interdisciplinary (teachers plan unit, teach ideas related to a theme in separate subjects—example: Study the golden age of Athens in social studies, read Greek myths in language arts, study Archimedes and density in science, etc.)
4. Integrated (teachers plan unit around central theme; concepts or subtopics, not subjects, are pursued; a flexible schedule and various student groupings are used—example: In investigating homelessness, examine reasons for homelessness, citizen attitudes, community programs, local housing policies, etc., in a flexible structure)
5. Integrative (like number 4, with one critical difference: Students are greatly involved in selecting the theme, planning activities, making decisions about time and materials, etc.)
6. Empowering (like number 5, with focus on helping students to understand how social forces affect their development and on engaging students in socially useful activity—example: Study media images of adolescents and explore the effects that *Seventeen Magazine*-type models have on the body image of girls)

2. Interdisciplinary Theme Unit Process
(Authors)

"starter" activity

▼

provide general information

▼

students select sub-topics/acticities
of interest to them and acceptable to teacher

▼

students work in small collaborative groups
to explore, gather data, develop projects,
"make and do"

▼

"tie up" activity

It is often advisable to set requirements such as all students must:

1. Read significant material about the topic and incorporate it into reports, projects or journals.

2. Engage in substantive writing related to the topic to seek information, give directions, report findings, questions, or hunches, etc.
3. Complete an arts/making project that illuminates the topic.
4. Use community resources such as relevant people, places, archives to explore the topic.

(Frequent checks, contracts, and timelines are needed.)

3. Involving Students in Integrative Curriculum
(From Brodhagan, Weilbacher, and Beane, 1994)

A four-day process designed to help students develop questions about themselves and their world and to derive from it a theme and related activities at Marquette Middle School, Madison, Wisconsin:

1. Questions/concerns about self (compiled individually)
2. Questions/concerns about world (compiled individually)
3. Search for joint concerns. Do these suggest themes? (Share individual questions in small groups.)
4. Share small-group findings (in the whole group)
5. Select one theme (done by the whole group)
6. Brainstorm possible activities related to theme (half group: personal concerns; half group: concerns about the world)
7. Select activities (whole group votes on these)
8. Determine knowledge or skills needed for activities (whole group)

4. Suggested Topics for Integrated Studies (not mutually exclusive)
(Authors)

- Topics related to adolescent development
- Topics drawn from your system's established curriculum guide
- Contemporary issues
- Neighborhood/community sites and events
- Conceptual contrasts (e.g., competition versus cooperation)
- Student interests and hobbies
- Teacher interests and hobbies
- School issues

5. Curriculum Options

Increased flexibility of program and time schedule enhances the possibilities for teamed teachers to introduce innovative approaches to curriculum. Brief descriptions of some of those options are included in this example. Detailed description of curriculum opportunities available to teams is well beyond the scope of this chapter. For further discussion and examples, see Arnold, 1990 and 1997; Stevenson, 1997;

Stevenson and Carr, 1992; and Beane, 1993. As already illustrated, learning that engages and empowers young adolescents does not always conform to traditional offerings of core subjects plus electives. Therefore, teams are encouraged to look beyond that traditional paradigm for structures that may prove more complementary to children's interests and readiness.

- ***Interdisciplinary/Integrated Studies***

Learning that is not restricted to often-arbitrary categories such as "science" or "math" shifts the emphasis in students' minds from covering or mastering discipline-specific content to making sense of a whole topic. Consider the study of Africa described in Scenario 2. Students generated lists of "things one ought to know" and conducted research into one region of that continent in order to address those topics. Although one might conclude that this was social studies, the students' work utilized skills and concepts from all disciplines. We do not propose that the entire curriculum must be "interdisciplinary" (drawing from all relevant disciplines) and "integrated" (combining students' questions, ideas, and interests with the teachers' content and skill agenda). However, if students are to truly grow in terms of personal initiative and responsibility that lead to a self-reliant, scholarly disposition, the curricular program must be generously disposed toward this kind of learning.

- ***Independent or Orbital Studies***

Students choose topics that they want to explore until they have developed expertise. Topics may range as widely as, for example, from the History of the Super Bowl to German Operas to Favorite Italian Recipes. Studies usually go on for two to four weeks. Teachers and often parents assist students in planning an investigation, locating resources, and organizing a presentation to classmates about their learnings.

- ***Competitions***

Spelling bees, geo bees, Math Counts, Odyssey of the Mind, and other such competitions are very appropriate to include in a team's curricular program. Numerous problem-solving activities, such as an egg drop or a paper airplane contest that can be located through modern technology education curricula are particularly effective ways of complementing students' various interests and cognitive strengths.

- ***Community Service***

Young adolescents benefit by contributing their energy, time, and expertise to projects that serve the community. Whether the service is reading to primary children or showing visitors around the school, the school is improved for their initiatives. Students can also give back to the taxpayers of their community by such services as shoveling snow from the walks of elderly citizens or adopting a street or park to keep tidy. Our students also respond positively to the appreciation that they receive from adults.

• *Apprenticeship/Internship*

Young adolescents' ubiquitous speculations and questions about how the real world works are directly satisfied by working alongside responsible adults. Serving a week or longer apprenticeship in a hardware store, radio station or a bank or working with a veterinarian or photographer or home decorator enables them to see the workings of the adult world at close range. Adding an academic dimension to such experiences captures the essence of what has long been highly regarded as "experiential education."

• *Book Talks*

Too few youngsters today elect to read rather than to watch television or to listen to music. By providing a half dozen or so paperback copies of a selection of the excellent literature available to young adolescent readers today, teachers can promote students' reading the same book together, especially when the students have some choice in the books and their fellow book group members. Two overarching goals should guide this option: First, members of a small group of students agree to read together at a pace that they believe works well for them; they take turns talking about what they have read. The familiar analytical agendas common to teachers should be postponed with book groups; the key is that students learn to sustain their reading and discussion together, independent of teacher direction.

• *Simulations*

Simulations are an excellent teaching device to use with young adolescents. Events from history and day-to-day community processes can be adapted in order that they can be taught through simulations that engage students in role playing, record keeping, reading and writing, planning, and evaluation. Whether the topic being learned is the Declaration of Independence or a community redevelopment plan, teams are an ideal grouping configuration for simulation. A rapidly increasing number of computer simulations of varying quality are becoming available.

• *Computer Technology*

Microcomputer technology has revolutionized our capacity for writing, record keeping, communicating around the world, and conducting research of many kinds. We know students at Ligon Middle School, Raleigh, NC, who solicit material on a topic worldwide, edit it, and publish an electronic magazine, *Midlink,* that has had over one hundred thousand World Wide Web log-ons; we know others who have E-mail tutors in the community who mentor their writing on a regular basis. A computer facility within a team space can become a center for all of these activities and more. There are rapidly developing CD-ROM resources to advance students' independent interests, academic curriculum, and self-sufficiency with a technology that is quickly becoming as common in their lives as the telephone.

• *Reading/Writing Workshops*

Accommodating the diverse levels of student proficiencies in terms of reading and writing skills and taste is a substantial challenge to teachers in classes where every student is expected to learn a single curriculum. Fixed class schedules further frustrate attempts to adapt instruction to diverse learners. Reading and writing workshops, in which students daily interact, read, and write about a variety of topics (Atwell 1987, Rief 1992), are perfectly accommodated by the flexible scheduling possible in teams.

• *Theme Studies*

Because of the relative ease with which teachers and students are able to collaborate, teams are particularly well suited for carrying out integrated studies of themes such as adolescence, exploration, flight, citizenship, and careers. Sometimes themes are prompted by special events, such as a major election or the NCAA basketball tournament (see Stevenson 1997, Beane 1993). Theme studies generally span several weeks, and they culminate in some kind of special event in which students present their work to parents and friends.

• *Inquiries*

What are the recreational preferences of families? Their television-watching habits? Favorite recipes? What do students and parents think about the team's homework policy? Team rules? A team trip being considered? Creating systematic ways to gather information from one's constituents is a natural advantage for a team. Virtually any question of interest to students and teachers invites research that produces data for both statistical and subjective analysis.

• *Community Field Studies*

Every team has a community outside the school walls. What do we know about it? What questions might we explore? How could we give something back to the community that supports our education? Whether the community is rural or urban, the essence of "exploration" is achieved when teachers and students explore their community firsthand together, gathering a wide assortment of information and producing a new collection of knowledge to be shared with community members.

• *Personal Improvement Projects (PIP)*

Everyone has a need to improve in known ways. Whether the need is for improved handwriting, mathematics, fitness, eating habits, or knowledge in any discipline, every student has needs that can be addressed through PIPs. In the best of circumstances this fact is established as a distinct component of the team's curriculum. All students and teachers continuously set goals and assess their progress in a shared quest for self-improvement.

• *Expert Studies*

Every youngster wants and needs to feel that he or she has expertise in areas that are deemed worthwhile by others. Charity James (1974) shows how a team curriculum could accommodate this need by providing students with choices about topics about which they wish to develop individual expertise. For one student that might be something esoteric; for another it might be more mundane. Fly fishing, a sports team, ham radio, stamps, a particular career—anything that a student wishes to investigate is possible. Students keep careful records of their progress, and to bring closure to a study they teach their parents and classmates what they have learned.

• *Home-School Studies*

Ideally parents and their young adolescent children share some interests and develop them together. Often, however, this ideal does not exist in families. A team has a special leverage in developing projects that family members are expected to do together: writing a family history, collecting family stories, cataloguing household artifacts, or describing travels, careers, or ancestors. Sometimes standard curriculum units such as the Civil War or health practices invite parent participation. Of course, the prudent team invites parent reaction and participation prior to finalizing such studies.

• *Shadow Studies*

What does an actuary do? What happens during a typical day in a lawyer's life? A shopkeeper? A store manager? Shadowing is an excellent way for students to conduct highly organized observations of adults at work. In so doing they actually carry out a form of research that involves observing, recording (writing), analyzing, interviewing, and creating a summary that identifies major and minor occurrences (Stevenson 1997).

• *Direct Instruction*

It is important to note that direct teaching retains a very significant place in a team's program of curriculum and pedagogy. Where the purpose is to teach a specific concept or skill such as latitude and longitude or photosynthesis or quadratic equations, good direct teaching is often the most appropriate way for a teacher to present information and for students to understand it. Where inquiry, collaboration, or creative endeavor is the primary goal, direct teaching is less effective. Although many of the examples offered here could be regarded as "indirect instruction," there is still a crucial need for effective pedagogy via direct instruction.

• *Programmed Learning*

Computer software programs for individual learning have proliferated in recent years at a staggering rate. Students who are gifted in terms of learning mathematics as well as those who struggle with spelling can benefit from well-developed programs. Such programmed instruction usually removes participating students for a time from the social mix of students, and sometimes that is also a benefit to others. As long as the learner is developing mastery in an area of need, however, everyone benefits.

- ***Peer Tutoring***

All students benefit when the team climate embraces the value of readiness to help each other. Sometimes students' friends are better able to help them than is a teacher. Peer tutoring at its best happens organically, that is, when students seek each other out for clarification of an explanation or critical feedback or other assistance. Sometimes there is a formal arrangement by which students who have expertise in spelling or mathematics or writing may be designated as "peer tutors" who are on call at particular times to their teammates.

- ***Minicourses***

Short courses taught for only a week or two provide young adolescents with the variety that so many of them need. This arrangement also enables teachers to give time to topics that might not ordinarily be in the curriculum, such as "History of Rock and Roll" or "Mysteries of the Universe" or "History of Comic Strips"—three examples that our students have very favorably received at no cost to their other studies. Minicourses also enable teachers to teach particular personal favorites that they might not otherwise be able to share with their students.

- ***Advisor/Advisee Curriculum***

Because team members are advisors and have common planning time, they can jointly plan advisory activities that build on students' group/individual needs and interests. Although commercial materials can at times be helpful, the best activities result from advisors having meaningful discussions with students about aspects of adolescent development, getting along with peers, significant school policies, or community events, television shows, and so forth. Team members who share insights about their students and particular topics can greatly facilitate advisory curriculum.

- ***Intramurals***

Middle level schools strive to achieve students' participation in a wide variety of activities for all students, and intramurals are especially effective at accomplishing this goal. Intramurals involve everyone and avoid the "star system" of conventional schools that requires tryouts that inevitably result in cuts that deny participation. Good intramural programs frequently include individual and team sports, outdoor education activities, and "new games" as well as more academic games or ones based on television shows. The very best programs engage teachers and students in inventing imaginative games or contests. Teachers usually serve as organizers and coaches, but intramurals present an especially good opportunity for students to also take responsibilities for serving as referees, scorekeepers, arbitrators and leaders. In order to accomplish full participation, intramurals are usually organized schoolwide. Sometimes they are organized so that interdisciplinary teams or teacher advisory groups compete with each other in sports and other activities. Events usually result, of course, in one team winning and the other losing. It becomes important, therefore, for educators to be attentive to how well students are learning to handle these outcomes. Learning in healthy ways how to deal with being a winner or loser is a particularly appropriate goal in middle level schools, because individual identity formation is such a profound developmental task of early adolescence. The aphorism that "winning is everything" must not overwhelm the higher principle in middle level education that "participation comes first." A vivid example of lost perspective in this regard is presented in chapter 3, Scenario 5. Sometimes critics argue that when a school is organized by teams, students will spend so much time with their teammates that they want to get to know the rest of the school. If this concern exists, it would be wise to organize intramural teams so that members come from multiple teams. However intramurals are organized, the abiding emphasis should be on *participation* by all students.

• *Team Identity Activities*

As chapter 6 indicates, teams need to plan specific activities to build team identity and a sense of belonging, such as camping trips, musicals, field days, and so forth. Example 6 in chapter 6 gives an extensive listing of such activities.

• *Teacher's Choice*

A teacher friend whose certification specialty is science happens also to love photography, poetry, bicycling, and song writing. In a departmentally organized school it was difficult, if at all possible, for him to draw from these personal passions in teaching his young adolescent students. His schedule consisted of five sections of earth science and life science. When he later became part of a three-teacher team, those earlier limitations no longer figured in his schedule. He and his teammates incorporated several of the preceding options, and he was able to do things with students that were not previously available for want of time and opportunity. What is more, he also enjoyed much richer and more satisfying relationships with his students. They saw him much more fully as the interesting, diversely talented person he is. He modeled exactly the breadth and depth of education and personhood that young adolescents so urgently need as they are forming their own personal identities. When schooling is at its best, teachers are able to learn and grow and become more fully themselves. A well-conceived and organized team helps make that outcome possible.

6. Modes by Which Students Can Demonstrate Knowledge
(Authors)

- Oral report
- Photographic essay
- Slide/tape show
- Shadow box
- Build a model
- Make a new product
- Charades, pantomime
- Animations
- Book making (illustrated report in homemade book)
- Ads
- Meet the press
- Commercials
- Cartoon strips
- Mobiles
- Dioramas
- Role play or dramatization
- Interview/talk show format
- Quiz show
- Videotape
- Puppet show
- Graphs, charts with interpretation
- Letter (to the editor, senator, etc.)
- Collage
- Invent a board game or simulation
- Painting or work of art
- Diary or journal
- Questionnaire/interview and write-up
- Experiment and write-up
- Demonstration
- Series of questions
- Poem
- Tests—essay, short answer, multiple choice, fill in the blank, rank order, matching, react to a statement, select the relevant questions

ACCOUNTABILITY

How is our team doing?
How well are our students learning? Developing?
How well are our goals being accomplished?
How can we best evaluate?
What evidence is available?

Scenario 1

Sixth, seventh, and eighth graders on the Alpha team at Shelburne, Vermont, Community School individually assess their personal progress in relation to "Essential Behaviors for Learners," their school system's statement of educational philosophy and goals. Their teachers, Linda and Than, have adapted this formal document into lists of skills and concepts that their students can easily understand and use to take stock of their own progress (see Example 1). The teachers guide the students as they peruse their portfolios and daily records in order to assemble data on which an objective self-appraisal depends. These assessments occur at eight- to nine-week intervals throughout the three years that students are members of Alpha, and they comprise students' perspectives on their growth over the middle years.

Scenario 2

Teachers and students of the Knowledge Seekers team in Dallas, Texas, are considering an extensive, fourfold schema of evaluation: Teachers evaluate students and themselves; students evaluate teachers and themselves. Portfolio reviews, goal-setting and review conferences with advisors, journals, written comments, skills checklists, questionnaires (see Example 2), peer assessment, videotape review, and a host of other procedures are being considered within this framework.

It is the "students evaluate teachers" component of this schema that concerns Audrey. With twenty-five years of teaching experience, she wonders about the qualifications of a thirteen-year-old to assess her. Moreover, she is a bit apprehensive because she has difficulties with some students. However, she is persuaded by her team arguments that because students are the "primary clients" of education, it is crucial to know their thoughts and feelings about their teachers. Reluctantly she agrees to have students fill out a teacher evaluation questionnaire, designed by teachers and students (see Example 3), at the end of each grading period.

When her first set of student questionnaires contains some negative appraisals, Audrey largely dismisses them. After a second set yields the same results, including a few comments indicating that students feel that she does not always respect them, she becomes quite perturbed; she has always prided herself on her care and concern for students' well-being. Although it is a difficult task, she decides to discuss matters with the students. She does, and to her astonishment finds that students feel that she is quite sarcastic, that students take seriously things she says in jest. With this knowledge in hand, she changes the nature of her give-and-take with students. Her third set of evaluations is dramatically better, containing numerous comments about how much students appreciate the way she talks openly with them. Audrey now says that students' evaluations have helped her teaching more than anything else that has occurred in the past ten years.

Scenario 3

Members of the Songadeewin Family in Swanton, Vermont, Central School District have articulated lofty goals through their creed and "Nine Ways of Knowing" (see chapter 7, Scenario 4). However, from time to time they fail to live up to their lofty goals. When it appears that the team needs to refocus, members engage in a Songadeewin Family Retreat. During these two days, with an amended class schedule that may include an overnight at the school, they revisit their purposes and examine their progress. For these assessments, the teachers depend a great deal upon older students to serve as small-group leaders because of their prior retreat experience. On this year's retreat, the first day's emphasis is on students' reflections on the meaning of their creed and "Nine Ways." In small groups the sixth-grade leaders guide a webbing process that identifies team accomplishments and stumbling blocks. Students also write anonymous completions to three sentence stems, responding to "I wish all the students in Songadeewin knew: how happy it makes me when . . . how much it hurts my feelings when . . . how good I am at . . ." Teachers then read aloud selectively and anonymously from those offerings. Finally, students are regrouped with new leaders and asked to list on large sheets of easel paper: (1) what they think is going well, (2) what students and teachers can work on together, and (3) ways they can accomplish changes. Overnight the teachers analyze these self-appraisals and the next morning distribute a summary to the students. After a thorough discussion to ensure that everyone understands this summary, the team engages in a process of individual planning and goal-setting tied to the revisited Songadeewin philosophy. Once again in small groups, students brainstorm the extent of their progress, using specific criteria. For the final activity of the retreat, students craft essays about what they are learning about themselves and about working together toward the ways of Songadeewin.

Scenario 4

People in the community have expressed interest since the Skowhegan, Maine, Middle School has changed from a familiar departmental organizational structure to multigrade seventh- and eighth-grade teams. No parents have had any experience with such a design, and the principal, Jerry Lynch, is frequently questioned about the rationale and evidence that support it. To respond to legitimate concerns for accountability as well as to enrich their own professional understanding, Lynch, Assistant Principal Judith Enright, and the faculty establish a system for easily tallying some pertinent data. They examine overall and individual daily attendance patterns; total number of office referrals and patterns of office referrals for individual students; student, faculty, parent, and visitor surveys; and comparisons of standardized test scores before and after the teaming innovation. This data is systematically collected over a three-year period. By every single measure the school's multigrade teaming arrangements show evidence of progress.

Scenario 5

Principals of the three middle schools in High Point, North Carolina, meet regularly for assessment and planning with Associate Superintendent Dr. Bill Anderson, who has led the system's transition from junior high schools. At a session in the late spring of the first year, they review three sources of evaluative data: regular school records (test scores, attendance, discipline), the Connecticut Survey of School Climate, and questionnaires designed in-house that ask specific questions about the functioning of teams, advisories, and curriculum. It is the results of the questionnaires, filled out anonymously by parents, teachers (see Example 4), and students and coded by schools, that catch their eye. Although the overall results are quite positive, the data reveal that all three of the constituent groups feel that teaming has had little positive effect upon curricular integration.

This information is shared in each school with the teams, who discuss it during common planning time. After numerous discussions about the difficulties in making significant strides toward integrative curriculum, all of the teams express a need for staff development in this area. The principals relay these findings to Dr. Anderson, who, in conjunction with them, sets up a series of interdisciplinary workshops for faculty in the spring. In addition, procedures are developed so that the assistant principals responsible for curriculum can work more closely with the teams.

Scenario 6

The reputation of the Unit Team at Fayerweather Street School, Cambridge, Massachusetts, for innovative practice has generated numerous requests from educators outside the school for appointments to observe the team over a school day. Although it is flattering to receive the attention, the team is increasingly distracted by having strangers wandering in and out, asking questions, and sometimes getting in the way. At a Unit All-Team Meeting, the teachers and students decide to establish a two-hour visitors' schedule for Tuesday, Wednesday, and Thursday mornings, with a student committee organized to debrief the visitors for a half-hour at the end of their visit. The Unit teachers, Willy and Chris, also recognize that these visitors are a useful source of fresh insights about the team. Thus they create a "Unit

Visitor Questionnaire" (see Example 5) to gather information that is used as part of their team evaluation. This data becomes useful curriculum material for student mathematical analyses and the writing of summaries. Because the visitor reviews are overwhelmingly complimentary, students' confidence in themselves and their educational program is enhanced.

COMMENTARY

Responsibility is the price every person must pay for freedom.

Edith Hamilton

Because everyone has attended school, each of us holds opinions about what constitutes "good education." Therefore, teachers who undertake the change from subject matter departments or self-contained classrooms to team organization can be certain that they and their efforts will be observed and judged by others, both inside and outside the immediate school community. Given the certainty of such critiques, it becomes very important to incorporate a method for demonstrating team accountability into the team plan. We need to know more fully and be able to show to others just how well our innovations are working.

In most settings, educational excellence is increasingly equated with students' high test scores and grades. Although such indicators may have value, they are wholly inadequate for assessing the overall quality of an educational program. Something as complex as teaming begs for multiple forms of assessment, several of which have been indicated in the preceding scenarios.

An important element in any plan should be helping students to assess themselves because they will not have teachers to weigh their efforts when they become adults. Indeed, much human misery is due to inadequate self-assessment. Consider, for example, those who talk on and on, unaware if others are interested, or those who feel that they have completed a job but have not. Although self-assessment is important at any age, it is especially so during early adolescence, when independence, self-definition, and knowing where one stands are of paramount concern. Self-assessment does not replace teacher assessment but augments it in a powerful manner. Wise teachers teach students ways to grow in self-knowledge.

The Alpha teachers in Scenario 1 engage young adolescents in assessing themselves in a unique way: Students examine their progress in relation to the criteria found in formal declarations by their school system. Such assessment is not easy. Yet, when such criteria are edited into a form and language that young adolescents can understand, they are quite capable of taking personal stock as long as teachers help them with the process. By editing the criteria in this manner, the teachers assume more ownership of them. In addition, they become more aware of ways to combine their own criteria, and those of their students, with external demands.

In Scenario 2, the Knowledge Seekers' "fourfold" process of evaluation sets forth a full approach to classroom evaluation that goes well beyond the usual practice of limiting assessment to teacher evaluation of students. Here both students and teachers engage in assessment of self and one another, and the team has developed multiple ways of examining each area. Note that it was a big step for Audrey to agree to having students evaluate her, and that the support of her teammates enabled her to take this risk. Audrey's experience with students assessing her teaching illustrates one of many ways that student feedback can be of great help and is a reminder that well-conceived evaluation is not an indictment, but rather a means of improvement.

Team accountability must go beyond the classroom to assess the functioning of the team as a whole. When a team is built around clear statements of belief and reasoned policies to guide day-to-day operation, as is the Songadeewin Family in Scenario 3, those beliefs and policies become highly appropriate benchmarks for such assessment. Songadeewin involves students deeply in evaluating team performance, as well as in their own contributions relative to these standards, in an exemplary manner.

Because the public (and often professionals) has a penchant for evaluating education in terms of quantified, numerical data, it behooves teams such as those at Skowhegan Middle School in Scenario 4 to construct a system by which such data can be gathered and used. If, for example, the incidence of disciplinary referrals to the principal or assistant principal decreases, or if the daily attendance of team members declines from previous levels, these facts bear examination. We must ask, "What is happening in the team that could explain these changes?" Because these kinds of data are already maintained in the school office, it makes good sense to use them as part of the overall team evaluation. It also makes good sense to invite students to speculate about aspects of the team that might cause such changes. Teachers on a highly organized and purposeful middle level team should expect to see over the first two to three years certain evidence of improvement in attendance, citizenship, and academic measures. Because team organization stands as a way to *improve* the education of young adolescents, given time for evolution and growth of the program, one should see concomitant improvement in students' lives and accomplishments.

Scenario 5 illustrates the manner in which an enlightened school system can help teams. By gathering and summarizing perceptions about teaming from teachers, parents, and students and then sharing them with principals and teams, Associate Superintendent Anderson provides valuable information for teams to consider. And by responding quickly to team requests for help, he enables teams to improve their efforts in behalf of their students.

Although few teams may be as heavily visited as the Unit, described in Scenario 6, news about such successful programs has a way of generating curiosity. When teachers and students are willing to share their program with visitors, it is reasonable and fair to ask visitors to provide something useful in return. In this case the feedback is formally organized with an easily completed Lickert-type questionnaire built around the team's stated goals and policies. Whenever a team accepts visitors or presents its program to others, an opportunity exists to gather data that will contribute to the important work of demonstrating multidimensional accountability.

An important area of team accountability not touched on in the scenarios involves the manner and quality with which teachers work together. A form for team self-assessment is displayed in Example 6. The interpersonal aspects of teams working together are addressed in the next chapter.

PRINCIPLES

- **The team takes the initiative for gathering data.**
  A comprehensive team plan includes a commitment to and a process for gathering data that can be used to guide a team's evolution. That information may also be used over an extended period (two to three years or more) to make judgments about the influences of the team in promoting student progress. It is particularly important that teams gather data about things they wish to know. The team teachers' desires and dispositions, not simply those of the school or school system, must be reflected in demonstrating professional accountability.
- **Students help determine a team's effectiveness.**
  Teams, like other aspects of schools, are most authentically defined and explained by the students who experience them. For example, if we wish to know about the social studies program or the quality of our teaching, we should ask students. Their responses may constitute the actuality of the program in a far more believable manner than do curriculum guides, texts, and the like. Again, students may be in the best position to judge whether or not the team is following its goals and philosophy. Therefore, students must be brought into the accountability functions of their team as trusted, respected partners.
- **Useful, pertinent data are comprehensive and come from multiple sources.**
  A team is far too intricate to be judged by a single criterion. Formal and informal information about student achievement, growth, and development, teacher and student perceptions of selves and one another, appraisal of overall team performance in relation to team vision and philosophy, school records, and evaluations from those outside the team should be used whenever feasible. Data from multiple sources should reflect the teachers' assessment of what is most available and useful in their particular context.
- **Information gathered is used for team improvement.**
  In an age when evaluation is often used to make political hay or to cast stones, it is important to keep in mind that the real goal of assessment is to improve the team so as to foster student academic and personal growth. Therefore, mechanisms must be in place to analyze the data gathered, understand implications, and modify old ways or develop new strategies for working together.

PLANNING GUIDELINES

1. *Determine what information you would like to know/need to know, guided by team philosophy and goals.*

Bear in mind school and school system requirements but do not be limited by them.

2. *Determine what sources of useful information are available and develop a plan for obtaining it, being sure to involve students in the process.*

   Because so much material is potentially of value, it is judicious to prioritize needs as well as to consider what is readily available. Data from regular classroom procedures may include such things as portfolios of students' work; team discussions of students; student assessment of self (Examples 1 and 2), teachers (Example 3) and projects; skills checklists; advisory conferences; parent conferences; grades; diagnostic tests; and achievement tests. In addition to these data, some minimal information that should be kept from the very beginning includes:

   – Overall team attendance records by month or term
   – Attendance patterns of individual students who have a history of high absenteeism
   – Overall team referrals to the office for disciplinary reasons
   – Office referral frequency for students who have a history of frequent office referrals
   – Periodic student assessment (discussion, inquiry, survey, etc.) of team effectiveness according to its stated goals

   Through the principal be sure to enlist the help of the office staff in gathering quantifiable data.

   Finally, it is quite helpful to have students and teachers formally assess the team from time to time. (See also Example 7, chapter 6; and Example 7, chapter 11. Example 6 provides an extensive format for students to evaluate their teams.)

3. *Develop procedures for carefully analyzing and making modifications based on findings.*

   Although the team leader may often initiate various steps, other team teachers and students should assume significant responsibilities. Common planning meetings, all-team meetings, advisory sessions, and team retreats or special meetings are some of the occasions when the needed tasks can be discussed and undertaken.

4. *Share your findings appropriately.*

   Obviously, where results are positive, share the good news with administrators, parents, and the community at large. Where improvement is indicated, seek out those who can offer sound advice or give help.

ADDITIONAL POSSIBILITIES

- Use advisors to report student progress to parents. Such reports might include grades and comments about students' strengths, weaknesses, and overall growth, plus a student-written self-assessment. Because an advisor usually has about 15 students, such in-depth reporting is quite feasible.
- Carry out shadow studies, which have long been used successfully to clarify practices in middle level education (Lounsbury 1991, Stevenson 1997). College stu-

dents, parents of former students, and professional friends are often available to help out for a day or so observing an individual student's activity at five-minute intervals throughout a school day and sharing a report on the observation (often with student anonymity) with the team teachers.

- Invite carefully selected colleagues to visit, work with students, interview them, and report insights and impressions.
- Evaluative data may lead to establishing team goals or to a team mission for a coming term or school year. Thus improving attendance, adopting a theme, planning a community service project, or writing the history of the school might be decided upon. Ideally, the experience with setting team goals should be augmented by students setting personal goals and assessing their progress toward them.
- Encourage the school system, where appropriate, to gather information about team practices that can lead to team improvement. (See Example 4.)
- In time it may become appropriate to undertake a formal team evaluation that gathers data reflective of the team's progress in light of its stated educational goals and those of its school system. That evaluation can be reflected in a formally published report that is shared with administrative superiors and the elected school board.

CAVEATS

Keep good records, and keep them consistently! There are so many issues for teachers to consider when creating a team plan that accountability often slips to the background if teachers are not diligent.

Bear in mind the big picture and take a long-term perspective. The overarching goal is to create an educational experience for young adolescents that matches better with their nature and needs than does the traditional alternative. Although day-to-day judgments will in all likelihood be driven by immediate and short-range considerations, it is extremely important at the outset to put mechanisms or systems in place to gather data about the team's influence on students. Teachers who team should remember (and remind each other) that as they and their students accrue experience with their organizational plan, their version of teaming will evolve. Likewise, as the program becomes increasingly familiar, everyone—including outsiders—will become increasingly confident in the process. As teacher confidence grows, teachers naturally become more comfortable with opening up to additional sources of evaluation.

EXAMPLES

1. Alpha Team Adaptation of Essential Behaviors of Learners

(Shelburne, Vermont, Community School, adapted from Chittenden, Vermont, South School District)

- ***Effective Learners Think/Work Creatively and Critically***

I am growing confident of my creative and critical abilities because I . . .

– plan a strategy to accomplish a task.
– adapt information and ideas to solve problems.
– inquire when I want to find out.
– use a variety of learning styles.
– present my work in a variety of ways.
– make predictions based on available information.
– apply my understanding and knowledge of the past.
– evaluate and interpret information.
– recognize concrete and abstract relationships.

- ***Effective Learners Collaborate with Others***

As part of my continuing development toward working collaboratively with others, I . . .

– respect other individual and cultural points of view.
– respond constructively to support others.
– compromise when appropriate.
– provide leadership.
– work to bring about successful resolution to a question.
– recognize when the group goal is more important than the individual goal.
– offer solutions and express my opinions constructively.
– communicate my needs.
– make an effort to get to know the people I work with.

- ***Effective Learners Communicate with Others***

I am developing the ability to communicate because I . . .
– choose appropriate forms of communication.
– express myself orally.
– express myself visually.
– express myself through performance.
– express myself in writing.
– express my opinions.
– express myself logically/mathematically.
– express my feelings.
– listen and reflect on what is being communicated.

- ***Effective Learners Function Independently***

As part of my continuing development as an independent learner, I . . .

– assume responsibility for my own learning.
– am able to follow through on commitments.

– am challenged by new opportunities.
– have abilities and skills I am confident about.
– identify priorities and budget my time.
– learn from my successes and my mistakes.
– know how, when, and where to ask for help.
– recognize skills and abilities that need improvement.
– take care of my personal, social, and emotional needs.

2. Student Self-Evaluation Questionnaire
(Hawley and Hawley, 1983)

This self-evaluation form is to help you know more about yourself as a learner. It is for your own benefit and will not be used as a basis for your grades or comments on your work.

1. How satisfied were you with your learning this week?

1	2	3	4	5	6	7
very dissatisfied						very satisfied

2. What things contributed to your satisfaction?

3. What could you do to make the class more satisfactory for you?

4. How well did you concentrate in class?

5. How much did you participate?

6. How carefully did you do assigned tasks?

7. Open comment:

3. Student Evaluation of Teacher Form

Please check the column that best fits your opinion for the statement below:	Almost always	Sometimes	Not often
1. The teacher respects students and treats them fairly.			
2. The teacher really understands and knows the subject(s) he/she teaches.			
3. The teacher presents and explains things clearly.			
4. The teacher uses many different techniques.			
5. The teacher makes students feel that learning is really important.			
6. The teacher encourages students to ask questions and discuss ideas.			
7. The teacher makes clear what is expected of students.			
8. The teacher gives students choices & involves them in significant decision making.			
9. The teacher listens to and tries to help students who need special help or come to him/her with problems.			
10. The teacher grades fairly and is willing to listen when students disagree.			
11. The teacher keeps good discipline without threatening students.			
12. The teacher is a pleasant person to be around & creates a sense of community.			

The teacher is best when he/she:

The teacher would be better if he/she:

COMMENTS (Use back if necessary)

4. Teacher Assessment of Teams/Block Scheduling
(High Point, North Carolina, Public Schools)

How do you feel about the effect of teacher teams/block scheduling on	Significant Effect				Little/ No Effect
1. Enhancing the flexibility in groupings?	1	2	3	4	5
2. Integration of subject matter?	1	2	3	4	5
3. Promoting student achievement?	1	2	3	4	5
4. Discipline?	1	2	3	4	5
5. Student attitudes toward school?	1	2	3	4	5
6. Improving opportunities for staffing?	1	2	3	4	5
7. A more positive attitude on your part about teaching?	1	2	3	4	5
8. Improving opportunities for planning?	1	2	3	4	5

9. How would you recommend improving the teacher teams/block scheduling organization?

10. Please use this space to make comments on any of the items on teacher teams/block scheduling organization.

5. Unit Visitor Questionnaire

(Fayerweather Street School, Cambridge, Massachusetts)

Name (optional) ____________________

Home address ____________________

Position ____________________ Years in education ________

Why did you visit our team/school?

How did you hear about us?

* * *

1. Please describe/list what impressed you most favorably about the Unit:

2. What concerns do you have as a result of your visit?

3. What are your ideas about ways we might improve the Unit?

* * *

Please rate the following:	Students					Teachers				
	Low				High	Low				High
Intellectual Intensity	1	2	3	4	5	1	2	3	4	5
Academic Quality	1	2	3	4	5	1	2	3	4	5
Interpersonal Relations	1	2	3	4	5	1	2	3	4	5
Initiative	1	2	3	4	5	1	2	3	4	5
Responsibility	1	2	3	4	5	1	2	3	4	5

If you are willing to be telephoned for elaboration, please complete:

Name ____________________ Telephone (   )____________________

6. Jungle Gem Team Evaluation
Griffin Middle School, High Point, NC

Now that the year is almost over, we'd like your views on how things have gone for you. Please give each section careful consideration. We're interested in your observations and suggestions!

1. Rank each item from 1–5 with 1 being TERRIBLE and 5 being EXCELLENT (obviously that means that 3 is AVERAGE).
2. Beside each + write something that you liked about that activity/policy. Beside each – make a suggestion for improvement or tell something that you didn't like.

TEAM POLICIES/PROCEDURES/ACTIVITIES

Team Meetings _____

+ ____

– ____

Intramurals _____

+ ____

– ____

Team Improvement Teams _____

+ ____

– ____

Classroom arrangement/seating _____

+ ____

– ____

Citizen of the Month luncheons _____

+ ____

– ____

Field trips _____

+ ____

– ____

Is there a field trip you would suggest for the future? ____________________

____

Advisory activities _____

+ ______________________________

– ______________________________

Knowledge Bowl _____

+ ______________________________

– ______________________________

CUBS/Bearbase _____

+ ______________________________

– ______________________________

Interdisciplinary activities _____

+ ______________________________

– ______________________________

Team Discipline Policies _____

+ ______________________________

– ______________________________

Auctions _____

+ ______________________________

– ______________________________

Jungle Jack _____

+ ______________________________

– ______________________________

Can you suggest additions for the purchase list? ______________________________

____

Should any changes be made to the purchases/fines options? ______________________________

____

ACADEMIC AREAS

Think about your academic classes. Tell us one thing you liked about each class and one suggestion for change.

Math

+ ______________________________

– ______________________________

Language Arts

+ ____

− ____

Science

+ ____

− ____

Social Studies

+ ____

− ____

What did you like most about being on the Jungle Gem Team? __________

____

____

Can you offer ANY suggestions that will help us make this a better team?

____

____

We appreciate your time and suggestions.

INTERPERSONAL RELATIONSHIPS

How do we get to know and trust each other?
How do we create a positive environment?
How do we solve conflicts in constructive ways?

Scenario 1

Overheard in a faculty lounge:

"*These kids are crazy. All they want to do is fight and be rude . . .*"

"*Middle school kids don't want to learn anything. They are brain dead.*"

Heard at national conventions:

"*Early adolescence is the range of the strange. . . .*" "*Young adolescents are hormones with feet. . . .*" "*Young adolescents can't deal with new concepts easily. . . .*"

Overheard at a cocktail party:

"*Oh, you teach eighth grade? My hat's off to you. It's such a difficult age. . . .*"

Conversation at a team meeting:

Heather: "*Why, Ralph, I'm surprised you feel I'm prejudiced. When I look at people, I don't even notice whether they are black or white.*"

Ralph: "*Suppose I told you that I don't notice whether you are male or female?*"

Scenario 2

Three of the teachers on "the Family" team, Galad, Kay, and Vivian, have worked together for the past ten years. Lance, the fourth team member, has been with the Family for three years. The team members meet daily in their small office, which includes a telephone, microwave, and small refrigerator. On the walls are a Family logo, photographs of team members and activities, a large calendar annotated with the Family's events, and a bulletin board with reminders and announcements.

As the teachers enter the office, Kay and Lance rib each other about their less-than-outstanding performance in a faculty-student basketball game, and Vivian inquires about Lance's wife, who fractured a bone in a minor car accident. Galad serves popcorn that he has just prepared. As the four teachers settle into their prepared agenda, their demeanor changes because the first item is discussion of a just-announced systemwide plan to evaluate all teachers on the basis of their students' progress as measured on standardized tests. The teachers are united in their outrage over the plan: They object to such a misuse and overemphasis on test scores, and they resent the fact that they were not involved in any way in a matter that so severely affects their day-to-day efforts. Furthermore, they know how unfair the proposal is because some teams have been assigned a preponderance of high achievers, whereas others, such as the Family, have more low achievers.

Yet, the teachers are divided over what their response should be. When the conversation begins to get heated, Galad suggests that they list possible responses and try to reach a consensus in a logical fashion. All agree. Alternative responses include writing an acidic note to the school board, going immediately to the principal's office to protest, contacting an attorney, staging a sick-out, raising the issue to the school's Program Improvement Committee, or doing nothing. After much discussion, they decide to go to the principal. Galad says he will schedule a conference as soon as possible.

Near the close of the meeting, Galad observes that in light of their having just completed such a volatile session, this would be a good time to assess their group process, a procedure that they follow once a week (see Example 7). They agree to do so, and after reviewing the results are particularly pleased that they have been able to listen to one another without interruptions, an issue they have been concerned about.

Scenario 3

Ross and Nancy want to develop an "intentional context" for Team 8–1 at Shoreham-Wading River Middle School in New York, addressing the question, "How can we create and maintain an environment where kids can feel good about themselves and others, have good relationships with us, celebrate one another, and learn to become more responsible people?" In so doing, they develop activities that build upon and flesh out "the Distinctions," the values/characteristics that they wish their team to embrace (see Scenario 2, chapter 4).

On the first day of school, students enter the room to the Beatles' "Birthday" ("Today's your birthday, we're gonna have a good time. . . . I would like you to dance. . . . Take a cha-cha-cha-chance . . ."). Ross reads his poem, "The First Day," and Nancy reads another, "Desiderata," both of which the students seem to like. After an amicable tone has been established, the teachers introduce themselves by talking about their spouses, kids, pets, experiences, and passions. They also show photos of themselves as eighth graders, which add even greater interest. Then students are randomly paired for introductions, and after time to converse they introduce one another to the rest of the team. The session closes with Ross reading Robert Frost's "The Road Not Taken" and leading a discussion about the importance of the choices that we make.

The next day students come to class with a written definition or description of two of the twelve "Distinctions" (cooperation, responsibility, appreciation, etc.). At the close of the previous day they had drawn one Distinction from a bag and were told to choose a second one that they'd like to write about. Their descriptions are read aloud, posted on the walls, and become a basis for frequent references during the course of the year.

During the third week of school, the team goes to the Pocano Environmental Education Center (PEEC) for three days of outdoor education and community building activities. Students write brief essays expressing what they learned about the "Distinctions" while at PEEC. The essays are collected, photocopied, and bound for distribution to all team members.

Just prior to Thanksgiving, students write notes of acknowledgment and appreciation to two teammates, again one name drawn from a bag and another that is chosen. Each statement of acknowledgment is read aloud and presented to the individual being acknowledged. Furthermore, Nancy and Ross organize a variety of group acknowledgments. "Everyone stand up who is on the soccer team . . . in the band . . . made 100 on a math test . . . didn't make 100 on a math test . . . helped with the Special Olympics," and so on.

In January students are asked to describe "three important lessons I have learned" this year: one in math or science, one in language arts or social studies, and one in any topic. Again, student writings are read, posted, and frequently referenced.

Twice during the year, students write and send letters of appreciation to people who are important to them, but these letters are not read or graded by the teachers. During the December holidays, the letters are sent to anyone whom the students choose; parents and best friends tend to be their most frequent choices. At the end of the year, the recipient is any teacher whom students perceive as having made a difference in their lives during their three years at the school.

These sessions are held during a double-period all-team meeting that Nancy and Ross adjust to their daily schedule. Students' "tickets of admission" to these sessions are their completed assignments. The rare student who comes unprepared has to sit outside the room until the assignment is completed.

To bring closure to the year, Nancy and Ross sit in a circle with their students for "Memory Minutes"—reminiscences and reflections about their year together. Amid smiles and tears, kids and adults talk about what individuals and the team as a whole have meant to them.

Scenario 4

As the second All-Team meeting of the newly formed Flyers Team convenes, we hear the following banter among students:

Mike: *"Hey, Madonna, your lipstick is about an inch thick. How about getting rid of some of it on me?"*

Doris: *"In your dreams, Fat Face. I'd rather die."*

Ronnie: *"Oooooo, I guess she told you, Blubber Boy."*
Erica: *"Why don't all you guys shut up? You make me sick."*

Marlene and Tim, the Flyers' teachers, remark on the number of put-downs that they have heard recently and ask the students how they feel about them. Mike immediately says that "cracking on people is a great way to have fun." Another student, Martha, retorts, "It may be fun for you, but it sure isn't fun for everybody. Some people get their feelings hurt." Several others nod in agreement, including Mike, who responds with a knowing shrug. Ronnie bursts in, "Aw, come on, get real. Don't be so serious. Nobody means anything by cracking on people. We're only kidding. It's just having some fun."

After a moment's hesitation, Maggie, one of the more mature eighth graders, glances at a couple of her friends and says, "I think some people are being mean to each other. There's too much dissing and too many put-downs. Some people are really getting their feelings hurt. And it sure doesn't help team spirit." Tim nods and observes, "Maybe a few of us are *intentionally* trying to hurt others, but I wonder how many people think that put-downs are a real problem for our team. What do the rest of you think?" There's concurrence that even though they know that teasing is something that kids do in fun, they haven't liked it. Marlene then points out, "This looks like an important issue that probably won't go away unless we choose to do something about it. What do you think about breaking into small groups to see if we can come up with some solutions?" Noting their agreement, she continues, "Okay, sit with whomever you wish and talk about the specific things being done that some of us see as put-downs, how you feel about it, and what we might do to make things better. Let's take fifteen minutes now, and if need be, we can continue the discussions in TAs [Teacher Advisory groups] tomorrow morning."

Scenario 5

Harvey, a social studies teacher, arrives at the Mercury team's common planning meeting ten minutes late. His teammates have begun a discussion about planning a three-week interdisciplinary unit for the next semester. As others express enthusiasm for developing a unit, Harvey voices concern that his students will not do well on the year-end standardized tests if they spend so much time on what he sees as just an "extra" project. When assured by teammates that any unit selected will involve numerous concepts related to history and geography, Harvey counters that students will get behind in the specific content of their textbook. Mary, a science teacher, then suggests that the theme of "flight" might be selected to coincide with the time of year when Harvey's classes begin learning about the Wright Brothers and continue with looking at the evolution of flying. The rest of the teachers concur.

After a period of silence with everyone waiting for Harvey's assent, he states that he has a lot of other obligations in the spring and doesn't think he can find time to work on the unit. Mary explodes, "For crying out loud, Harvey. You never want to do anything that involves working together. Everybody's busy, but all we are talking about is a simple three-week unit that ties in well with what we are already teaching. When we formed this team, we all agreed that we wanted to do a lot of integrative work. We'll never do *any* with your attitude!"

Hank, the team leader, has been listening anxiously and intervenes, "I think we ought to mull this over for a while. There's nothing to be gained by forcing someone to do something against his will. I'll put it on our Friday agenda, and that will give us some time to think it over. Now, let's move on to the next topic."

Scenario 6

When Mr. Huggins arrives Wednesday morning for a conference that he has requested with the Enterprise team to discuss the work of his son, Jimmy, he gets right down to business. "I don't get it," he says. "I thought teams were supposed to space kids' assignments out so they wouldn't have a lot of big things due at the same time. Now I find that Jimmy has two tests on Thursday plus a fifteen-page project due on Friday. He's panicked and sure he's going to fail the term. I don't think that is a smart way to handle things, not to mention unfair. If I treated my customers that way, I'd be out of business in a flash. What's going on here, anyway?"

Jenny and Will, the Enterprise teachers, listen intently while Mr. Huggins talks. When he finishes, Jenny calmly acknowledges that she can understand why he is so upset, given his understanding of the situation. She and Will then go on to explain that although Thursday is earmarked for math quizzes, they never schedule more than one test on a given day. Jimmy himself has chosen this Thursday as the day to take a makeup test in social studies. They further explain that the project due on Friday had been announced three weeks ago, that much of the work for it had been done in class and in previous homework assignments, and that the suggested number of pages was five to fifteen, including illustrations.

Rubbing his chin, Mr. Huggins slowly says, "I see. I see. Jimmy didn't tell me all this. I'll need to have another talk with him." After suggesting that Jimmy postpone his makeup test until Monday, the teachers suggest some strategies for Mr. Huggins to help Jimmy become clearer about assignments and his work. At the close of the conference, Mr. Huggins smiles, shakes hands with Jenny and Will, and thanks them for their time and concern about Jimmy.

COMMENTARY

If you treat an individual as he is, he will stay as he is, but if you treat him as if he were what he ought to be and could be, he will become what he ought to be and could be.

Goethe

The way that interpersonal relationships are formed and handled will make or break a team. No matter how bright and industrious teamed teachers are, no matter how ingenious their plans, if they cannot relate positively to each other and to their students and in many instances to administrators, parents, and colleagues, most of their efforts will amount to little. By the same token, if students do not develop a strong sense of community and respect for one another, team life will be miserable and unproductive for all concerned.

It is often difficult, especially at first, for teachers who have been accustomed to working alone to become comfortable with always being supportive team members. After all, few if any of us were prepared to teach as a member of an interdisciplinary team. Jan Robinson, a team teacher at London Middle School in Buffalo Grove, Illinois, states the case well:

> All I had known up until this point was working by myself in the classroom. What I did I was very good at. I hung my hat on being an excellent math teacher. I had to let go of the fact that I was no longer queen of my classroom, but an integral part of a team. Suddenly, we were experiencing what we were asking students to do. . . . You simply must learn that diversity builds a better product. (1995, 1)

Where team members are engaged in power struggles, disrespect, bickering, sarcasm, and such, it is virtually impossible for them to work together effectively. Where students are put down, treated harshly, and not listened to, they will become sullen and withdrawn or rebellious. Motivation and true intellectual endeavor will wane, and there will be no sense of "team." Where teachers are at odds with parents, administrators, and colleagues, the resulting lack of trust and respect will surely undermine the kind of support that strengthens the team.

Conversely, where understanding, respect and trust, and goodwill are prevalent, teaming becomes a rewarding experience for all concerned. Positive relationships do not *guarantee* that teaming will flourish, of course. A great deal of commitment, planning, and hard work is still required, as previous chapters have made clear. However, positive relationships are the single most important element in the development of an effective team organization.

A plethora of research, theory, and recommended practice has been published about interpersonal relationships, some of it dealing specifically with various types of teams in business, industry, and schooling. Unfortunately, very little of that data is devoted to interdisciplinary team organization in schools. We have had to draw primarily from our own empirical experience as team members and consultants working with teamed teachers in writing this chapter, and we recognize that in so doing we have just scratched the surface of a complex, multilayered issue. Later in this chapter, however, we will explain initiatives that will serve all teamed teachers well.

Scenario 1 portrays two types of attitudes that can destroy teaming if not overcome quickly. The first is the all too prevalent, stereotypical view of young adolescents that sees ten to fourteen year olds as *innately* irrational, ravaged by personal storm and stress, in conflict with parents and adult values, dominated by peer pressure and social concerns, and uninterested in intellectual endeavors. While parts of this description may depict some young adolescents, there is solid research to support the fact that it is not characteristic of the vast majority. And the aberrant behavior that does occur is not the inevitable result of pubertal changes young people are experiencing. Social factors such as isolation from the adult world, insufficient guidance and support from parents and adults, and lack of meaningful roles and opportunities to contribute to society contribute much more to the adolescent malaise that does exist than do biological factors (Arnold, 1993). The critical point for teams to grasp is that if team members believe this stereotypic "popular wisdom," their efforts are largely doomed from the start. Young people quickly sense when they are viewed negatively and are therefore unlikely to cooperate with those who see them in a bad light. Thus a self-fulfilling prophecy is established instead of seeing the potential in students and trying to ameliorate the societal conditions with controlling and coping with students. Moreover, they will trivialize many of the crucial issues that young people face in striving to become adults. The starting point for everyone working with young adolescents is to appreciate them—their directness, idealism, off-beat humor—and to understand that they are capable of far more than they are usually given credit.

The second destructive attitude in this scenario is that of racial insensitivity. In claiming not to notice whether Ralph was black or white, Heather obviously thought she was manifesting an enlightened view. What she was doing, of course, was denying a basic part of Ralph's identity—his blackness. And Ralph let her know! (Ralph's response is cleverly appropriate because many of the prejudicial attitudes, including denial, that plague race relations are similar to those that involve gender relations.) This encounter is but one small incident in the huge realm of racial misunderstanding, prejudice and injustice that engulfs society. Teachers such as Heather, while perhaps well intentioned, seem oblivious to these realities. They want to see themselves as "good people" and believe that race relations are getting better and better. Their solution to diversity is to make everyone the same, not to recognize and honor differences. One of the chief barriers to racial understanding is that relatively few black and white people know each other well. They may work in the same business or school, but they don't work together . . . they don't socialize outside the workplace . . . they don't share hopes and fears . . . they don't talk frankly about racial differences. Teaming provides a great opportunity to overcome racial (and gender) barriers, for teachers and students who take this process seriously are inevitably drawn together in a personal manner. They cannot hide from one another; the structure of teaming does not allow it. Teams that are successful in promoting positive race relationships are generally those that face racial issues—often awkwardly, falteringly—but they face them.

In Scenario 2, the Family illustrates how a mature team promotes highly positive human relationships. Members of this team are true professional colleagues; they genuinely like and respect each other; they enjoy kidding one another; they take an interest in each other's lives outside of school; they share values and principles about their work. Their efforts are enhanced by a cozy, well-appointed meeting room that manifests their "Family Values." They stay focused with an agenda. When the important issue of evaluating teachers on the basis of their students' test scores arises, they freely speak their minds. Significantly, however, they do not passively accept a policy that they abhor. When emotions flare, they move to a formal problem-solving approach that is calming and effective.

In Scenario 3, Ross and Nancy do not leave the development of positive interpersonal relationships to chance. They have agreed about the importance of teaching specific values, and they have created a deliberate plan for building community spirit in their team. Drawing directly from their vision and philosophy statement, they carefully craft a series of activities that encourage students to practice the values embodied in "the Distinctions." Their expectations and standards are very clear and agreeable to their students and parents.

The tone is set on the first day and is powerfully reinforced by daily reviews and a dedicated outing away from school on the third week: Students know that their teachers are responsible adults who genuinely care about them, that their feelings and ideas are unequivocally valued, and that everyone on Team 8–1 is expected to acknowledge and appreciate each other. Having students write frequently about important values in this context causes them to relate these values to their own lives. Having teammates speak appreciatively about each other helps build trust and togetherness, using peer pressure to a positive advantage. Posting student definitions of "the Distinctions" and referring frequently to them reinforces the whole process. It is important to note that as students are asked to acknowledge their peers, the procedure of selecting names by chance ensures individual choices and guarantees that no one is left out. The intentional context that Ross and Nancy created to end the year by allowing students and teachers to reflect on their time together and to say good-bye to each other closes the year in an appreciative, *meaningful* way.

Dealing with put-downs, the focus of Scenario 4, is an all-too-familiar and vitally important issue for virtually all teachers of young adolescents. Sometimes put-downs are mild, humorous, and obviously done with no malice, and they may be of little consequence. But it is also very easy for them to get out of hand and become hurtful and divisive. Many young adolescents like Mike simply do not realize that insults can really hurt other people. Lots of youngsters have not grown into the realization that demeaning others does not elevate anyone and that continual criticism of others affects one's own character.

Fortunately Marlene and Tim, the Flyers teachers, as well as a number of their students, do realize these truths and are unwilling to let the put-downs pass unchallenged. They further recognize that indulging permissive attitudes toward put-downs will likely poison the ambience of their newly formed team. Thus they call attention to the issue and work on creating plans to address it. Most noteworthy is the considerable attention and time given to students' concerns about the interpersonal climate of their "family" within the school. Their confronting the various issues associated with put-downs stands as a model of responsibility to team climate and to each other. It also teaches personal integrity: When you see injustice that you can change, do it. Marlene and Tim's leadership acknowledges contrasting feelings and ideas and gives direction for students to develop their own solutions to their problems. In their so doing, their students learn empowerment.

In Scenario 5, Harvey is the classic example of a minimalist team member—someone who won't pull his own weight. This scenario depicts a situation that regrettably is faced by far too many teams. He has an excuse for anything and everything that involves team effort. Though his Mercury teammates make every effort to accommodate his "concerns," he will not budge. Understandably, his teammates are put out with him, and Mary lets him know it.

Harvey's attitude and behavior raise serious questions. Why was he placed on the Mercury team? Any team? Should he be teaching in a middle school? At any level? What should teams do when faced with a Harvey?

In this particular dilemma, nothing is resolved at the moment of confrontation. Hank, the team leader, elects to postpone the issue for a couple of days, allowing time to defuse the emotion and to provide some buffer time for reflection and informal talk about the curriculum issue. Obviously ignoring the problem over a longer time will intensify emotions rather than resolve them. For the sake of students and teachers, however, teams *must* deal directly and deliberately with the Harveys of this world.

A first step might be sending "I" messages to Harvey—describing how his behavior affects their work and their feelings about it and him—then listening to his reasoning. Assuming that a breakthrough occurs, a next step might be jointly formulating a concrete plan with Harvey that clarifies his participation and contributions to overall team efforts. If Harvey still balks, then the team members are justified in telling him that they are unwilling to work with him next year and will inform the principal of their decision.

The importance of listening and keeping cool under fire is evident in Scenario 6. Like many parents of middle schoolers, Mr. Huggins accepts his son Jimmy's story as the whole truth and is incensed at the Enterprise teachers for loading Jimmy with so much work due at once. Instead of immediately defending themselves against Mr. Huggins's attack, Jenny and Will hear him out and acknowledge that his feelings are justified based on the information he has. They then explain the situation fully and make some constructive suggestions for Mr. Huggins to work with his son. They also volunteer to follow up with Jimmy. Their sensitivity and skill in dealing with Mr. Huggins allow him to speak his piece and to learn from the teachers, leading to a promising plan and what will hopefully become a happy resolution.

We must also note that this circumstance could have provided an important learning opportunity for Jimmy, had he been present at the conference. His presence would have ensured everyone's understanding of the problem and the strategies for avoiding it in the future. It might also have provoked some profitable discussions between him and his father.

PRINCIPLES

- **Mutual respect, goodwill, and an attitude of cooperation are the bedrock of teaming as well as of personal growth and development.**

Without living out these core values, the best-laid plans will falter, relationships will deteriorate, and students will be robbed of opportunities to learn what are truly among the most basic of "basic skills." Gandhi's words, "Be the change you seek," capture the essence of this outlook. (See Examples 1,2,3 and 4 for attitudes and behaviors that block or foster positive relationships.)

- **All human beings have a great need to belong, to be part of a meaningful group.**
  Creating a warm and accepting sense of community is a team's first order of business because a basic need of young adolescent youth is to belong to schools, teams, programs, groups, and individuals whom they like and respect. Groucho Marx's one-liner that "I don't want to be a member of any group that would have someone like me as a member" does not apply to young adolescents; they yearn to belong, to be connected to others they appreciate, and to be certain of their membership status and interpersonal relationships.
- **Active listening is an essential interpersonal skill.**
  Showing interest in others' views through attentiveness to body language as well as to spoken language communicates respect. Listening for feelings as well as for ideas, avoiding distracting or defensive comments, and showing understanding through nods or reflective comments convey that one is attuned to the speaker.
- **Taking responsibility for one's problems shows individual maturity.**
  "Owning" other people's problems is emotionally draining and nonproductive. Showing concern, clarifying, or mediating is helpful, but trying to directly change other people is futile. Quick-reflex attempts to solve another person's problems rob that person of initiative. Especially in working with students, the *process* of learning how to deal with interpersonal and personal problems can be more important than actually resolving a particular quandary. When facing conflict, Gordon's (1974) advice is helpful: When you own the problem, send "I" messages—how the problem affects me—not "you" (accusatory) messages. (See Example 3.) When you and others own the problem, you can engage in the six-step problem-solving strategies shown in Example 5.
- **Conflict is inevitable and can often be healthy.**
  Indeed, growth is virtually impossible without successfully resolving and moving beyond conflict situations. It is important to acknowledge and to respond to differences as they arise, not allowing small irritations or contraries to mushroom into large ones. Sound, preconceived procedures for dealing with inevitable differences can often reduce or entirely eliminate potentially noisome friction and yet manage it effectively when it does arise. (See Example 6.)

PLANNING GUIDELINES

1. *Develop a plan for encouraging and reinforcing positive interpersonal relationships.*
   Create whatever rituals, activities, and procedures best suit your vision of community spirit. After they are under way, draw on students' ideas and initiatives for making the team safer and stronger and, in their vernacular, "more fun." Creating a positive climate can head off many problems before they start.

2. *Discuss your team agreements, expectations, procedures, and guidelines as frequently as necessary, making sure that they are clearly understood and supported.*

   As has been discussed in chapters 4 and 7, coming to agreement about a team's vision, values, and procedures grounds a team's position. That foundation is best used continuously as a reference for dealing with unforeseen problems. When those agreements are insufficient or are not working, they must be amended.
3. *Become more knowledgeable about interpersonal relationships, listening skills, and conflict resolution.*

   In addition to learning about how to cultivate effective interpersonal relationships, include that knowledge in the evolution of the team's procedures, the curriculum, the advisory program, and in working with parents.*
4. *Establish specific guidelines and structures for dealing with conflict that may arise during common planning, all-team meetings, or mediations.*

   Identify conflict directly as it arises and don't allow it to fester.
5. *Engage students in discussing and assessing team relationships on a regular basis.* (See Example 7.)

   Periodically assess the professional interpersonal climate.

ADDITIONAL POSSIBILITIES

- Teams of four or five teachers should occasionally invite a group process observer to attend common planning and all-team meetings. Often an administrator or guidance person can perform this service and provide constructive feedback to the team.
- Offer workshops for parents, perhaps led by a developmental psychologist or other specialist, to teach strategies for helping parents in their relationships with their young adolescent children.
- Establish a peer mediation program within your team, if not in conjunction with the whole school. Such programs offer students the opportunity to have conflicts and problems mediated by peers who have been appropriately trained, rather than by a teacher or administrator. Students who are not satisfied with the results may have the matter decided by an administrator. Mediation is especially compatible with the approach to governance and human relations espoused in this book. It allows students to accept responsibility for their own actions, provides opportunities for leadership and growth, teaches students in concrete ways about human differences and commonalities, and enables them to learn a problem-solving process. In addition, it can substantially reduce the amount of time that adults spend on discipline problems and create a more positive ambience in the team and school (Schrumpf, Crawford, and Usadel 1991). Some useful resources for establishing peer mediation programs are the National Association for Mediation in Education, 425 Amity Street, Amherst, MA 10002; School Mediation Associates, 72 Chester Road, No. 2, Belmont, MA 02178; and Conflict Resolution Resources for Schools and Youth, 149 Ninth Street, San Francisco, CA 94103.

*Excellent strategies for working successfully through interpersonal conflicts are available through published approaches to mediation. (See reference suggestions below.)

CAVEATS

Make community development between students and with adults your top priority. Be careful not to get into such a hurry to do so many things at once that team spirit is neglected.

Acknowledge individual preferences and points of view but remember that team goals must come first if you are to progress at all. Be especially wary of letting your own priorities get in the way of team solidarity.

Be ready to compromise. Disagreements are inevitable, so don't be surprised when conflict arises. Remember that compromise is often the key!

Where fundamental principles are in conflict and are not open to compromise, seek professional mediation from a guidance counselor or a community person trained in mediation or conflict resolution.

EXAMPLES

1. Team Participation: To Sabotage or Support?

(Authors)

Sabotage Strategies	*Support*
meetings: come late/leave early	be on time for meetings
grade papers during meetings	participate fully in team meetings, volunteer
interrupt teammates	listen attentively, giving everyone a chance to speak
disregard others' ideas	acknowledge differences
insist on having own way	support equitable decision making
do your own thing	seek and support synergy
complain, whine, sulk, blame others	emulate the qualities you admire in others
criticize colleagues' work in private to teammates	discuss each other's work only in team meetings
use sarcasm	use language you want others to use with you
be a killjoy ("50 Reasons Why It Won't Work")	fully support teammates' initiatives, be patient, and remember that teaming is an *evolutionary* process

2. Twelve Roadblocks to Active Listening

(Adapted from Gordon, 1974)

1. Ordering, directing, commanding
2. Warning, admonishing, threatening

3. Moralizing, preaching, obliging
4. Advising, giving suggestions or solutions
5. Persuading with logic, arguing, instructing, lecturing
6. Judging, criticizing, disagreeing, blaming
7. Praising, agreeing, evaluating positively, approving
8. Name-calling, ridiculing, shaming
9. Interpreting, analyzing, diagnosing
10. Reassuring, sympathizing, consoling, supporting
11. Probing, questioning, interrogating
12. Withdrawing, distracting, humoring, diverting

3. Three Components of "I" Messages
(Adapted from Gordon, 1974)

1. A nonjudgmental description of the behavior that is unacceptable to you
2. The tangible effect that the behavior has on you
3. The feelings generated in you as a result of the tangible effect of the behavior

Example: "When you interrupt me, I am not able to express my ideas coherently. I feel very frustrated."

4. Behaviors That Promote a Negative Racial/Ethnic Atmosphere
(Adapted from Love, 1978)

1. Low expectations for academic performance
2. Using inappropriate instructional materials
3. Poor teacher-student interpersonal relationships
4. Not valuing students' contributions
5. Biased grouping practices
6. Biased counseling practices
7. Biased institutional practices
8. Failure to treat students as individuals
9. Bias in discipline procedures
10. Lack of honesty in interactions with students
11. Miscellaneous

5. Six Step Problem Solving
(Adapted from Gordon, 1974)

1. Clearly define the problem or conflict, including feelings about it.
2. Brainstorm possible solutions.
3. Evaluate possible solutions.
4. Make a decision (by consensus, not vote).
5. Determine how to implement the decision.
6. Assess the success of the solution.

6. When Conflict Arises

(Adapted from Harvey and Drolet, 1994)

- Keep cool. Choose the time and place to deal with conflict; give only amount of information that one can receive.
- Use active listening; don't try to resolve an issue before hearing it fully.
- Focus on behavior, not the person; give descriptions, not judgments.
- Send "I" messages, not "you" messages.
- Diagnose the situation and match the solution sought to the type of conflict that is involved.
- Seek alternatives, not answers.
- Search for win/win, not win/lose solutions.
- Don't confront "difficult persons," and remember that they usually speak only for themselves.
- When receiving criticism, focus on what is said, not on why it is said.

7. Team Self-Assessment

Source Unknown

Do We:	Very well	Just O.K.	Needs Work
1. Use active listening skills in communication?			
2. Express feelings openly and honestly?			
3. Allow each member equal opportunity to contribute?			
4. Stay on task/topic?			
5. Allow for clarification when needed?			
6. Support and encourage each other?			
7. Explore all possibilities before deciding?			
8. Strive to achieve consensus?			
9. Strive to apply standards for effective groupwork			
10. Deal with conflict appropriately?			

POSTLOGUE

As we mention in several places in this book, we hope that many teams will use this work to develop a written plan or planning outline to guide their teaming efforts. By committing ideas to writing, teams must necessarily grapple with issues and make some commitment; they cannot gloss over or postpone important decisions. In our experience, teams who begin with a written plan are considerably more successful, especially the first year or two of teaming. They have a clearer idea of what they want and how to accomplish it; they hit the ground with their feet moving. In addition, a written plan enables a team to share its ideas more easily with others, making it more possible to obtain feedback that may refine or improve the plan. Of course, the plan will change over time as team members gain insight from their experience working together with young adolescents.

To provide additional guidance for teams who will develop written plans, we conclude this handbook by reproducing the actual planning outlines of two teams (pseudonyms are used) which were developed during the course of summer institutes on teaming we conducted. The reader will note that the format they used is slightly different than the one set forth in this book. We do not present these outlines as ideal plans, but as first, real-world efforts that may be useful to others who are in the planning process.

Good luck in your planning. Teaming is a great adventure. If you pull together and keep your eye on the prize—the full development of young adolescents—you will grow personally and professionally in untold ways. And you will make great strides in pursuing the goal that attracted you to teaching in the first place: making a significant difference in the lives of kids.

1. TEAM PLANNING OUTLINE

"The Trail Blazers"
Grades 7-8 Multiage
Roosevelt Middle School
Team Members: Rhonda Collins,
Doris Wells (Team Leader)

1. VISION/PHILOSOPHY What do we believe? What are our values?

MISSION STATEMENT: The mission of the Trailblazer program is to help students become confident, independent learners. They have many opportunities to make decisions in a consistent, secure setting.

We will encourage involvement with new experiences, ideas and people through our academic studies, class meetings, and community service projects. Recognizing the inherent grouping/strengths/weaknesses of the developing adolescent, we wish to help them develop self-confidence, necessary interpersonal skills, academic skills, and leadership skills in order to more effectively mesh with their peers and world in general.

Our MISSION for the academic year will be to develop leadership skills in our students through a variety of experiences which will include the peer mediation program and class meeting opportunities.

2. GOVERNANCE How do we make decisions?

- Establishing/clarifying policies

Our SHARED ACADEMIC GOALS encourage the direct participation of all students in experiencing concepts in math, science, humanities, writing process, and reading skills which are appropriate for their interests. We also will encourage further development of skills in these areas. It is also expected that we will incorporate the district-wide curriculum guide materials.

There are UNIFORM MINIMAL STANDARDS which apply to 90% of all students. Each teacher identifies these standards within her own teaching disciplines and as well identifies those shared in overlapping responsibilities, such as reading, writing, work completion, etc.

STUDENTS' PARTICIPATION includes their role in determining the use of block time for units of study and subsequent evaluation criteria. Students will directly participate by developing learning contracts. Student chores may include: bulletin boards, cleaning of chalk boards, putting up chairs at the end of a school day, coordination of the student calendar of activities, assignment board, etc. As the year progresses, students will assume complete responsibility for student/teacher awards, Triple Dare activities, etc.

CITIZENSHIP STANDARDS (class rules) will be developed during a class meeting (individual → larger group consensus).

LONG-TERM ASSIGNMENTS AND TESTING SCHEDULES will be posted on the bulletin board along with the calendar of STUDENT ACTIVITIES on a weekly basis.

INTERPERSONAL DIFFERENCES among students/teachers will be handled through a conflict resolution program called "Peer Mediation" to be taught throughout the school year.

- Leadership roles and functions
  - Team leader –Doris Wells
  - Timekeeper–Rhonda Collins
  - Scribe/historian– Rhonda Collins
  - Newsletter mentor–parent/teacher
  - Mediation committee–students through Peer Mediation program
  - Liaison to off-team colleagues, other teams–Doris Wells
  - Liaison to parents–Rhonda Collins
  - Service project coordinator–Doris Wells
  - Special event/project overseer–both Rhonda and Doris

– News media specialist–Rhonda Collins
– Representative to school-wide committees–shared by both Rhonda and Doris

- Common Planning Time
  One period per day is reserved for this, using a specific agenda structure for efficiency. Twice each month one of these periods will also include a representative from guidance, special services, and teaching assistant. Rhonda Collins will keep the team book up to date.
- All-Team Meetings
  One period per week will be reserved for class meeting. Skills in leadership will be emphasized, as will the modeling of participatory democracy and conflict resolution.

3. PROCEDURES How do we function day to day and week to week?

- Time management
  Our academic schedule includes daily block time of two, sometimes three periods. Usually, science and the humanities will be taught at this time. We share our math time with another team, so that period is not flexible. Our schedule includes the exploratory subjects, physical education, and music, as determined by the master school schedule. We are concerned about the number of periods per week our students are separated into seventh and eighth grade groupings, and we'll continue to lobby to change this. We plan to develop a year-long schedule of units which we will share with other teams in the school.
- Organizing students
  Our classes are heterogeneously grouped for everything but math class. We prefer, also, that our classes are multiage. For science, the humanities, and math we have seventh and eighth graders together. Because of our schedule, students are separated into seventh and eighth grade groupings in reading, spelling, and expertise. We have a TA program in place presently and student groups are mixed among the different seventh and eighth grade teams. We collaborate with other teams in a variety of ways, such as: the annual school-wide interdisciplinary study, T.A. activities, informal activities, etc.
- Student Responsibilities/Assessment/Evaluation Strategies
  Students are responsible for: class participation, timely completion of classwork and homework, maintenance of academic notebooks and assignment pads, maintenance of evaluation notebooks and completion of mid-quarter progress reports. Student goal setting will be a high priority this year with time set aside each week in order to complete this. We will conference regularly with students as they set realistic goals for the quarter.

4. IDENTITY Who are we and what do we stand for? How do we celebrate?

- Representations/traditions
  TEAM NAME: Trailblazers
  Students will determine: team LOGO, COLORS, t-shirts . . . .

SPECIAL EVENTS/TRADITIONS: Trailblazers Night, Teddy Bear share, community service day during the holidays, end of year share, Dude/Dudette awards,Trailblazer magazine of student writing,Trailblazer scrapbook.

- Awards

  A birthday bulletin board section will be established for student/teacher birthdays. A balloon/pencil/"A" grade in any subject, etc. will be considered as special birthday gifts from the team. We are in the process of negotiating with our principals in a way in which academic successes can be rewarded by them, as well, in a direct manner. Recognizing accomplishments in citizenship, special initiatives, etc. will take place during class meeting ("take a bow"). Students-of-the-week Recognition (2–3 students/week) will include the students' pictures and artifacts which represent the students.

- Activities

  We plan to initiate a regional celebration (involving towns that feed our school). Triple Dare activities and team records will be incorporated on a fairly regular basis. Many other activities have already been described: team picnics, community service projects, novel groups,Trailblazer nights, etc.

- All-Team Meetings

  Student leadership will be emphasized in our class meetings. A program which teaches conflict resolution will enable students to have the necessary skills in place in order to practice reaching consensus on issues of interest to them during these class meetings. The sharing of student interests and accomplishments will take place at this time on a regular basis, as well as planning future activities for our program.

- Team's physical environment

  We will arrange the room to accommodate large-group instruction, individual work spaces, and places for socializing. Students will be invited to make regular contributions to a special section of our bulletin boards. Displays of students' academic work, projects, etc. will continue on a regular basis. Theme bulletin boards will be directed by the students whenever possible and often (perhaps in teams). Team colors and logo will be determined during our earliest class meetings by the students on the Trailblazers team.

5. COMMUNICATION How do we keep everyone informed?

- Professional colleagues

  Our special service representative and team guidance counselor will be invited to our CPT(Common Planning Time) every other week. Once per month, our principal and assistant principal will be invited to our CPT. If possible, a representative from the exploratories will be in attendance at our CPT meeting once per month. Once a week, we will communicate current and future plans to our special service representative, principal/assistant principal, guidance counselor, and exploratory representative. Once we develop our program newsletter, we will disperse copies to each team in the school and to a ninth grade contact teacher. We also will send a copy to Jack Gordon, assistant superintendent, and to the chair of the school board.

- Students

 For academic information, we will use our daily assignment board, a posted weekly calendar, and regular classroom announcements. Our eighth grade students will be participating in a mentor program with the incoming seventh graders. A student/parent picnic will be held in August with mixing activities and dinner planned. In September, a parent dessert/orientation will be held. October will include a school-wide Open House in which student portfolios and work will be shown by the students to their parents. A parent "get-together" will be held in November, hopefully directed by one of our parents. In the past, parents used this evening to discuss common issues of concern about their adolescents. Two or three of these may be planned for the year.Trailblazer volleyball night, inviting parents and students, will be held in January.

- Parents

 A student-parent handbook will be developed by our students beginning this fall with our guidance. Parent/student conferences will be held on an as-needed basis. Parents will be utilized to a greater extent as resources. We again intend to have parent involvement in our novel groups. Parent involvement with a regular newsletter (including parent contributions) is planned, as well. Thank you notes will include all student signatures on our Trailblazer logo.

- Community

 We will continue our contributions to the school paper. We will attempt to publish news in the local paper. We will continue and augment our community service projects and involve the communities in our area.

6. CURRICULUM What and how do we learn?

- Goal-setting

 Our SHARED ACADEMIC GOALS encourage the direct participation of all students in experiencing concepts in math, science, the humanities, writing process, and reading skills which are appropriate for their interests and needs. It is also expected that we wil incorporate the district-wide curriculum guide materials. The overall goal for our students this academic year is in teaching/practicing leadership skills. We will have a sense of its success if individual conflicts decrease in frequency, skills are utilized during class meeting as consensus is approached on decisions, and the decrease in the number of times students are sent to the assistant principal due to inappropriate behaviors. Individual students will set goals concerning leadership behaviors, writing/ math portfolios, as well as in other academic areas. Teachers' personal goal-setting will directly integrate these student goals with the emphasis on guiding students to success. Mandated curricular requirements (through scope and sequence) will be monitored/incorporated by the teachers as appropriate.

- Academic Program

  We have seven skill areas within our academic instruction: 1) public-speaking, 2) research, 3) writing, 4) problem-solving, 5) reading, 6) study skills, and 7) interpersonal skills. These will be taught across the courses of science, math, humanities, reading, and other curricular activities.

  Through coordinated classroom instruction, we will collaborate in teaching journalism (writing process), conflict resolution, cooperative learning, decision-making/goal-setting.

  The "hows" of implementing this curriculum are:

  –Direct Instruction will be used in humanities and science; skills and concepts taught will be integrated as well in math, writing, and reading.

  –Reading & Writing Workshops will continue, as will "novel groups."

  –Orbital (Special interest) Studies: We will sharpen our format, forms, research process, and topics in our present expertise program.

  –Interdisciplinary Units: There will be a minimum of two integrated/interdisciplinary units during our academic year. Possibilities include: Lake studies, Industrial Revolution/Machines. One building-wide IDU (Interdisciplinary Unit Themes) will probably focus on careers.

  –Theme studies may include the study of the national election (leadership) and TV advertising/programming.

  –Minicourses will be offered periodically for students to choose from topics of their interest, for example, studying the physics of amusement rides during the Central Valley Fair.

  –Inquiry projects will be integrated into the core curriculum, for example, a parent survey may lead to a student engineering project.

  –Field trips will continue and will include an emphasis on experiential activities.

  –Problem-solving: A weekly problem-to-solve will be introduced.

  –Community Service: We will continue our holiday service project, and hope to expand to one service activity each semester.

  –Simulations will be continued in our core curriculum.

7. ACCOUNTABILITY How do we know what is being accomplished?

- Student progress

  Both teachers will continue to monitor students' academic progress (homework, classwork, quizzes, tests, projects, etc.), attendance, and behavioral concerns. Our records are typically very current and recorded in an efficient manner (we have both taught for twenty years).

  This next academic year we are initiating a new organization for our students' records. Each student will have a personal binder which will be stored in a drawer of the filing cabinet with easy access when appropriate. Within each student's binder, the student will enter: any homework sheets for a given academic area, the mid-quarter progress report once it is signed and returned from home, and graded quizzes and tests. At the end of each quarter, the binder may be sorted out by the student if desired . . . a "clean slate" for the new quarter. Stapled to the back will be the student's: learning style inventory, study skills inventory, interest inventory, goal-setting form, the student's homework contract, standardized test scores, and any behavioral/discipline reports.

- Record-Keeping

Portfolios for writing and math will be stored in a drawer of the filing cabinet where students will have easy access when appropriate.

Learning contracts for special research reports, etc., as well as mid-quarter progress reports will be stored in the student's personal binder which will be stored in a filing cabinet at school (as mentioned above). Student/teacher conference reports, as well as peer/group evaluations, will also be stored in this student binder. Standardized test records will be stapled on the back of this binder.

The detailed evaluation notebook in which a student tracks his/her separate grades on homework assignments, classwork, quizzes, tests, and projects will be stored in this binder as well.

A separate teacher record-keeping notebook will be stored in the filing cabinet and will contain student reports from special services, any profile sheets completed by previous teachers which helped determine current team placement, and any notes from parent/teacher conferences.

- Team/Program Evaluation

An informal evaluation within the team will continue to take place as we evaluate and verbally communicate how we are progressing at the end of our CPT meetings. Input from our exploratory representative, our guidance counselor, and special service representative will be asked of them on a quarterly basis and any necessary adjustments made as a result. Student surveys and parent surveys will be conducted and also seriously considered, on a semester basis and adjustments to our program made as needed. We will be asking our visitors to share with us any of their perceptions of our team/program on an open-ended questionnaire as the occasion arises. When possible, we will ask teachers from other teams to observe/evaluate our program and make changes when needed. Our administrative team will be asked to observe and evaluate our program from time to time and, again, we will make adjustments as needed. In order to make comparisons to research-based standards, we will read middle level education journals (state and national level) and make observations regarding our program. Changes will be made as needed.

Team record-keeping concerning daily attendance patterns will be included in each student's evaluation notebook and reviewed on a weekly basis. Perhaps we will graph the attendance pattern at the end of each semester. Actually, attendance has been very good in the past for this program so no particular concern in this regard exists at this time. Of course, this speaks well for the program, its students, and parent support. In order to encourage and reinforce reading habits, we will have a reading tree with the names of books read by each student and a blue sticker next to the title of any book considered superior by the student placing the leaf on the tree. Evaluation of student performance (grades, standardized tests) was addressed earlier in this section. Disciplinary incidences will be handled and recorded in cooperation with the assistant principal, also considered in an earlier section.

8. TEACHER EFFICACY What's in it for me? for us?

- Personal priorities

  Feeling the need for a sense of accomplishment through documented successes, we will give more direct attention to tracking the short and long range accomplishments of our students. We both struggle to balance our commitments to school and home and more systematic use of in-school time may help. Both of us enjoy teaching a variety of subjects which requires effective time management. Because we now have CPT scheduled daily, the frustration of lack of daily communication will decrease. It enables us to make short- and long-range curricular plans. We will also be able to regularly assess and evaluate the program more effectively. We recognize the need to spend more time outside of school together and also plan to attend some professional conferences together.
- Professional Priorities

  We plan to continue our course work in conjunction with our individual professional development plans, filed with our school district. Both of us plan to pursue middle level certification this fall. As stated earlier, we plan to attend conferences related to our program and professional development. We will incorporate newly learned ideas and systems in our team plan, as needed. It is also a function of both our personalities that we question, re-evaluate, and adjust our teaching methods and the program. Because we will be surveying students, parents, and other staff members more regularly, we also hope to incorporate their feedback in our evolution process.

  We both have actively participated in school-wide leadership through membership on the Steering Committee, Communication Committee, Math Committee, Scheduling Committee, and others. We plan to continue our participation, but also balance time commitments to school-wide leadership and to our own program. We both coach intramural sports activities and share the staff responsibility for meeting students' extra-curricular needs. We will continue our participation in our state-wide professional organizations, and welcome the opportunity to present at state conferences. We also will make an attempt to contribute to the state Journal and Newsletter.

2. TEAM PLANNING OUTLINE

"The Champions"
Grades 4-6 Multiage
Westfall Elementary School

Team Members: Mary Toles, Marcus Reiner
Pauline Henderson, Dot Wilburn, (Team Leader)

1. VISION AND PHILOSOPHY

The Madison Central School Philosophy Statement is mentioned in the ABLE Plan as follows:

"We at MCS wish to foster successful development of each child in terms of academic performance and social skills in order that he or she will be a thoughtful and informed young person learning and interacting positively with their peers and adults."

MISSION STATEMENT: We will hold students to high standards, teach them at their level of ability, listen to their concerns as individuals, provide opportunities for children to develop social and problem-solving skills and maintain a consistent standard for all, staying in communication with parents.

Theme: "Accepting the Challenge"

Motto: "I Can Do It!"

Student goal-setting will include social, physical, and academic goals that will be reviewed monthly with team advlsors. We will set quality standards through use of portfolios, project criteria, and the A.B.L.E. plan.

The all-team handbook will be given to all team members and parents during the first month of school.

Our pledge is as follows:

We're the Champions from Madison
We do our best to make learning fun.
When I come to class, I have a pencil and a book.
My assignment's on time–Hey, everybody look!

I listen to the one who's doing the talking,
I'm doing my work, I'm not up walking.
I'm fine, I'm funky, I'm full of fun.
I show respect for everyone.

Cooperation makes us ABLE
To deal with anything on our table.
How I behave is up to me;
I accept full responsibility.
I'm fine, I'm funky, I'm full of fun;
I am a Champion from Madison!

2. GOVERNANCE

- Team Policies:

  Goals–Revise and update A.B.L.E. (Academic and Behavioral Learning Expectations); modify spelling programs to integrate subject area vocabulary;

standardize expectations for written work; establish a panel of peers for mediation of chronic homework or behavioral issues.

Theme–"Accept the Challenge!"

Citizenship standards–The team will adhere to the standards set by the A.B.L.E. plan.

- Leadership Roles and Functions:

Team Leader–Dot Wilburn
1) Set the agenda.
2) Act as the team liaison to the administration.
3) Enforce team rules.

Recorder–Mary Toles
1) Keep minutes for each meeting. Maintain log.
2) Take care of team correspondence with staff and parents.

Liaison–Pauline Henderson
1) Surveys and informs off-team staff of team decisions and activities. (Since Emily is half-time at ACS, Maurice Lussier will share this responsibility.)

Activities Coordinator–Marcus Reiner
1) Arranges field trips.
2) Notifies appropriate school personnel of plans which affect school procedures.
3) Takes care of special activities' financial arrangements.

Team Rules:
1. Meetings will begin on time.
2. Team discussion will be restricted to items on the agenda.
3. Members should be sensitive to the positions of others.
4. Members should be honest about positions held.
5. Members should follow through on responsibilities.

Common Planning Time:
- MTWF 8:00–8:20
- Tuesday 11:45–12:20, IEP/IST
- Wednesday 9:50–10:20 October-February while D.A.R.E. is in session
- Friday 1:15–2:00 (occasionally)

- All-Team Meetings:

The first All-Team Meeting will be held the first day of school with kick off activities involving cooperative games and snacks followed by group discussions on team values. Thereafter, the whole team will meet at least once per month. During this first meeting, teachers will model participatory democracy. Thereafter, the meetings will be run by the students on a rotating basis.

In addition, students will be selected to be on P.O.P., Panel of Peers. The purpose of P.O.P. is to enlist peers in a cooperative manner to help students who are consistently having difficulty in academics or behavior. One of the advisors for this group will be the guidance counselor who has been working with students on conflict resolution.

Volunteers will be sought for peer tutoring to aid those students who are having trouble with any academic subject or organizational needs.

Small team meetings, or crews, will meet weekly on Tuesdays 2:00–2:45. The purposes of these meetings are: 1)To participate in a team activity such as the newsletter, hall bulletin board, a science/social studies unit, or a math investigation unit. After four weeks, crews will rotate to another project. 2)Create cooperation and team spirit by a common goal.

Crews will meet twice per week for 3–4 hours in order to work on interdisciplinary units. These time blocks will be on a rotating basis.

3. PROCEDURES

- Time Schedule:

  Within the perameters of the master schedule, the attached schedules attempt to address the matters of 1)Common Planning Time 2)All-Team Meeting time 3)Small group or crew meetings 4)IDU meetings and timing of the units during the year 5)prep time 6)IEP/IST meetings.

- Student Organization Strategies:

  Students will meet in the All-Team Meeting and in their crews to discuss personal goal setting. Each month the student will meet with their advisor to review and modify their goals.

  Student progress will be communicated in several ways: 1)Phone calls to parents with both positlve and/or negative comments. 2)Mid-term progress report to parents of all students noting progress in all academic as well as behavioral areas. 3)Report cards distributed quarterly. 4) Parent conferences held twice per year unless needed more often.

The A.B.L.E. Plan defines the expectations for the MCS students in grades 4–6:

1. Be prepared for class.
2. Listen attentively; stay on task.
3. Be respectful towards peers and adults.
4. Cooperate with students and adults.
5. Take responsibility for your social and academic behavior.

In order to maintain a consistent enforcement of student expectations, a daily class log will go with the class throughout the day so that all teachers have an opportunity to note both positive and negative achievements or behaviors.

- Goals:
  C–capA.B.L.E. of succeeding
  H– for the high expectations we have for ourselves
  A–for being A.B.L.E. to meet any challenge
  M–for mediating our differences
  P–for pride in what we are and what we can become
  I–for idealism, helping others
  O–for open minds
  N–for neighbors, being friends
  S–for self-respect, the most important ingredient

Throughout the year there will be many opportunities for students to share their activities and accomplishments with their parents. For example: At open house in September, the team could present their pledge. The winter holiday program will highlight the IDU on holidays of the world. The spaghetti-eating utensil invention will culminate with a spaghetti dinner provided by the PTO. At the Fly into Spring demonstration, parents are invited.

- Assessment/evaluation calendar and strategies:
  Students will develop a greater sense of self-assessment in their daily work and projects. The writing process is one good example. In addition, they will cooperate in peer conferences. All IDU's will be shared with the other crews during an All-Team Meeting. During at-home projects a project log will be kept which reflects the amount and kind of research, and type and amount of corroboration with parents. This log is an integral part of the project.
  At CPT, assessment of IDU's according to goals and time available will be accomplished.

4. IDENTITY/RECOGNITION

The team name will be the CHAMPIONS. These students will be divided into four smaller groups called CREWS based upon the colors in the team logo: Emerald, Purple, Blue, and Yellow. The logo will incorporate the regional characteristics of lakes, mountains, sun, and a bear. Our mascot is Champion, a stuffed bear.

The banner will be constructed by students with a parent advisor. This committee will meet before or after school to complete the design.

Physical Environment: Student work and projects will be displayed in the classrooms and on the team's bulletin board. Pictures taken of crew work will be displayed on a bulletin board and then placed into a scrapbook that will be passed down to Grade 5 at the Grade 6 Graduation Ceremony.

Two students will be chosen on a weekly rotating basis to display some personal artifacts to others in the school. These will be called Students of the Week. Team advisors will model this in a display at the beginning of the school year. Team historians will be chosen from Grade 6 on a rotating basis.

Team buttons and pencils sporting "I can do it!", "Accept the challenge!", and "I am a CHAMPION!" will be available for student rewards and recognition. T-shirts with the team's logo will be available for purchase.

- Traditions:
  Fly Into Spring (Project and Contest)
  Myths (Interdisciplinary Unit)
  Great Ice Cube Melt (Project and Contest)
  Young Scholars (Academic Effort and Behavior Recognition)
  Honor Roll (Academic Excellence)
  Snow Sculpture/Winter Carnival
  Graduation (Grade 6 Ceremony)
  Jane Morris Memorial Essay Contest (All School Civic Theme)
  Canadian Trip (Grade 6)
  Academic Banquets (Bi-Annual Recognition for Honor Roll)
  Pizza Parties (Quarterly Recognition for Young Scholars)

- Awards:
  Students will be honored with a birthday cupcake at lunch. Mini-awards will be presented frequently to students to recognize their successes. As listed under identity, the team will feature two students of the week for special recognition. At All-Team Meetings, students will comment on another's successes and ask them to "Take a Bow." Likewise, teachers will award Shining Star certificates to those who have made a contribution to the team. As listed under procedures, mid-term progress reports will be mailed to all students celebrating the many successes, as well as those areas needing improvement. Recognition after completion of a project is often done with the use of ribbons and certificates.

- Activities:
  According to the A.B.L.E. Plan, "Young scholars" will be honored with a pizza party each quarter. Honor Roll is posted in the hall each quarter, and academic banquets honor achievement twice per year.
  All-Team competitions, holiday parties, IDU culminating events, Memorial Day program, visits to nursing homes, All-Team musicals, (*Pinocchio, Don't Smoke that Cigarette!*), waddees, field trips, winter carnival, welcome back barbecue and family fun night are all activities which highlight effort, success and teamwork.

- All-Team Meetings:
  At the monthly meetings, work of each team will be shared. Conflict resolution and problem solving will be a focus while two sixth graders will be the chairperson and the recorder. In order to speak, the baton must be passed. These leadership positions will be rotated to other students on a monthly basis. The team pledge will be recited and team songs will be sung.

- Team's Physical Environment:
  A special bulletin board for pictures, another bulletin board for upcoming events, and team colors decorate team areas. Champions our team mascot. "I

CAN DO IT!"–aphorism. Artwork decorates halls. Good work is displayed in classrooms as well as at the Art, Science, and Writing Fair and the Christmas Program. The team scrapbook will be assembled by student historians. Samples of monthly newsletters will be assembled as an ongoing history of the team.

5. COMMUNICATION

Communication with our professional colleagues will be handled in the following manner:

1. Invitation in mailbox or by verbal request to off-team colleagues.
2. Recorder will write up the agenda and action taken to be distributed to other staff through Action Minutes.
3. Team liaisons will distribute Action Minutes to off-team colleagues, Principal and Central Office Staff.

Student communication will occur during weekly crew meetings. All-team meetings will occur at least once a month for awards and recognition, solving community issues, and for sharing and competitions. Orientation will take place during the morning of the first day of school (see below).

The student handbook will be distributed to students and parents during the first month of school. Weekly Specials and Class Schedules will be included in the Student Handbook. Student-created Bulletin Boards will announce upcoming events and schedules. A weekly calendar of tests and events will be posted after team collaboration on Fridays.

- Orientation Day:

  1. Introduce teaming concept to all-team.
  2. Brainstorm "Things that cannot be done alone."
  3. Cooperative games.
  4. Cooperative snacks. (Each crew to prepare and provide a part of the whole snack.)
  5. Divide into crews with their teacher advisor.
     a. Discuss goal-setting.
     b. Discuss student roles and responsibilities.
     c. Discuss mediation procedures.
     d. Discuss ABLE changes and homework expectations.

Parents will be kept informed through the monthly team newsletter and through the student-parent handbook. Notes home will be sent as needed. Two parent-teacher conferences will be held; one to take place in November with grade level teachers at the end of the first quarter, the second to take place in the spring with Teacher Advisors rather than classroom teachers.

Communication with the community will be facilitated through the teams' newsletter and the local media (Madison Independent, Valley Voice, WFLT, WMOX, WCAL). Community Service Projects are as follows: Reading to Grades K/1/2; and Kidscards to Elders.

6. CURRICULUM

The goals are threefold: The CHAMPIONS goals (see under procedures): student academic, social, and physical goals to be set and self-assessed with their Crew Advisor on a monthly basis; teachers personal goals similar to those of the students (i.e., sharing and teaming goals).

The curriculum is mandated by the Madison Northwest District as evidenced by the individual scope and sequence for each subject area. MCS is departmentalized for Math, Language and Social Studies. Though these lines are disappearing with teachers teaching all disciplines through interdisciplinary units.

Interdisciplinary Unit Themes (IDU's)

1. Elections
2. Holidays Around the World
3. The Wonder of Snow
4. Myths (Greek, Norse, Native American will rotate yearly)

Home-School Projects

1. Hanger Inventions
2. Great Ice Cube Melt
3. Fly Into Spring
4. Spaghetti-Eating Utensil Inventions

Themes

1. Literature-based connections with Science and Social Studies
2. Civil Rights/Grade 6 (year-long)
3. Inventions/Grade 5 (year-long)

Community Service Projects

1. Kidscards to the elderly and homebound
2. Reading to the K/1/2

7. ACCOUNTABILITY

Student progress will be monitored as follows:

1. The Grade book
2. Criteria Grading Sheets (checklists for projects)
3. Individual Goal Sheets (revise with advisor monthly)
4. Portfolios (Math and Writing)
5. Academic Logs (for student self-assessment of progress)
6. Homework Folders (kept by teachers/distributed monthly)

Record-Keeping Systems:

1. Portfolios
2. Standardized Test Scores in Files
3. Peer/Group Evaluations (in Crews and in Writing)
4. Contracts (includes academic and behavioral goals)

5 Interim Tests and Progress Reports
6. Contact Log (parent contacts with teachers by phone, conference, notes)

Team Program Evaluation:
1. Common Planning Time (CPT) will be used to evaluate program goals.
2. Student self-evaluation of Interdisciplinary Units personal goals
3. Parent Survey in January to evaluate program
4. Off-team specialists who work at other schools will help evaluate the program in relation to others they have observed (through goals' checklists)
5. Principal evaluation of team goals
6. Book Log of books read and book reports
7. Daily attendance is kept for the entire week and we have a small student population, so attendance can easlly be monitored.
8. ABLE offenses (time outs and homework sheets, are monitored by the office)
9. Panel of Peers (POP) will meet with chronic offenders of rules–the frequency will help us determine whether the program is working.

8. TEACHER EFFICACY

Our personal priorities as a team deal with:
1. The impact we have on students/making a difference
2. The fun and camaraderie with students and with teachers
3. The opportunity to observe students grows toward their full potential through Grades 4, 5, and 6
4. Support for and from other colleagues who team

Our professional priorities include developing expertise in teaming, being part of an innovative area in education, integrating technology, and developing community partnerships.

REFERENCES

Alexander, W. M. (1995). *Student-oriented curriculum: Asking the right questions.* Columbus, OH: National Middle School Association.

Alexander, W. M., & McEwin, K. (1989). *Schools in the middle: Status and progress.* Columbus, OH: National Middle School Association.

Allport, G. (1959). *The nature of prejudice.* New York: Bantam.

Arnold, J. (1993). *A curriculum to empower young adolescents* (occasional paper). Columbus, OH: National Middle School Association.

Arnold, J. (1990). *Visions of teaching and learning: 80 exemplary middle level projects.* Columbus, OH: National Middle School Association.

Arnold, J. (1997). Teams and curriculum. In T. Dickinson & T. Erb (Eds.), *We gain more than we give: Teaming in middle schools.* Columbus, OH: National Middle School Association.

Atwell, N. (1987). *In the middle: Writing, reading and learning with adolescents.* Portsmouth, NH: Heinemann.

Beane, J. A. (1993). *A middle school curriculum: From rhetoric to reality* (2nd ed.). Columbus, OH: National Middle School Association.

Brazee, E., & Capelluti, J. (1995). *Dissolving boundaries: Toward an integrative curriculum.* Columbus, OH: National Middle School Association.

Brodhagen, B. L. (1995). The situation made us special. In M. W. Apple & J. A. Beane (Eds.), *Democratic schools.* Alexandria, VA: Association for Supervision and Curriculum Development.

Brodhagen, B., Weilbacher, G., & Beane, J. (1992). Living in the future: An experiment with an integrative curriculum. *Dissemination Services on the Middle Grades, 23,* 9, 1–7.

Carnegie Council on Adolescent Development (1989). *Turning points: Preparing youth for the 21st century.* New York: Carnegie Corporation.

Damico, S. (1982). The impact of school organization on interracial contact among students. *Journal of Educational Equity and Leadership, 2,* 238–252.

Dewey, J. (1938). *Education and experience.* New York: Collier Books.

Dickinson, T. S., & Erb, T. O. (Eds.). (1997). *We gain more than we give: Teaming in middle schools.* Columbus, OH: National Middle School Association.

Epstein, J. L., & MacIver, D. J. (1990). *Education in the middle grades: National practices and trends.* Columbus, OH: National Middle School Association.

Felner, R., Kasak, D. T., Mulhall, P., & Flowers, N. (1997). The project on High Performance Learning Communities: Applying the land grant model to school reform. *Phi Delta Kappan, 78,* 7:520–527.

Garvin, J. (1989). *Merging the exploratory and basic subjects in the middle level school.* Rowley, MA: New England League of Middle Schools.

Gatewood, T., Cline, G., Green, G., & Harris, S. (1992). *Middle school interdisciplinary team organization and its relationship to teacher-stress.* Research in Middle Level Education, 15 (2), 27–40.

George, P. S., Spreul, M., & Moorefield, J. (1987). *Long term relationships: A middle school case study.* Columbus, OH: National Middle School Association.

George, P. S., & Alexander, W. M. (1993). *The exemplary middle school* (2nd ed.). New York: Harcourt Brace Jovanovich.

George, P. S., & Schewey, K. (1994). *More evidence for the middle school.* Columbus, OH: National Middle School Association.

George, P. S., & Stevenson, C. (1989). The very best teams in the very best schools as described by middle school principals. *Early Adolescent Magazine, 33 (5),* 6–14.
Gordon, T. (1974). T. E. T.: *Teacher effectiveness training.* New York: Wynden.
Grillo, T. (1992). Attleboro keeps teacher, class together. *Boston Globe,* 27 October, p. 24
Harvey, T., & Drolet, B. (1994). *Building teams and building people: Expanding the fifth resource.* Lancaster, PA: Technomic.
Hawley, R., & Hawley, S. (1981). *Evaluation.* Amherst, MA: ERA Press.
Holland, H. (1997). The challenge of teaching: New report suggests major changes in training, organization and practice. *High Strides,* 9, 4, 12–13.
James, C. (1974) *Beyond Customs.* New York: Ageathon.
Johnson, S. (1990). *Teachers at work: Achieving success in our schools.* New York: Basic Books.
Kayzenbach, J. R., & Smith, D. K. (1993). *The wisdom of teams.* New York: HarperCollins.
Korinek, L., & Walther-Thomas, C. S. (1994). *Co-teaching: The nuts and bolts.* Unpublished training materials. Williamsburg, VA: College of William and Mary.
Larson, C. E., & LaFasto, F. M. J. (1989). *Teamwork: What must go right/what can go wrong.* Newbury Park, CA: Sage.
Lickona, T. (1988). *Raising good children.* New York: Bantam.
Lounsbury, J. H., & Clark, D. C, (1990). *Inside grade 8: From apathy to excitement.* Reston, VA: National Association of Secondary School Principals (NASSP).
Love, B. (November 1977). Desegregation in your school: Behavior patterns that get in the way. *Kappan,* 168–170.
Lynch, J. (1990). *Evaluation report for Skowhegan Area Middle School.* Skowhegan, ME: School District 54.
McKewin, C. K., Dickinson, T. S., & Jenkins, D. M. (1996). *America's middle schools: Practices and programs—A 25-year perspective.* Columbus, OH: National Middle School Association.
National Middle School Association (1995). *This we believe: Developmentally responsive middle level schools.* Columbus, OH.
Rayer, S. R. (1993). *Recreating the workplace: The pathway to high performance work systems.* Essex Junction, NJ: Oliver Wright.
Reif, L. (1992). *Seeking diversity: Language arts with adolescents.* Portsmouth, NH: Heinemann.
Robinson, J. (1995). The tenets of teaming. *Middle Ground, 1.*
Schrumpf, F., Crawford, D., & Usadel, H. (1991). *Peer mediations: Conflict resolution in schools.* Champaign, IL: Research Press.
Schwarz, Paul (1997). "Central Park East and School Reform." Talk given at North Carolina State University, Raleigh, N.C. on April 23.
Stevenson, C. (1997). *Teaching ten to fourteen year olds* (2nd ed.). New York: Addison Wesley Longman.
Stevenson, C., & Carr, J. F. (1993). *Integrated studies in the middle grades: Dancing through walls.* New York: Teachers College Press.
Strahan, D., Bowles, N., Richardson, V., & Hanawald, S. (1997). Research on teaming: Insights from selected studies. In T. Dickinson & T. Erb (Eds.), *We gain more than we give: Teaming in middle schools.* Columbus, OH: National Middle School Association.
Valentine, J. W., Clark, D. C., Irvin, J. L., Keefe, J. W., & Melton, G. (1993). *Leadership in middle level education: A national survey of middle level leaders and schools* (2nd ed.). Reston, VA: National Association of Secondary Schools.
Vincent, P. F. (1994). *Developing character in students.* Chapel Hill, NC: New View.
Wolfgang, C., & Glickman, C. (1986). *Solving discipline problems.* Boston: Allyn & Bacon.

ADDITIONAL RESOURCES

Print Resources

Arcaro, J. S. (1995). *Teams in education: Creating an integrated approach.* Delray Beach, FL: St. Lucie Press.

Carnegie Council on Adolescent Development. (1995). *Great transitions.* Waldorf, MD: Carnegie Corporation.

Erb, T. O., & Doda, N. (1989). *Team organization: Promise—Practices and possibilities.* Washington, DC: National Education Association (Analysis and Action Series).

Gardner, H. G. (1988). *Helping others through teamwork.* Washington, DC: Child Welfare League of America.

George, P. S. (1985). *The theory z school: Beyond effectiveness.* Columbus, OH: National Middle School Association.

Lipsitz, J. (1984). *Successful schools for young adolescents.* New Brunswick, NJ: Transaction Books.

Merenbloom, E. Y. (1991). *The team process: A handbook for teachers.* Columbus, OH: National Middle School Association.

Parker, G. M. (1990). *Team players and teamwork: The new competitive business strategy.* San Francisco: Jossey-Bass.

Peters, T. J., & Waterman, R. H. (1982). *In search of excellence: Lessons from America's best run companies.* New York: Harper and Row.

Rottier, J. (1996). *Implementing and improving teaming: A handbook for middle level leaders.* Columbus, OH: National Middle School Association.

Video Resources

Becoming the Very Best Team. (Available from Teacher Education Resources, 1–800–617–2100.)

Interdisciplinary Team Organization. (Available from Teacher Education Resources, 1–800–617–2100.)

Interdisciplinary Team Teaching: Cornerstone of the Middle School. (Available from Orange County, Florida, Public Schools, 1–407–317–3263.)

Partner Teaming. Vermont Association for Middle Level Education and Vermont Department of Education. (Available from National Middle School Association, 1–800–528–6672.)

Student Directed Learning: The Alpha Program, a Middle School Approach that Works. (Available from the Resource Center for Redesigning Education, 1–800–639–4122.)

Associations and Agencies

Association for Supervision and Curriculum Development, 1250 N. Pitt Street, Alexandria, VA22314 (1–800–933–2723).

National Association for Secondary School Principals, 1904 Association Drive, Reston, VA 20191 (1–703–860–0200).

National Middle School Association, 2600 Corporate Exchange Drive, Suite 370, Columbus, OH 43231 (1–800–528–6672).

National Resource Center for Middle Grades Education, College of Education, University of South Florida, Tampa, FL 33620 (1–407–317–3263).

New England League of Middle Schools, 460 Boston Street, Suite 4, Topsfield, MA 01983 (1–508–887–6263)

Various state middle school associations. A list is available from the National Middle School Association (see preceding address).

GLOSSARY

Advisor/Advisee Program (also called "Teacher Advisory Program" or "Homebase Program")—A program designed to insure that each student has at least one faculty member who knows that student well. All teachers serve as advisors so that the student-teacher ratio is 15–1 or less in advisory groups. Ideally these groups are organized on the basis of teams and meet daily for at least 25 minutes. The advisor serves as friend and advocate to advisees, meeting with individuals and leading group activities that deal with adolescent concerns, citizenship, academic guidance, school issues, etc.

Affiliated Team Member—A special subjects teacher assigned to a team to collaborate with team teachers to the extent possible and to serve as an advisor for students. The chief limiting factors in collaboration in most schools is that special subject teachers do not share Common Planning Time with the team, and they teach students on several teams.

All-Team Meeting—A meeting of all team students and teachers to build community and to address team plans and concerns. Meetings should be held at least once a week, most often during an extended advisory session. Small teams often meet on a daily basis.

Common Planning Time—Time designated on the school's master schedule for team teachers to meet to discuss team matters. Ideally, this time is allotted on a daily basis for at least one period in addition to the time allotted for individual teacher planning. Students are in special subjects during Common Planning Time.

Core academic subjects—Language arts, social studies, mathematics and science, which are typically taught by team teachers.

Departmentalization—The conventional way of organizing secondary schools into academic departments so that teachers teach their specialties to students during fixed periods on the schedule. The antithesis of teaming, departmentalization does not allow teachers to share the same students and schedule, or to have Common Planning Time.

Flexible Block Schedule—A way of organizing a school so that team teachers have a great deal of autonomy as to the use of time. Teams are assigned large blocks of time which they control. They may "flex" their schedule by lengthening or shortening periods, adding extra periods or merging them in order to facilitate curricular activities and student needs. They may also group and regroup students within this framework. Typically teams operate on a schedule that delineates (a) a large block or blocks of core academic time, (b) lunch time, and (c) special subjects (or exploratory time). (See Example 5, chapter 2)

Integrated Curriculum—Curriculum that draws from the knowledge of relevant disciplines, the teachers' skills and purposes, and the students' questions, interests, and initiatives to explore a theme or topic in depth.

Special Subjects(Often called "Exploratories")—Subjects that are non-core academic subjects and taught outside the team. These usually include, but are not limited to, the arts, vocational education, physical education, foreign language, and special education pull-out coursework. In relatively few circumstances, one or more of these subjects is taught within a team.

Teaming(shorthand for Interdisciplinary Team Organization)— Two or more teachers who represent the core academic subjects—language arts, social studies, math and science—who share the same students and same schedule, have Common Planning Time, and who usually have their rooms in adjacent spaces.

Team Leader—The designated leader of a team who facilitates team development, helping the team to function in a purposeful, organized fashion. Major duties include helping to forge and monitor a team vision; leading team meetings; communicating with administrators and others; coordinating curriculum planning and teaching; monitoring student and team progress; and providing a safe, positive climate. Team leaders may be appointed by the principal or elected by team teachers. Except in situations where faculty do not know one another well, we favor the latter approach.

Team Leaders' Meeting—A meeting of Team Leaders with the principal and assistant principals, and often guidance counselors and a special subjects teacher/leader which is held at least once a month and ideally, bi-weekly. This meeting provides times for team issues to be aired so that planning can be facilitated and teams can learn from one another. Also, it enables the principals and other key personnel to be informed about team matters so they can be supportive of team endeavors.

Team Teaching—A form of teaching where two or more teachers join together solely for instructional purposes (e.g., co-teaching a traditional subject or an interdisciplinary unit, sometimes in the same room) but do not necessarily share the same students or schedule the rest of the day. Thus team teaching is not synonymous with teaming, though the two terms are often confused. Teachers engaged in interdisciplinary team organization may or may not employ team teaching, depending on circumstances.

INDEX